PRAISE FOR *TALENT AC*

'With *Talent Acquisition Excellence*, Kevin Wheeler and Bas van de Haterd offer a timely and astute look at how we are in a revolutionary period in recruiting. Blending keen insights with compelling examples, this book illuminates the future for talent leaders seeking to drive innovation and results. Required reading for anyone aiming to master modern recruiting's tools and tactics.'
Toby Culshaw, Head of Talent Intelligence, Amazon Stores

'People teams worldwide are wrestling with the implications of divergent yet intersecting trends in the gig economy, shift to remote, cloud and collaboration, profound social and cultural change, the arrival of transformation technology in generative artificial intelligence, all amidst an unstable and increasingly worrisome geopolitical environment. This is a timely book from Kevin Wheeler and Bas van de Haterd, two of the most original and iconoclastic thinkers in the world of TA/HR, who pull together these diverse threads into a concise, imaginative and persuasive narrative.'
Hung Lee, Curator, Recruiting Brainfood

'This book is an insightful exploration of how the world of work is evolving, and how the field of recruiting needs to adapt alongside it. Few authors can bring this to light with the credibility and bonafide of Kevin Wheeler and Bas van de Haterd. The depth of their collective experience is on display throughout each page as they explore the evolving dynamics of the workplace, seamlessly blending insights on technology, human psychology, and the art of recruitment. The book covers an impressive spectrum, from exploring the role of algorithms and analytics in shaping recruitment strategies to the human-centric aspects of workforce planning and talent attraction. It is a guide, a reflection of decades of earned wisdom, and a strategic tool all rolled into one.'
Lars Schmidt, Founder and CEO, Amplify Talent

'In *Talent Acquisition Excellence*, Kevin Wheeler and Bas van de Haterd set out a compelling and powerful template for talent acquisition in the age of AI, analytics and complex talent ecosystems. I particularly enjoyed the

scenarios laid out in the book, which provide a compelling treatise on how strategy, technology, process, and data can be interwoven together to build a world-class talent acquisition function. A must-read for recruiters, HR professionals and business leaders alike.'
David Green, Managing Partner at Insight222, co-author of *Excellence in People Analytics*, and host of the Digital HR Leaders podcast.

'*Talent Acquisition Excellence* is a pragmatic guide for a TA or HR leader on what to consider when building a future-proof TA function from scratch. The authors use results and scientific data to understand what's integral to a best practice TA function and are not afraid to conjecture on how this will play out in the future with a mixture of recent real-life examples and near future projections to inspire HR and TA leaders. I welcome the thought-provoking discussion this forward-looking book will inspire and influence Talent Acquisition development for years to come.'
Andrea Marston, Senior Director Global Talent Acquisition, VMware

'Kevin Wheeler and Bas van de Haterd offer a balanced perspective that underscores how the universal themes and best practices of Talent Acquisition transcend industry sectors, languages, and borders across the globe. It's a treasure trove of wisdom, filled with real-world examples and insights. A must-read for TA leaders seeking practical answers and thought-provoking insights.'
Shelley Billinghurst and Serge Boudreau, The Recruitment Flex Podcast

'Embark on a transformative odyssey alongside the visionary insights of Kevin Wheeler and Bas van de Haterd, the oracles of talent acquisition. In their meticulously crafted guide, business leaders will discover the strategic power of talent acquisition, gaining profound insights into the future of recruitment. Peer into the crystal ball of emerging trends, technologies, and strategies that will sculpt the hiring landscape. Stay ahead, triumph in the war for talent, elevate your leadership, make informed decisions, and propel your organization to unprecedented success!'
Tash Johnston, Talent Acquisition Leader

'A timely and profound exploration of how to attract and retain top talent in today's rapidly evolving work environment. *Talent Acquisition Excellence* offers a masterclass in recruitment strategy, providing state-of-art perspectives and guidance.'
Ross Dawson, Futurist, Keynote Speaker and Author of *Thriving on Chaos*, Chairman, Advanced Human Technologies Group

'In an industry typically heavily influenced by vendors setting the tone for what TA excellence means, Kevin Wheeler and Bas van de Haterd have curated an independent and refreshing take on navigating our ever-evolving landscape of recruiting and hiring practices. Your new 'go-to' recruiting resource is a blueprint for innovative approaches for success in sourcing, engaging, and securing top talent. This book is packed with punchy narratives, cool charts and contemporary insights that have practical application. Leveraging real-world scenarios, useful tools and meaningful data. It's a comprehensive guide that will resonate and provoke thought, as well as enable recruiters and hiring partners.

Must-read for anyone aiming to keep ahead of the curve or elevate their recruitment game in the times ahead!'
Tracy Quinn, APAC Regional Head of Talent Acquisition

'*Talent Acquisition Excellence* is a masterful orientation to the current state of the art in TA with a big look at what we can expect next. Kevin Wheeler and Bas van de Haterd combine their broad knowledge of international trends, and Kevin Wheeler, as always, considers the grand sweep of history before making predictions about the future. It's practical, smart, and full of concrete examples. I wish I had this book ten years ago!'
Dart Lindsley, Strategic Advisor, People Experience, Google, Speaker and host of Work For Humans

'This is a vital book for any talent acquisition professional looking to get ahead of the curve. These are incredibly disruptive times for the recruiting function with challenging talent markets, exponential technological advances, and fast-changing business needs that make it impossible to know what skills will be needed and when. *Talent Acquisition Excellence* provides a roadmap to the radically changed talent acquisition function of the future. The book is visionary but at the same time also accessible, pragmatic and practical.'
Matt Alder, Host, The Recruiting Future Podcast

'*Talent Acquisition Excellence* provides a clear roadmap for building a more effective and efficient talent supply chain that is capable of meeting your organization's current and future talent needs. This book is a must read for any HR leader looking for practical advice and real-world examples for how to transform the recruiting function into a strategic capability.'
Thomas Bertels, Founder and President, Purpose Works Consulting

'*Talent Acquisition Excellence* is a game-changer in recruitment literature. It stands out with its clear, no-nonsense approach, directly addressing how digital tools and analytics can revolutionize hiring. The book offers unique insights and real-world case studies, making complex concepts accessible and applicable. This book is especially valuable for HR professionals and recruiters looking to leverage technology for smarter, more effective talent acquisition. Readers can expect to gain practical strategies and see tangible improvements in their recruitment outcomes. It's a concise, impactful read, essential for staying ahead in the modern recruitment landscape.'

Felix Wetzel, VP of Product Management, Cielo Talent

Talent Acquisition Excellence

*Using digital capabilities and analytics
to improve recruitment*

Kevin Wheeler
Bas van de Haterd

KoganPage

First published in Great Britain and the United States in 2024 by Kogan Page Limited

2nd Floor, 45 Gee Street	8 W 38th Street, Suite 902	4737/23 Ansari Road
London	New York, NY 10018	Daryaganj
EC1V 3RS	USA	New Delhi 110002
United Kingdom		India

www.koganpage.com

Kogan Page books are printed on paper from sustainable forests.

ISBNs

Hardback	978 1 3986 1418 5
Paperback	978 1 3986 1416 1
Ebook	978 1 3986 1417 8

British Library Cataloguing-in-Publication Data

A CIP record for this book is available from the British Library.

Library of Congress Cataloging-in-Publication Data

2023949950

Typeset by Integra Software Services, Pondicherry
Print production managed by Jellyfish
Printed and bound by CPI Group (UK) Ltd, Croydon, CR0 4YY

CONTENTS

ABOUT THE AUTHORS

Kevin Wheeler

Kevin Wheeler is an author, teacher, consultant and speaker. Kevin is President and founder of both The Future of Talent Institute and Global Learning Resources, Inc. The Future of Talent Institute is an educational and research organization focused on researching the future of work, talent acquisition and learning. The Institute works with firms globally to help them better understand and adapt to future trends. Global Learning Resources, Inc. is a consulting company that helps organizations attract and build talent through improvements in their human resource strategies, talent management and recruiting functions. Kevin has worked globally with numerous Fortune 100 and 500 firms.

He is a well-known public speaker on talent management, recruitment and learning with a focus on identifying emerging trends and issues. Kevin is co-director of the Australasian Talent Conference which produces conferences, seminars and workshops on talent and recruitment in Australia and New Zealand. He is also the author of hundreds of articles on talent management, career development, recruiting, human capital, leadership and on corporate universities and learning strategies. His weekly newsletter, *The Future of Talent Weekly*, is read by over 5,000 recruiters. He also authored a book on corporate education entitled *The Corporate University Workbook: Launching the 21st century learning organization*.

Before embarking on his consulting career, he was the Senior Vice President for Global Staffing and Workforce Development at the Charles Schwab Corporation in San Francisco. In this role, he was responsible for worldwide recruiting and for developing talent through a variety of programmes including those delivered through Schwab University.

Prior to Schwab, Kevin worked in Thailand as the Vice President of Human Resources for Alphatec Electronics, Inc. He was responsible for expatriate and local recruiting, training and development, policy, and government and educational relations. Kevin spent seven years in Thailand as a Peace Corps Volunteer teaching English at the secondary school level. He is proficient in the Thai language. He also spent 18 years at National Semiconductor Corporation in various human resource roles. He founded and served as Director of National Semiconductor University. NSU pioneered distance learning technologies and forged alliances with universities to provide employees with degree-track education.

Kevin has served as a member of the Board of Directors for the American Society of Training and Development (ASTD) from 1995–97 and was chair of the San Francisco-based Academy of Business and Finance from 1997–98. He is on the advisory boards of several technology firms focused on using artificial intelligence to improve employee recruitment and development.

He has served as adjunct faculty at the University of San Francisco, San Jose State University and on the business faculty at San Francisco State University.

Kevin has a master's degree in organizational development from the University of San Francisco.

Bas van de Haterd

Bas van de Haterd is an author, international speaker, consultant and entrepreneur. He has published several books in Dutch on the future of work. He has been a consultant for many major corporations as well as local and national governments and universities.

His Dutch publications include books on *The New World of work*, *(R)evolution of Work*, *The Societal Impact of Self-driving Cars* and *10 Jobs That Will Appear and 10 Jobs That Will Disappear*. He's also written hundreds of articles for many different publications.

He is the founder and managing director of Digitaal-Werven, a well-known Dutch research, award and events company on candidate experience. He is a well-known speaker on talent acquisition and the future of work and has spoken on conferences all around the world. He's also an often-seen guest on Dutch national radio and television with regards to the changing labour market or recruitment innovation.

Bas holds a Bachelors degree in marketing and became the managing director of a remuneration research and consulting company very early on in his career, which was his first step into the world of HR. After this he worked for an event and training organization, where he started training on 'the new ways of recruitment'. He was the first Dutch person to train recruiters on using LinkedIn, when most of them didn't even have an account. He was briefly on the management team of an IT company, but soon found out managing people wasn't his thing.

Having tried every assessment tool he could access on himself, close to a hundred at the time of this book's publication, he might be the most assessed person in the world (joking!). Once a year he visits at least one conference that he has no reason to visit in order to be inspired by a totally different world – for example, an academic conference on big data and refugees, a conference on the future of shoes and the national convention of non-executive board members.

ABOUT THIS BOOK

An Introduction to the Scenarios

In this book we've written several fictional stories about fictional companies. In these scenarios we show how different ideas, developments and technologies could work in practice; how these ideas and technologies might evolve and work together. One important thing we want to highlight with these fictional stories is that there are several roads that lead to Rome. There are more ways to excel at talent acquisition and thrive as a company in this new era of AI and algorithmic-driven recruitment. The main thing you will read in all of these stories is that these companies succeed by sticking to their strategy (and often heritage) when it comes to dealing with talent. Whether it's hiring top talent or developing talent internally, global or local approaches, or internal talent departments or RPO (recruitment process outsourcing), everything can succeed if done right. There is no one right way to do talent acquisition in general, but for every company there is a right way to do it for them.

FOREWORDS

This book captured my interest because of a number of experiences.

[1] A Fortune 50 company made the statement that every new professional hire was a $9 million dollar investment (perhaps hyperbole) which included cumulative total compensation, training and development investments, and cost of support requirements for any employee who worked with them for 30 years.

[2] A senior executive pronounced to his team that they could make any financial investment required to run their business on their own, but if they wanted to hire above a certain level, they had to have his approval (again, perhaps hyperbole).

[3] In our research from the Organization Guidance System (OGS), we examined which of 10 talent initiatives had the most impact on employee, business, customer, financial, and community value. Talent acquisition was number 1 (not hyperbole).

This book focuses on talent acquisition, perhaps the most critical talent decision any organization makes. Kevin Wheeler and Bas van de Haterd have the experience to offer unique insights into improving the talent acquisition process. They have broad consulting experience in global firms where they have designed and delivered talent acquisition processes. They astutely observe what does and does not work. They access relevant literature and share first-hand stories of talent processes. They turn ideas into tools and actions. This book captures their collective wisdom.

They wisely start by discussing the future of work with changes in the business context (technology) that affects organizations (more dynamic capabilities), that shapes where and how people will work in the future. This context reinforces employees as investments, not assets, with a focus on skills more than degrees.

Talent acquisition requires clarity about what makes an employee. They offer new definitions of what comprises the workforce (full time, part time, contract, temporary) coupled with technology (robots, AI). Workers in this new talent ecosystem have primary responsibility for their careers and skills to create their careers. Skills for the future are more about learning, adapting, and motivation than merely technical expertise, all of which can be found in a global context.

Technology will not only change how businesses operate, it will change how talent acquisition is done. Information about a potential employees' skills and fit for today and tomorrow can be more readily examined though analytics about employee background and job requirements. Algorithms can help source, screen, assess, secure, and onboard candidates. Technology enabled stages of recruiting exist to ensure that the right candidate is hired by managers who will work with the candidate. Supply of talent can be crafted as a process that can be managed and improved at each step. With a supply-chain logic, plans can be made to identify and recruit individual who met expectations. These individuals are attracted to a company because of the opportunities and promises a company makes.

A positive employer brand becomes a magnet to attract the right people because of what the company offers the employee. An employee makes a personal choice to join an organization and personalizing the job offer for an employee improves attraction.

Selection is more than an interview which may include biases and could lead to mis-hiring. Using technology again, candidates can be assessed on their ability to do the work required to be effective. A selection process can be established with a focus on character, talent, and ambition that offers a template to screen potential candidates. Screening comes by defining and assessing specific traits of the potential candidates. Interviews can be complemented by using validated assessments, and tests help screen candidates.

Deciding to insource or outsource recruitment processes becomes a key decision. In many cases, Recruitment Process Outsourcing can enable talent acquisition because of access to latest technology, in-depth expertise, and lower costs. In other cases, when talent is a differentiator, companies may spend extensively on recruiting to get the right talent.

They propose a new ecosystem or network model for talent acquisition centered on data and technology, then populated with experts in the domains of talent acquisition (employee development, marketing/branding, self-service, performance, and analytics). When experts in these hubs collaborate, they create a dynamic and high performing recruiting function. For the future, creating positive brand images for both the hiring organization and the potential employee allow both to be more aligned. The six recruiting skills for the future anchor their work (analytics, networking, relationships, flexibility/agility, market intelligent, and technological acumen).

This book is for both the talent acquisition devotee who wants to dive into the disciplines and actions for improving talent. The specific ideas, tools, and actions will help any talent enthusiast improve. The book is also written for those who recognize that talent matters and talent acquisition is the first step to better talent. The melded case studies inform what any leader can do to upgrade talent.

As I read through the book, I took notes. Some of the detailed ideas will show up in what I teach and advise others to improve their talent acquisition process. Many of the ideas will shape what I share about the importance of talent and how to become more excellent.

The three vignettes I started with are no longer hyperbole, but reality.

Dave Ulrich,
Rensis Likert Professor, Ross School of Business, University of Michigan
Partner, The RBL Group

If you are a recruitment professional or in HR generally, you'll find that this book gives you a comprehensive overview of what's new and what works for talent acquisition. But it is also much more than that. Authors Kevin Wheeler and Bas van de Haterd have shared their deep understanding to give you a big picture vision of how work is changing and where it is going.

The book is full of insights in managing talent and organising the workplace. Talent acquisition is of course at the cutting edge of market dynamics, where supply and demand are always changing. What the authors help us understand is that today's employee value proposition has become very complex. First, because the digital and social media technologies used for recruitment are more and more sophisticated and full of risks. Second, despite the importance of technology, it's the human dimension that is more important than ever when competing for talent. Getting talented people to join you and stay with you is largely how you answer the human questions. What work-life balance benefits are you offering and how much flexibility do people have in deciding the time and place where they work? How much empowerment and voice do workers have with management? Are managers capable and committed to developing their team members? Does the organisation itself have a purpose, and does it respect its ethics? The classic foundations of remuneration and career mobility are very important in choosing an employer but you compete for talent on a host of issues.

I find that Wheeler and van de Haterd are at their best when they explain why the human relationship between the individual worker and the employing organization has changed from the industrial model of work. They show how technology and gig work are combining to create a new labour market with large range of contractual possibilities. Kevin Wheeler gives an excellent overview of the American workforce today, where after more than thirty years of stagnation in real wages workers resulted from the shareholder first model of capitalism. Bas van de Haterd describes Europe's different model where social policies guarantee human development in areas such as affordable health care, unemployment compensation and retirement. Neither of these models are perfect. As founder of the ASEAN Human Development Organisation working in Asia these past 20 years, a different model has taken shape. ASEAN is the world's fastest-growing economic region. The policies and practices of the workplace are very different from one country to the next. At the same time, however, this region is unique – it is unlike Europe and the US but it is also unlike China and India. Across ASEAN the culture of work, and therefore talent management, uses its own concepts. For example the Philippine malasakit (caring for people), the Indonesian gotong royong (collaboration), the Vietnamese kiên cường (resilience) and the Thai sanook (fun, interesting) have influenced the culture of work across ASEAN.

For practitioners and policy makers in the world of work, this means that talent acquisition is not a one-size-fits-all function using standardised technology. On the contrary, technology now enables organisations to be culturally sensitive and adapt the work experience to individuals.

When it comes to understanding how this changes the function, van de Haterd and Wheeler actually deconstruct the current HR model of talent. They replace it with a radically different function made up of hubs for recruiting, talent management, employee development and internal mobility. The big advantage of their new model is that it does not assume that work is based on the full-time job as the core foundation. Their model works equally well for different working relationships between individuals and organisations in all types of contractual configurations.

As with any book that describes the present, it becomes obsolete by the time it is published because events and innovations, even wars, change the context of business. Nevertheless, the historical vision described by Wheeler and van de Haterd gives us a good look at the future of talent. I particularly like how they propose a new skillset for professionals while emphasizing the long-term evolution of work as a human development experience. That's quite an achievement and makes the book well worth a read.

Bob Aubrey
Founder of the ASEAN Human Development Organization

Introduction

What's happening to work?

Work ain't what it used to be! You can work anywhere. Starbucks can be your office. Even your job is probably something that didn't exist a decade ago. New careers have emerged; old ones are dying – maybe as many as 50 per cent of all current jobs will disappear within 10 years, according to some studies.[1]

As these studies are either hyped or downplayed, it's essential to understand what it means when we say jobs are disappearing. A good example of this is the bank teller whom the ATM has largely replaced. But that doesn't mean banks no longer have branches with employees; there are just fewer than there used to be. It also means the people working there have very different skill sets. The workers in a branch are selected on their interpersonal and communication skills, while a teller needed to be meticulous and precise.

Organizations are also changing. Hierarchy is shrinking in favour of smaller and flatter organizations that are more widely distributed. Jack Welch, the former CEO of General Electric, once created a stir at a human resource conference by stating: 'There's no such thing as work-life balance. There are work-life choices, and you make them, and they have consequences.'

He was addressing women specifically and speaking about their opportunities for promotion and growth within traditional corporate America. And, of course, he was criticized for taking this attitude, even though it accurately reflects traditional corporate America. He did not recognize how rapidly emerging trends would force corporations to change their thoughts about women, workers and work. He was right that there are work-life choices and workers are making a choice. They are pressuring corporations to change their hiring and employment practices by turning down offers and demanding higher wages and more flexible working arrangements. Things that in certain countries, like the Netherlands, have been normal for decades. The culture of part-time work is very country-dependent. The pandemic has cemented the thinking that work and life must be balanced and that employers and workers need to create mutually beneficial relationships.

The concept of work and life being somehow distinct is a recent construct. There was no work-life balance in the 17th, 18th, 19th or most of the 20th centuries. No one would have even thought to separate what portion of farm life, for example, was 'life' and what portion was 'work'. Wives, husbands and children worked as family units, producing food and clothing or operating small businesses. Roles were assumed and cast off as needed, and whoever had the ability or skill needed at a particular time did what was needed. Interestingly enough, many societal constructs built on this world of work are still present in our daily lives. For example, the typical long summer holiday in the northern hemisphere was designed so that children could help with the harvest. And although in this book we will primarily look at what organizations can do themselves, governments that are willing and able to change their country's labour laws and societal structures to accompany this new world of work better will flourish above those that do not.

It was only in the industrial era, an era we are leaving, that the artificial distinctions between work and life arose to meet the needs of factories. Everyone had to be in a physical place for specific times to make things. It took decades to get people accustomed to working at a particular time and staying for a fixed amount of time. Working from eight or nine in the morning to five or six in the afternoon for five days a week is an artificial construct that served employers but was unnatural and stressed workers and families. Neither corporate nor factory work has ever been natural, and younger workers realized years ago that there are more flexible and fulfilling ways to achieve goals.

Remote and hybrid work

People are thinking differently about work because the Coronavirus forced them into virtual work and because the nature of work itself has changed and allows a large portion of the workforce to be located anywhere. The advent of the internet, video communication tools, artificial intelligence (AI) and the shift from physically making things to processing data and providing services has transformed how we think about work. It is not necessary to be at an office to do most of the world's work, nor is it essential to stick to fixed hours or days of work. Research shows that over 37 per cent of all American jobs[2] can be done remotely all the time, while 58 per cent say they can work remotely at least some of the time.[3] With tweaks to job requirements and automation, that figure could grow substantially.

According to Global Workplace Analytics, just 3.6 per cent of the US workforce worked from home in 2018. Now, 'Our best estimate is that 25–30% of the workforce will be working-from-home multiple days a week by the end of 2021.'[4]

Once people are accustomed to virtual work, they tend to resist going back to the office full time with its daily commute and hours spent in meetings. There are many advantages of working from home including more time with the children or spouse, less time travelling to and from the office, money saved by using less fuel in the car, needing fewer clothes and the ability, in many cases, to adjust working hours to meet the family's needs.

Some employees prefer a hybrid model of work where they work two to three days a week at home and the other days in the office or in a satellite office nearer their home. During the pandemic, many companies made hybrid or remote the norm, with some claiming that this would be permanent.

Issues arising with remote and hybrid work

However, many leaders are concerned about the longer-term consequences of hybrid work and the right balance will be decided per company. Back to the office mandates have led to resignations by top talent at several firms, signalling the importance of remote work. The difference in success and policies has made clear that nothing is more important for the success of remote and hybrid work than your company culture.

There is validity to this – there is no question that when people are working in proximity and share their personal experiences, they bond. And by sharing work experiences, challenges and how they overcame them they pass on the culture and values of the firm. Fully remote companies like Elastic and Gitlab have shown this can happen in a remote environment, but organizations need to be much more explicit about arranging this. The question is whether organizations will embrace this, which also requires hiring people that have a natural fit with company values or will rely on the implicit bonding that happens in an office environment.

There was an effort to move to more virtual work well before the pandemic. The Global Talent Trends 2019[5] survey conducted by Mercer, a human resources consulting firm, based on responses from over 7, 300 HR professionals, managers and employees from 16 countries, showed that 51 per cent of employees said they wanted more flexible work arrangements. Additionally, 84 per cent of employers reported that they offered some form of flexible work arrangements, such as flexible start and end times, part-time work and telecommuting.

But the resistance from leadership was strong, except in a handful of firms. Many leaders believed (and still do in some cases) that innovation only occurs when people are working physically near each other. They also believe that teamwork needs proximity to others and that it is hard or even impossible to recreate this virtually. But there is also recent data showing that innovation has not diminished during the pandemic and that people are adapting to working virtually in teams.

Several studies have attempted to examine the impact of remote work on innovation. For example, a study published in the Harvard Business Review (2020) found that patent examiners who worked at the US Patent and Trademark Office (USPTO) who worked remotely from within the United States saw a 4.4 per cent increase on individual productivity measured by the number of patent applications examined per month after the pandemic began,[6] indicating that remote work did not have a negative impact on innovation. However, in another published study it was found that remote work was associated with lower levels of creativity and innovation in a sample of software developers.[7]

Overall, the impact of remote work on innovation is likely to depend on various factors, including the nature of the work, the industry and the specific individuals and teams involved.

But there are other concerns. Managers worry that workers will slack off or be unavailable during normal working hours. Some worry that a worker might be doing another job simultaneously or, worse, running their own business. There was, and still is, a belief that 'if I can't see them, they aren't working'. Although the pandemic has dispelled many of these beliefs, they still linger, and in some cases this turned out to be true. As Forbes wrote in an article in 2021,[8] some people were working two full time jobs at the same time. For some this was a hassle, but others were able to do two full time jobs in just over 40 hours a week. This of course either means their talents are under-utilized to begin with or that they are much more productive working remotely. Some employees prefer to get away from home, socialize with their peers as they miss the office environment. This is especially true for employees who live in crowded conditions or do not have the tools to

work remotely. Elon Musk's 'you can pretend to work from home for someone else' remark clearly showcases some leaders' belief that work is done in
the office and nowhere else.

There are several reasons why employers believe this. One is simply old
ways of thinking and a desire to return to the way things were pre-pandemic.
In some cases, the leaders who desire their workers to be back in the office
don't have the skills to manage a team remotely. For others, it is a feeling
that collaboration, innovation and teamwork only happen when people are
physically together. And for a few, it is because they have invested millions
in buildings and real estate and cannot imagine a business without a physical presence. What would they do with those buildings they must pay taxes
on and maintain? Cities and governments are concerned that if these buildings are not occupied, they will lose vital money in tax, and small businesses
that depend on workers who spend money on food and such would go out
of business, further depleting tax coffers and raising unemployment.

We have already seen this happen. Restaurants have been hit hard as
fewer people eat out for lunch during the workday. In addition, many
companies have reduced their catering budgets and no longer order food for
meetings or events, further impacting the restaurant industry. Some small
businesses and restaurants have adapted to the changing circumstances by
offering delivery or takeout services, expanding outdoor dining options or
pivoting to new business models. However, many have struggled to stay
afloat, and some have had to close permanently. San Francisco has been one
of the cities hit hardest by the pandemic. Many small businesses struggled to
survive due to reduced foot traffic and increased operating costs.

Remote work also challenges corporate culture and raises some interesting and, as of yet, unanswered questions. What happens to the culture when
people are spread all over the world? When very few ever meet each other
face to face? And perhaps most fundamental, is corporate culture as important as we think?

Remote work also is reported to increase turnover as people feel less loyal
to an organization and have few if any close friends or colleagues. Some
firms experienced high levels of turnover during and after the pandemic –
often referred to as the Great Resignation. High levels of turnover also
increase the likelihood of management opting to automate more work.

Remote work may increase loneliness and damage corporate culture as
people are separated and lack interpersonal communication.

Perhaps with the advent of augmented and virtual reality, virtual work-
places can resemble the physical one. But this is likely several years away. In

the meantime, work will remain confused and different firms will experiment with many alternative work arrangements.

Employees are not assets

Companies often say that people are their most important asset. We have always found this term disingenuous, and when we hear it we feel that we are all being disrespected. Are we making too much out of a word? We don't believe so. Words are powerful and convey hidden meanings and create behaviours, sometimes ones we don't wish to convey.

The dictionary defines assets as resources owned or controlled by a business. Usually, assets are considered to be physical objects or financial assets. They can be sold, rented, depreciated or discarded. We don't put people in this category. But we often, inadvertently, impersonalize our candidates and employees and treat them as anonymous, impersonal objects.

When we think of employees as assets – as things we control and dispose of as we see fit – behaviours emerge that create many of the loyalty and engagement issues employers have. When we care more about stockholders than employees, we are disrespecting them. When we care more about our quarterly profits than employees, we are disrespecting them. When we treat candidates impersonally and often dismiss them perfunctorily, we are disrespecting them.

Many employees are leaving their employers or would like to leave because of lack of respect and lack of development opportunities or the ability to use their skills to their fullest.

We should think of employees as the most important investors in our organizations. They have freely chosen to share their expertise and skills with us expecting a return on their investment. We should think of candidates as those deciding whether to invest in us.

The return on an employee's investment may be a paycheque, security, meaningful work, relationships or a combination of some or all of these. Each employee has a built-in return on investment meter that is constantly sampling the atmosphere and deciding if (s)he is gaining or losing from a continuing association with the firm. If the employee feels that they are gaining, they don't look for different jobs and they remain engaged. But whenever the balance shifts even slightly, employees become vulnerable to any offer that may present itself. That is why having firms and managers with a history of employee loyalty and low turnover are so desired by job seekers.

Reid Hoffman, co-founder of PayPal and founder of LinkedIn, suggested a new model for this in his 2014 award-winning book *The Alliance*. His concept of work is forming an alliance between the company and the worker to achieve common goals and to separate when those goals are met. He calls them tours of duty where both parties are committed to an outcome, the support needed to produce that outcome and the timeframe to produce the results. They also agree to negotiate a potential new future before the tour of duty is up and leave if their new futures aren't aligned. He suggests that as long as the organization is contributing to the goal the employee has, the employee will be motivated and committed. At LinkedIn the first question that is asked of a new employee when they join is 'What do you want to do when you leave?'

The gig workforce

One result of the disrespect employees feel and the impact from the pandemic is the rise in the number of self-employed. As of September 2021, in the United States there were approximately 10.6 million self-employed workers, which represents around 6.7 per cent of the total workforce, according to the Bureau of Labor Statistics. However, it is worth noting that this number may have been impacted by the pandemic, which has led to significant job losses and changes in the labour market.[9]

In the United Kingdom, there were approximately 4.9 million self-employed workers as of January 2021, which represents around 15 per cent of the workforce, according to the Office for National Statistics. Again, this number may have been impacted by the pandemic.

Globally, it is estimated that around 400 million people are self-employed, according to the International Labour Organization.[10] However, this estimate includes a wide range of workers, from those who are highly skilled and earn high incomes to those who work in informal or precarious jobs and earn very low incomes.

The corporate environment is often bureaucratic and stifles creativity. It can be tough to get ideas accepted or even to have your ideas heard. There is favouritism, unequal pay and a lack of recognition for many. With the advent of the internet and a much lower barrier to entry for those wishing to start their own business, fewer are attracted to work in typical corporations. There is a changing mindset about work where people see earning money not as their major life activity. Rather, they right-size their lives and find a balance between providing enough income to sustain themselves and freedom to develop their own ideas.

For a small proportion of workers gig work is about the ability to be rewarded for their talents. Through platforms such as Kaggle and Wazoku gig workers from all around the world can work on challenges and get rewarded for the right or the best solutions. Very talented individuals can often gain large rewards in a short amount of time, also independent of their location. Very talented individuals from low-cost, low-wage areas of the world, like remote parts of Eastern Europe, are able to earn tens of thousands of dollars solving, for example, chemical or data analysis challenges on these platforms. This way of working unlocks possibilities for remote workers as well as the ability to attract very talented individuals that would otherwise not be 'hireable' for many western companies because of their location or nationality.

Work has become for many a mosaic woven from a variety of work experiences and types. Some choose to work full time for a while, then part time or not at all. Or they may have two or three part-time jobs that are very different (e.g. fast-food worker in the day and musician in the evening and bartender on weekends) and use the rest of their time to work on developing a product or service.

The challenge for the self-employed is income they can count on and, in many countries, the benefits that employment provides such as coverage for healthcare, unemployment benefits and retirement plans. These can be expensive and hard for a gig worker to provide for themselves. In some countries there are other systems, like the ability to get a mortgage for a house, that are primarily built on a traditional employee relationships. Several countries are creating laws that prevent employers from using gig workers without providing these benefits, although they are finding out this is harder to do than they expected without stifling entrepreneurship. Some are requiring organizations to treat gig workers as if they were permanent employees.

Many workers are trapped, in a way, between seeking flexible work and finding the security and the social security they need for a family. In much of Europe the social security structures are based on the employer-employee structure which is now breaking down as more and more people are moving to become gig workers. This doesn't just affect the gig workers, but also those that do not want to become one. A massive overhaul of labour market economics and laws are on all political agendas to adjust the system to the new reality, but no easy solution is in sight.

The war for talent

Most employees find themselves in a job with a job title and fixed set of skills. They are constrained by their title and function from using any additional skills they may have or from working cross-functionally except in circumscribed instances or when assigned to a special project. Pay is based on the job title and is usually calculated based on education and experience.

This is beginning to change. Organizations are realizing that they need a flexibly skilled workforce to meet changing demands and uncertain strategic directions. In the industrial age, which began fading in the 1980s and has now become the services age, strategic direction was predictable, and work could be divided into functional areas such as manufacturing, finance and human resources. The work within these functions was also carefully broken down and codified into a set of skills called a job. Over the past several decades jobs became specialized and narrowed in scope. The skills required to do them increased and credentials became essential to qualify. This served organizations well for decades, but things began to change with the advent of the internet, global supply chains, constant market shifts, and the rise of competitors never imagined. Organizations needed to adapt and quickly develop new services or products. They had to move faster, improve quality and omit older products and services more quickly than ever. Employees with fixed functional skills and deep expertise in narrow areas were not able to adapt quickly and became liabilities rather than the assets they had been.

Rather than find and hire people with fewer skills and experience but who were willing to learn, organizations began looking for people with impossible skill sets. Job postings became long lists of skills which very few possessed. This was soon called the war for talent by Steven Hanking (of McKinsey & Company) in 1997. The term was later adapted and popularised by Ed Michaels, Helen Handfield and Beth Axelrod in their book *War for Talent* (2001). It was a call for hiring more elite, highly credentialed and educated employees. It called for upskilling and better leadership.

This may sound like a winning formula and many organizations embraced it, but what was needed were agile, fast-learning, multi-skilled employees. In his groundbreaking book, *Work Rules* (2015), Lazlo Bock, who was the head of people operations at Google, dispelled the notion that graduates of elite schools were better at meeting the demands of innovation.[11] Based on data analysis and research conducted within Google, Bock learned that hiring for intelligence and adaptability were key and that empowering employees, not managers, increased innovation and improved employee retention and engagement.

From highly credentialed jobs to flexible skills

We understand that most of what anyone knows about a job is learned on the job. Informal and experiential learning are the primary ways that people achieve excellence and increase productivity. When we hire someone, we are hiring potential and a skill or set of skills, knowing that the person will learn the job and continue to learn and develop.

Perhaps, rather than focus on credentials, we should adopt these guidelines.

Hire for experience in doing something related to what the work requires. For example, if you are hiring for a software company, hire someone who has taught themselves to code or has written an app. If you are in human resources, perhaps someone who has worked with seniors or kids or who has shown empathy for and has experience in working with people. As Ginnie Rometty, Chairman of IBM (International Business Machines Corporation) says:

1 'Do away with specific college requirements and focus on a "skills-first" hiring approach.'

2 Look at a person's potential. Are they motivated to learn, do they have a pattern of learning new things and experimenting? Do they read? Are they curious? These are better indicators of future success than a degree. There are also specific assessment tests available to test for a person's learning agility.

3 Look for agility and flexibility. Have they shown that they can thrive in different situations? Have they faced adversity and overcome it? Do they have determination and a 'can do' attitude?

4 Do they have confidence in their abilities and are they eager for the job? Are they excited? This is why active candidates might be better than passive ones as they have shown interest in your organization. Often motivation is far more important than lazy expertise. It is, however, very important to notice that humans, and recruiters specifically, are very bad at predicting a candidate's motivation for a specific job according to research by the universities of Utrecht and Ghent.[12]

5 To bring in diversity and to assess capability, create and hire from apprenticeship or internship pools. And hire internally from those employees who are motivated.

Smaller, flatter organizations

Many organizations have become virtual and have global work teams. These are loosely led, but well connected and coordinated. Chinese-owned Lenovo, one of the world largest makers of computers, has no physical headquarters. Its staff is dispersed geographically and works wherever it makes the most sense. Other companies are following this model because technology makes it possible to tap into the world's most creative people, locate scarce skills, get a broad array of diverse thinking that crosses cultural barriers and provide everyone with a choice as to how, when and where they work. The work is moving to talent, rather than vice-versa. Mostly smaller companies have done away with their corporate headquarters altogether – including GitHub, DuckDuckGo and hundreds of others. And many large organizations are allowing their workers to choose where to work and how often.

Large, hierarchical organizations were necessary in the age of manufacturing. Making things required lots of people and space. Employees were generally semi-skilled or unskilled and required close supervision and direction.

Machinery and raw materials were expensive and required large amounts of capital to acquire. Only large organizations generated the cash and could take advantage of the economy of scale that volume created. The 20th century was the age of mass production and long product cycles. The longer a product could be manufactured without change, the more profit.

The 21st century dawned with new expectations and demands. Consumers look for personalized products and services, delivered instantly at a low price. Speed and variety are the watchwords. Large capital outlays are less and less the major requirement for growth.

The internet and new technologies, such as 3D printing, have made it possible to start a business with little to no capital and produce small quantities of goods on demand. Size is actually a disadvantage. It takes an organization that is nimble, responds to demands faster than a competitor and offers customizable products and services to be profitable.

In response to this, organizational structures are evolving. The trend is to shrink hierarchy, reduce the number of employees and distribute work differently.

Sharing, teams, networks and the workspace

These changes in structure are leading to changes in what the workplace looks like. The traditional workspace was designed for individual productivity with cubicles for privacy and to wall each person off from others. Today's new workspace is open and has shared space. Desks, tables and tools are designed to maximize socialization and the exchange of ideas and information. As these workspaces are functional for focus work, many new offices have different 'task-relevant' workspaces –there are different spaces for different tasks within the office.

As innovation comes from networks, particularly of diverse people with different points of view, organizations have been installing internal social networks and promoting the wider use of external networks such as Facebook and LinkedIn. The future is around sharing and building webs of interconnections that are limited only by objectives and desired results.

Some firms are focusing on finding people to work on projects rather than in functional silos. There is more willingness to think about roles as opposed to titles and specific functional jobs. Self-managed project teams are routine at places like Google but are still rare at more traditional companies. Several companies, from Schneider Electric to ABN AMRO, are working with internal gig platforms in order to optimally use the talent within the organization as well as give employees more opportunities to challenge themselves. Many people are more likely to feel productive and engaged when working on projects and the interplay of ideas and open discussions often leads to better products. In teams and networks, the more experienced members act as informal coaches and trainers to the less experienced members, thus accelerating learning and the transmission of tacit knowledge.

Design with data

Design can happen in an evolutionary and haphazard way, as it has for corporate recruiting, or we can deliberately design. Deliberate design involves challenging assumptions, learning more about the customer, developing and testing a variety of approaches to find the best one, and then implementing and continually improving that design.

We are at the beginning of a transformation in what we know and can know. We can collect vast amounts of data but have had until recently limited ways to understand the data, find patterns or integrate it into solutions. The improvements in AI, semantic search, voice recognition and other similar technologies have expanded our capability to see patterns, recognize associations and assign probabilities to events. By using data, we can design solutions that are more robust and effective than ever before.

More and more organizations are using data analytics, for example, to determine whether it is more efficient to hire a replacement for a position or to train someone internally. The decision is made on data, not on the opinions of HR or managers. Some organizations are calculating the impact one person has on profits versus another person with a different profile. Some are looking at the attributes of successful performers and tying their findings back into the recruitment assessment process.

In all cases, data is the key to good design. The more you know about your organizations, your candidates, past successes and failures, the costs involved and the impact of technology, the better your final design.

In 2012, the *Harvard Business Review* called the role of data scientist the 'sexiest job of the 21st century'.[13] Data scientists combine statistical analysis, probability theory and other sciences with qualitative research to help answer questions such as 'Which of these choices has the highest probability of success?' or 'What are the factors that lead to the highest performance?' They can help sort out the relevant data from the irrelevant and let us design better solutions.

We can lessen the mysteries around the impact of hybrid and remote work, performance, quality of hire, the best learning methods and much more by applying analytics and redesigning what we do.

A note of caution on designing with data does need to be made: as data reflects past decisions, especially in HR, this might include biases. To mitigate this risk it is wise to use a tool introduced by Professor Peter-Paul Verbeek of the University of Twente called 'design impact study'. Countries in the European Union can not start a major construction project without an environmental impact study that describes the impact on the environment, from animals to humans. A design impact study should describe the choices made and their impact based on behavioural science literature. We know, for example, that by making the choice of a retirement plan opt-in or by default results in a 90 per cent difference in participation. Every choice within a programme should be by deliberate design based on scientific studies.

Work will most likely continue to take up the biggest portion of our day, but it can be shaped to provide more enjoyment and fulfilment than in the past.

The winners of the future aren't the organizations with the best technology, nor with the best humans, but, as Professor Andrew McAfee describes it,[14] good humans with good technology and an excellent process design. This is based on freestyle chess tournaments where former world champion and the first world champion in chess to get beaten by a machine, Garry Kasparov, is involved. No human chess player can beat the best technology, but freestyle tournaments are usually won by a team of good chess players with a great strategy they've all agreed on beforehand, using mediocre technology with multiple algorithms that will generate different outcomes. Basically this means that having a clear strategic vision and making sure all employees actually believe and act upon this vision is the winning formula of the future. This makes hiring on value fit and vision alignment key to the future success of an organization as well as using multiple technologies that are not in agreement with each other. It's worth noting vision alignment is not the same as hiring 'yes men'; it means hefty debate on the tactical choices within the vision, but not going against the vision for short-term gains or because the employee doesn't really believe in the strategic vision of the organization.

Happy is (s)he whose work is also their passion. What you will be doing will change many times. The key success factors are developing a broad array of skills, being motivated to learn, thriving in a team, expecting constant change, keeping an open attitude toward the future and finding a place you fully align with the future vision.

Endnotes

1 Frey, CB and Osborne, MA (2013) The Future of Employment: How susceptible are jobs to computerisations, 17 September, www.oxfordmartin.ox.ac.uk/downloads/academic/The_Future_of_Employment.pdf (archived at https://perma.cc/R6R9-YV2U)

2 Dingel, J and Neiman, B (2020) How many jobs can be done at home?, Becker Friedman Institute, 19 June, bfi.uchicago.edu/working-paper/how-many-jobs-can-be-done-at-home/ (archived at https://perma.cc/67WQ-3BEF)

3 McKinsey &Company (2023) American are embracing flexible work – and they want more of it, 23 June, www.mckinsey.com/industries/real-estate/ our-insights/americans-are-embracing-flexible-work-and-they-want-more-of-it (archived at https://perma.cc/RNL5-99VN)

4 Global Workplace Analytics (2021) Telecommuting Trend Data, June, globalworkplaceanalytics.com/telecommuting-statistics (archived at https:// perma.cc/G7B2-B9VM)

5 Mercer (2019) Global Talent Trends 2019, www.mercer.us/content/dam/ mercer/attachments/private/gl-2019-global-talent-trends-study.pdf (archived at https://perma.cc/HR2C-JFGB)

6 *Harvard Business Review* (2020) Our Work-from-Anywhere Future, November–December, hbr.org/2020/11/our-work-from-anywhere-future (archived at https://perma.cc/Q3KH-GW2K)

7 Juárez-Ramírez, R, Navarro, CX, Licea, G et al (2022) How COVID-19 Pandemic affects Software Developers' Wellbeing, and the Necessity to strengthen Soft Skills, *Programming and Computer Software* 48, 614–31, doi.org/10.1134/S0361768822080047 (archived at https://perma.cc/2SEZ-V2QT)

8 Forbes (2021) The remote trend of working two jobs at the same time without both companies knowing, 15 August, www.forbes.com/sites/jackkelly/2021/ 08/15/the-remote-trend-of-working-two-jobs-at-the-same-time-without-both-companies-knowing/ (archived at https://perma.cc/WKQ2-MS83)

9 Bureau of Labor Statistics (2023), Self-employed workers (class of workers), www.bls.gov/cps/lfcharacteristics.htm#self (archived at https://perma.cc/ 4HTF-MTG9)

10 ONS (2023) Self-employment in the UK and its characteristics, Datasets, www.ons.gov.uk/employmentandlabourmarket/peopleinwork/employmentand employeetypes/datasets/selfemploymentintheukanditscharacteristics (archived at https://perma.cc/7ZZ3-P62W)

11 Bock, L (2015) *Work Rules!: Insights from inside Google that will transform how you live and lead*, Twelve, New York

12 Kappen, M, Naber, M (2021) Objective and bias-free measures of candidate motivation during job applications, *Scientific Reports* 11, 21254, https://doi. org/10.1038/s41598-021-00659-y (archived at https://perma.cc/3YM6-4PFF)

13 *Harvard Business Review* (2012) Data scientist: the sexiest job of the 21st century, October, hbr.org/2012/10/data-scientist-the-sexiest-job-of-the-21st-century (archived at https://perma.cc/2D3J-DC35)

14 *Harvard Business Review* (2010) Did Garry Kasparov stumble into a new business process model? 18 February, hbr.org/2010/02/like-a-lot-of-people (archived at https://perma.cc/U7KA-ACCC)

1

The emerging talent ecosystem

The employment market has become complicated, with multiple interests attempting to find a working balance. Employers are finding it necessary to negotiate the conditions of employment as employees are increasingly wary of accepting full time jobs that compromise flexibility or do not fully utilize their skills. The big resignation that was seen in the USA and other more Anglo-Saxon labour markets underlines the challenges employers face as they figure out how to thrive in this changing job market. Individuals are finding new freedoms and exploring their capacity and taste for change and entrepreneurism.

Perhaps the most fundamental question is, what is an employee?

In the United States, Black's Law Dictionary defines 'employee' as 'a person in the service of another under any contract of hire, express or implied, oral or written, where the employer has the power or right to control and direct the employee in the material details of how the work is to be performed'.

The alternative is to be classified as an 'independent contractor' who 'contracts to do a piece of work according to his own methods and is subject to his employer's control only as to the end product or final result of his work'.

The current definition of 'employee' assumes a person who wants to work (or should want to) on a permanent or regular basis with a weekly or monthly paycheque. There is also the expectation that they will receive benefits such as sick pay and have some level of job security.

History has shown that this definition is what most people and labour unions have sought over the past century. The desire for permanent work is deeply ingrained in the minds of people. Yet there are a growing number of people who are rejecting this and prefer the freedom and choice of an independent worker who works without a contract or regular defined hours or place of work. These people are called gig workers or freelancers.

They are willing to trade security, length of work, and guaranteed pay for flexibility and freedom. Figure 1.1 shows a sample of the various types of employment that now exist. Many of these are well established types of employment and are governed by a variety of laws. Others are not.

The tax authorities in different countries have created rules regulating temporary work and defining the difference between a contractor and a consultant. Yet some types of work are not yet well-defined, nor do they have legal status. Many countries are struggling to define whether a full time Uber driver is an employee, a contractor or a freelance worker, for example. In the United States, Uber drivers are considered independent contractors. This means they do not have taxes deducted from their earnings but are responsible for paying any taxes quarterly on their own. It also means they decide when, how often and how long to work.

FIGURE 1.1   Elements of a modern workforce

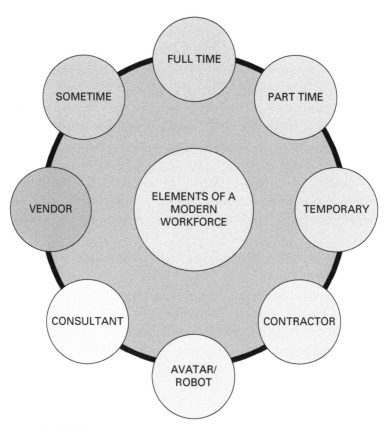

SOURCE Kevin Wheeler

In the European Union, however, new regulations are being drawn up that define Uber drivers and others, such as Amazon delivery drivers, as employees. A court ruling in the Netherlands stated that because Uber uses algorithms to allocate jobs to determine prices it showed that the drivers are indeed employees rather than contractors. The court stated that these algorithms constitute a 'modern relationship of authority' as an employer. Uber is now required to offer some sort of pay and benefits.[1] In France Uber had to pay riders 17 million euros in damages and lost salaries as they were falsely considered independent contractors.[2] As all EU countries have their own specific labour laws different countries have different situations, but one thing is the same, in every country there is a debate about the labour market and how to align the legal frameworks with the new labour markets that are emerging.

The (fictional) people described below are typical examples of modern workers that will emerge more and more around the globe, with the challenges for companies, governments and the workers themselves.

Sally

Sally is 32 years old and lives in a large urban area with three roommates. She has a degree in psychology and works as a customer relationship manager for a startup. Her work is varied and consists of everything from suggesting services a customer might like, helping customers with problems, to assuaging angry ones.

The skills she juggles include excellent communication capability, the ability to understand the context of her customers' needs and issues, and an understanding of how to influence and persuade. She works about half the time virtually and was doing this even before the pandemic. But she is already looking for something different. She is not married and has no interest in getting married, although she had been regularly dating before the lockdown. She doesn't know how to drive and uses public transportation, Uber or walks. Her social network is extensive, and she communicates primarily via messaging tools like WhatsApp. She is thinking of leaving the city to live in a more rural area where she can have animals.

She values independence and choice. Because she is young and healthy, she is not concerned with the cost of healthcare, nor does she worry about financial security. She has confidence in her health, skills and adaptability.

Tom

Tom is 35 and is considering a big move to either Portugal or Spain using the Digital Nomad visa they are offering. This is a new type of visa issued by more than 14 countries that allows anyone to work and live for up to two years in their country without paying local taxes. Tom works independently, doing a variety of things ranging from coding to writing fiction. He has technical and communications-related skills and spends as much time as he can writing a book. The coding job is primarily to make enough money to get by. All his work is project-based and freelance, which suits him perfectly. He uses a freelancer website to procure work and has a five-star rating which helps drive people to hire him. He has no desire to work for a company or be tied down to an office or regular working hours. Tom is unmarried, does not have a current girlfriend and prefers the freedom and independence of this lifestyle. He can live in Portugal or Spain cheaply and avoid paying local taxes with this visa.

Irina

Irina is 26, engaged to be married and lives in Bulgaria, near the Romanian border. She excelled in high school in chemistry and was granted a scholarship to Oxford University before returning home. She has a photographic knowledge of chemical components and their attributes and during her studies she was hunted by many chemical firms to join them. She, however, returned home to support her aging mother and while home fell back in love with her high school sweetheart. Having a creative mind on using different chemical formulas to give materials certain properties she decided to join crowdsourcing platform Wazoku. Here she submits proposals to challenges worth between $20,000 and $30,000 and wins on average two per year. With an average yearly wage in Bulgaria at $22,000 this is more than enough to sustain a really nice life in rural Bulgaria, where she spends most of her time taking care of her family.

Bill

Bill is 51 and is a programmer for a large tech firm. He has been working for this firm for 15 years, and he is worried that his skills are becoming obsolete. There is no convenient way for him to upgrade them and he isn't motivated to spend the time required to learn the new skills. He and his wife have discussed starting a gardening business, and he is contemplating leaving his employer and moving to the country. Bill's wife has a job where she can work anywhere. His children are teenagers and aren't excited about the possible new lifestyle, but they think he is cool for doing it. Their school has an optional virtual schedule, or they could home school. The internet has opened new options. He and his wife have saved a large amount of money and he is getting closer and closer to quitting his programming job and starting the gardening business. His only worry is the cost of healthcare for his family and that is the primary reason he has not already resigned.

The new worker

These examples represent the new worker: skilled, agile, flexible and wanting to be independent. They are not worried about security which they see embedded in their skills and ability to learn and not in a particular employer. They find work or projects through their social and professional networks and are always ready for a new experience.

Having a broad and ever-changing set of skills is the key to both their success and security. The concept of a job being relatively static with a fixed set of skills and competencies is fading. The historical attributes for success – college degree, GPA, experience or years of service and deep technical knowledge – are less and less important.

The computer and the internet have changed the landscape. With artificial intelligence (AI) augmenting our knowledge along with a vast array of tools and information sources online, it is quick and easy to look up whatever specific knowledge we need. For example, if I want to know about the changes in the tax code and how to apply those changes to my situation, I need only to search the internet. Not only will I find information from the government, but also videos and articles explaining the nitty-gritty of the changes and even guiding me through the process of completing tax forms. Therefore, we are less reliant on knowing or working with personal experts and more reliant on the shared knowledge embedded in the cloud.

Another example: a structural engineer can look up completed designs, find examples and consult with other engineers about any issue virtually. Artificial intelligence can augment and even completely do the required technical calculations, determine material strengths and identify potential weaknesses. Blueprints can be drawn, printed and checked automatically for code compliance. More and more knowledge, rules and advice will be available virtually. The primary engineering skills become design, creativity, adaptability and the ability to influence decisions and work with regulators and clients. More and more of the technical side of engineering can be embedded in online software, databases and AI.

This example underlines a shift in the skills needed for career success. While technical knowledge is still important, AI and automated tools are reducing the need, especially in routine situations. Notably different from the past, there is now little need for engineers or architects to design the standard home. Previously created plans can be modified and AI can diagnose potential issues. AI can help doctors diagnose many routine illnesses, aid in completing the average person's taxes, write standard software and take care of most bookkeeping duties. On a smaller scale Ikea now has its own 3D kitchen design tool online for all to use with great ease, while in the not-so-distant past the exact design and calculation of needed materials was a job for a kitchen planner which had to be double checked by a senior. Generative artificial intelligence is already capable of writing grammatically correct articles given a prompt from a human and designing completely new images from scratch to go with it.

Many firms, including some of the largest and best known such as Google and Microsoft, no longer require a college degree for employment in many jobs. Some firms prefer to buy whatever in-depth expertise they need from consultants rather than hire these skills on a permanent basis.

Over-credentialization

Perhaps requiring degrees and other credentials has led to what is commonly called credential inflation. Positions such as secretary or bookkeeper, which used to require only a certificate or two-year degree, now require a four-year degree or more. There are very few positions in high tech that do not call for at least a Bachelor of Science degree.

These requirements have become associated with the so-called 'A' players that firms seek in the belief that they will outperform those with lesser credentials.

But this belief is not validated by the research. Laszlo Bock, former head of people operations at Google, analysed and dispelled these beliefs. His book *Work Rules!* explains and documents the research that led Google to remove a four-year degree requirement from many positions.[3]

Now Facebook, Walmart and Accenture have also reduced their job requirements. There seems to be a trend to focus more on potential than on degrees and experience, especially as the talent shortage grows. Skills such as communication, general ability and motivation are becoming more important.

Lazlo Bock and others believe that 'A' players more often emerge from within your organization or are made by it because of the systems and processes you have in place.

One characteristic of the most productive and innovative employees is that they often are difficult to work with: Jeffrey Pfeffer, the co-author of *Hidden Value: How great companies achieve extraordinary results with ordinary people*,[4] and a professor at Stanford, records that Michael Jordon was cut from his high school basketball team. Other high performers have all sorts of issues when it comes to both performance and teamwork, but high GPAs are not a common characteristic.

The difficulty for recruiters and hiring managers is knowing who is or might become an 'A' player. We do know that it is almost impossible to find 'A' players outside your firm and then insert them successfully into it. Those who are hired because they were high performers at one company often fail at a new one. Companies that have spent huge amounts of money and time on competency analysis and developing complex selection systems, including a lengthy interview process, do not necessarily have more creative workforces. There are many analogies in the sports world. Many top major league players were considered poor choices or weak as rookies. They excelled, however, when challenged and when they were part of a well-functioning organization. Great players tend to emerge over time rather than appear fully formed at the interview.

When organizations combine rigorous development activities and provide continuous job opportunities, they produce exceptional employees. Historically, IBM and General Electric developed employees who were sought after by everyone. These firms spent billions on development programmes, established internal rotations and encouraged employees to move internally to gain knowledge and exposure.

New competencies

What is most important is to have the ability to understand the context of a situation and use human judgement to make a final decision. For example,

Netflix can make suggestions about which movies to watch based on your previous viewing habits, but suppose you had been watching movies starring children and then tragically lost your child, Netflix would not know that and might recommend, inappropriately, a movie about children. Unfortunately, computers and AI are not yet capable of understanding the context of a situation, nor do they have human empathy.

More and more people with broad general skills and the ability to make decisions based on knowing the context of a situation, having empathy and having the ability to learn will dominate the emerging talent economy. Many of these workers will not have traditional credentials but will be self-educated and will continuously learn from the internet, television, travel, social media and other sources. They will rely on augmented tools, online databases and social networks for guidance and support.

Firms such as Google are already hiring as much for motivation and the ability to learn quickly as they do for previously acquired skills. Formal education is useful, but it is not enough. People with the motivation and skills to learn and unlearn quickly are better able to adapt to change, new technologies and more likely to embrace the future.

The future workforce will be more independent, more broadly capable, better able to learn and adapt quickly, and more socially connected than any previous generation of workers. They will be less reliant on traditional jobs and ways of working and will construct their own work from the set of skills they have or can acquire.

Bo

Bo is a 41-year-old Chinese programmer who moved from a rural part of the country to Shanghai years ago and worked for over 15 years for two major IT firms on AI. The 9-9-6 work culture, working from 9 am to 9 pm six days a week has taken its toll on him mentally. Even though he has been very successful and belongs to the upper middle class, he is questioning his future. He is unmarried, as in his age cohort there are far fewer women than men because of the one child policy and the extreme amount of hours he has been working for so long. When both his parents recently passed away and his employer was pushing him to come back to the office sooner than he felt ready, he decided to quit his job and live off his savings until he found something with meaning. The time he spend at his parents' house in rural China gave him some perspective and he decided to try and make a living from there. He terminated the lease on his apartment in Shanghai and moved to his parents' old house. He quickly got a job teaching IT at the high school in the nearby medium-sized city and did some programming on the side via international gig platforms. He also quickly became a pillar of the aging community, helping many elderly people navigating the increasingly technological landscape the Chinese government mandates, something that doesn't make him any money, but gives him great satisfaction.

Somsak

Somsak was born in Thailand and lives there as well as in other Asian countries. He is widely travelled, and speaks Thai, English and Mandarin. He does not have a college education, but he has built a career establishing small restaurants and coffee shops. He now owns six of these coffee shops in three countries and spends his time mostly virtually overseeing their operation and advising and training staff. He travels occasionally to inspect them, but he finds that is increasingly unnecessary.

Over the course of his 38 years, he has learned the basics of international business law, finance, accounting, tax law, salary negotiation, recruiting, real estate negotiation, dealing with different cultures, managing and much more. All of this has been self-learned through the internet, his social network, a handful of experts he has consulted and from experience. In addition, he has sought out mentors and has several older and more experienced colleagues who help with difficult situations.

Somsak has a broad set of interests, including Asian art, traditional dance and literature. He is not married and does not own a house, but he is still close to his family and sees them regularly.

International talent

With the increasing acceptance of remote and hybrid work, talent pools also increase. Although of course for some organizations local knowledge is still necessary, like knowledge of the American tax code for developers of accounting software for the American market, for the majority of companies it is not.

Remote work allows companies to access a much larger pool of talent, regardless of where the candidate is located. By removing the requirement for employees to be physically present in the office, companies can tap into a larger pool of talent. The world is full of talented people, but many of them do not have the right passport to be eligible to work in the US or Europe. By hiring international talent and letting them work remotely, companies can benefit from a broader pool of skills, knowledge and experience.

With aging populations in many developed countries, and a reluctance, in many countries, to allow in more migrant workers, part of the skills challenge can be solved by sourcing that talent internationally and having them work remotely (preferably in the same time zone depending on the sort of work this is). Where we see many US companies looking at South America and EU countries looking at African nations like South Africa, other types of work can be done asynchronously or in some cases there's even a possibility of time zone arbitration (using the difference in time zones to avoid paying, for example, night shift rates for workers). Several Dutch contact centres set up subsidiaries in the former colonies in the Caribbean to be able to offer phone assistance until late at night without having to pay night time rates for overtime.

After the invasion of Ukraine by Russia (in 2022), however, several companies have revised their hiring remote policies to only include 'friendly nations'. Some organizations that had teams in Russia were left without those teams as major tech players cut off access to online tools within Russia, like Microsoft Teams and Slack, as part of the sanctions. This has led most major organizations to reevaluate their remote working policies.

The possibilities of tapping into international talent pools are not just dependent on the type of work, but also the country and mainly the language. As English is spoken in much of the world, German, French and Italian are much less common. So outsourcing, for example, customer service to another nation is much easier for an American, British or Australian company than a French, German or Italian one.

The qualities of a 21st-century worker

The worker of the 21st century has multiple skills, an entrepreneurial spirit and a thirst for learning. People like this do not find value in traditional educational models and are less and less interested in traditional corporate positions where depth of expertise is rewarded along with obedience and compliance.

While many might be comfortable working in a team, a team doesn't have to be colleagues on the same payroll. A team can be a network of associates and friends who share ideas and rewards.

Automation has already permeated various fields, including retail, transportation, surgery, medicine, bookkeeping, accounting, education and online learning. In addition, the pandemic has accelerated automation and proven that virtual work can be as effective and efficient as in-person working. As a result, the concept of work itself and how it gets done is changing rapidly.

When looking at talent needs, talent leaders need to anticipate which jobs will be phased out and which new ones will emerge. By narrowly defining jobs, we limit our ability to hire quickly and the potential for creativity and change. For example, IBM, Microsoft and many other organizations are already establishing apprenticeships and lowering the requirements for employment to attract a wider and more diverse workforce.

While some people are exceptionally capable and entrepreneurial, many others are not. What happens to the less capable, less motivated and less entrepreneurial people?

For the foreseeable future, many people will remain traditionally employed. The changes occurring are evolutionary and will over time encompass most of the world's workers. Today we have a smaller number of independent workers than traditional ones, but this might reverse over the next decade or two. Employers need to be aware that the talent they most desire and need will be the first to adopt an independent work style. Governments, especially in Europe where traditionally there has been a higher degree of social security, need to change their policies to be more contract-independent and serve their entire population. All benefits that are currently attached to traditional employment, whether it's health insurance in the USA, disability benefits in the Netherlands or maternity leave in France, need to become independent of the traditional employment structure in order to create a sustainable society in the new reality of the labour market.

TAKEAWAYS

- The definition of an employee is changing.
- A modern workforce includes all types of workers.
- Organizations are looking for employees with broad skills and that are agile, flexible and independent.
- Organizations have tended to overcentralize most jobs.
- The 21st-century worker will need new skills.

THE STORY OF BAZINGA*

Bazinga was founded as a casual gaming platform, combining standalone games with games played on social media platforms. The three founders had very different backgrounds and worked together on the first product while living on three different continents. Megha, who lived in India, was the CEO and responsible for marketing and the business model. Jarek, a Polish developer, was the CTO and responsible for the technical side. Bill, an American designer, was CDO (chief design officer) and responsible for the graphics. Bill's amazing designs were able to work on devices like phones and tablets because of Jarek's genius in development. Their first game, *Racing the Stars*, quickly became a hit, but unlike many others in the field they weren't a one-hit wonder and they weren't willing to sell to a major studio.

The massive success of their first game, financed by just a small round of seed capital, attracted the interest of major investors, but they were reluctant to take on too much money. As their first game generated a decent income and investors demanded growth plans they decided to not take the investment just yet. With much of the design work done Bill was looking for a new project, while Megha was enjoying every bit of commercial success of the first game. To be able to satisfy both founders, after many long virtual talks, at a physical get-together Bazinga decided to develop a 'cell' model. A second cell was created for the development of the new game. A new designer was hired to replace Bill to keep updating *Racing the Stars* and adding new features. When Bill's new idea and graphics were developed enough, Jarek also joined their new cell and as his team had already grown his second in command took over as the technical lead on *Racing the Stars*. When the second game launched Megha already had a marketing and sales team working under her so she could easily shift focus to the new game, while leaving the most senior people to run the operations for *Racing the Stars*. After the second game was also successful they copied the cell model to a third cell, but this time Megha became CEO, overseeing the entire company. They decided she would have a very small staff and the only centralized functions would be that of finance and HR. Marketing, sales, development and design would all be decentralized. A major role of HR was to help not just recruit the best talent for each role, but also help move people internally between units.

The early years

As with many startups at the time, from its beginnings Bazinga had a continuous improvement culture on everything, including recruitment and HR.

After the first few hires didn't live up to expectations this meant reviewing the entire process. Before Bazinga hired their 10th employee they had a framework in place to measure both technical ability with a work sample test as well as a motivational test that helped them determine fit with the startup environment.

Only when the third cell was formed and Megha became the CEO did she form a talent department. This meant processes starting to be formalized. So when Linda joined Bazinga as the head of talent she had a wealth of data on hires and performance, but no process in place. She quickly started working with data analytics to see if patterns emerged on the sort of employees that thrived in new cells opposed to existing cells. The data quickly revealed that certain personalities worked better in already successful games while others excelled in the creation of something new. But it also revealed that some employees' motives changed over time, often related to a life event like the loss of a loved one or parenthood, making their personalities more suitable for slightly different work. This is why Linda implemented not just very generous care facilities for employees, but also had an extensive check-in at the return of the employee to see if this employee would like to change roles or cells.

As Bazinga was a remote-first organization by design, with the three founders coming from different continents, talent acquisition has been global from the get-go. This allowed for Bazinga to recruit from a huge talent pool, but it also meant a massive number of applicants whenever they did open a vacancy. As they agreed to keep the centralized units small and HR was centralized, they needed a completely different approach to talent acquisition and candidate nurturing. Linda decided to create a talent community that also served as a gig platform. The platform was open for all to join and on the platform Bazinga would post challenges with awards for either the first person to solve it or the best solution depending on the challenge. The challenges ranged from data analytics on game play to bug fixing and from designing new game elements to developing a specific gameplay storyline. The winners of a challenge would be paid for their work, but it was also a way to show your talent and hence the perfect recruitment platform. When jobs opened, Bazinga wouldn't advertise them but would ask the best performing people in the community if they might be interested and if so they would be asked to take a psychometric test. The interview process was very short as they had already shown their quality on the gig platform and hires were made usually within a week after a job opening up.

When more and more games hit the market, Linda decided not just to have gigs by demand, but also have talent submit their own work. Designers primarily got the chance to submit new designs for an existing game. This could be new animals for a jungle-based game, new space ships for a space game or completely new levels. Bazinga supplied the platform to design these elements so they could be easily implemented in the game. If one was accepted a predetermined price would be paid and of course this would add to the chance of being hired. Bazinga also had a bug bounty programme, where people got paid for submitting bugs in the games, and another one for solving these bugs. It also had a programme for game improvements and potential commercial possibilities. These were harder to judge and took more time from the Bazinga team, but were also much less frequently submitted.

The second phase

After the implementation and success of the talent community Linda focused on internal mobility and retention. Linda believed that the best way to recruit was from within and so talent acquisition wasn't just about getting new people in through the external talent community, the internal talent pool needed to be used as well. So whenever a role opened, their talent management system would suggest internal candidates based on both their technical as well as their personality profiles. Only after these had been dismissed, either by the hiring manager or the employee, would Bazinga look at the external talent pool. To make this system work Bazinga used a combination of tools. First there was the work experience within Bazinga and evaluation of that experience. The work would be translated into skills and the quality evaluation of the work would influence the skill level. Workers would also be encouraged to do aptitude tests to look at potential skills they haven't been able to show in their day-to-day activities. Next to that, workers would be requested to do a personality test and can redo that whenever they feel like it. The combination of these data points helped fuel the internal mobility system and of course reports from this system were accessible for employees, even if they wanted to use it to get a new job somewhere else.

The next thing to be implemented was an AI personal coaching bot that would assess desires and wishes from employees and coach them to achieve them. This could be by looking for a mentor, suggesting training programmes and checking in on the achievements of these programmes. The AI coaching bot would also automatically make sure the talent management system was updated so when a new job opened, the employee would be mentioned as an internal candidate. From an employer brand perspective the internal mobility and growth was used as one of the key messages year in, year out. Bazinga had animations on how a candidate could progress internally in their career and had stories, both in video as in animated cartoons of actual employees careers. Bazinga didn't offer jobs; they offered careers.

The remote structure of the organization had major recruiting benefits, but of course also downsides as they had no hubs or places they met. The yearly one-week retreat with the entire organization wasn't enough to really build the trust within teams, so Bazinga added to the company-wide week a biannual physical team meeting. Some teams combined this with the company-wide retreat, having their additional retreat a week before or after the main one, while other teams had people that didn't want to be away from their loved ones for two weeks and so had three separate gatherings a year.

To support the team structure Linda also implemented an AI-based team coaching bot. This bot, which had no links with the personal coaching bot as they wanted to ensure the psychological safety of employees above all, had two tasks. First of all it was tasked with keeping up spirits within the team. It asked questions and got conversations between team members going. But they AI was also trained on noticing behaviours of individual team members. If a team member was all of a sudden less responsive in general or to a specific other team member it would notice and perhaps ask this team member if something was wrong. If the bot wasn't able to help fix the issue it could eventually escalate to the team leader to have a human conversation. Building on behavioural and linguistic analyses, it also measured the engagement of team members with the organization and it would connect with the employee if engagement dropped over a longer period of time. This AI bot was very helpful in detecting friction between teams or team members in the very early stages and so could solve small irritations before they got out of hand.

Bazinga never grew to be a company that employed tens of thousands of people but they never had that ambition, as they always looked at their total talent management and made good use of the community of freelancers that were part of their talent community. Linda made sure someone who rejected a job offer because they preferred staying freelance still had the same opportunity to get a gig as all the others. Using the community of fans that loved to develop new levels and units, but also loved to beta test and wanted to hunt and fix bugs, they were able to keep the headcount low. The cell structure made it possible to keep the team spirit really high and a maturity model of the cells helped get the right people with the right mindset working in each team.

This is a fictional scenario on talent acquisition in the near future.

Endnotes

1 Toh, J (2021) Another win for workers: uber drivers are employees, Social Europe, 22nd September, www.socialeurope.eu/another-win-for-workers-uber-drivers-are-employees (archived at https://perma.cc/XXT9-U7P6)

2 Hummel, T (2023) French court orders Uber to pay some $18 mln to drivers, company to appeal, Reuters, 20th January, www.reuters.com/business/autos-transportation/french-court-orders-uber-pay-some-18-mln-drivers-company-appeal-2023-01-20/ (archived at https://perma.cc/AU7Y-BLTG)

3 Bock, L (2015) *Work Rules!: Insights from inside Google that will transform how you live and lead*, Twelve, New York

4 Pfeffer, J (2000) *Hidden Value: How great companies achieve extraordinary results with ordinary people*

2

Technology and talent acquisition

There has been lots written about the impact of artificial intelligence (AI) on work and jobs. Thirty years ago, when Kevin was working in the semiconductor industry, AI was a hot topic but promised what could not be fulfilled. Computers were not powerful enough nor was there enough useable data to make good predictions. We made jokes about the poor performance of systems that purported to use AI such as Apple's early personal assistant, the Newton, that misspelled almost everything.

But in those intervening years computers grew exponentially more powerful and with the advent of the internet, data became abundant. The science of AI matured and rapidly advanced. The iPhone with its apps such as Siri and Alexa showed what was possible.

Inevitably, the convergence of AI, automation, design thinking, remote work, changing attitudes toward work and the move to more agile organizations has changed many aspects of corporate life and will require a complete revamp of how we do everything.

We have seen the rise of tools built on AI in many areas from chatbots that provide information and answer questions to e-commerce sites such as Amazon that anticipate our needs and desires and offer us products based on the data it can access about our interests and past actions and even adjusts the price according to demand and sometimes personal preferences. Things attached to the internet (the Internet of Things or IoT), which includes GPS trackers, blood pressure monitors, heart rate counters, smart watches, temperature sensors and more, provide continuous input for the machine learning and algorithms that lie underneath all of this.

Artificial intelligence has also made its entrance into human resources and recruiting. ChatGPT is one example, which we will discuss in detail later. Many tools will augment or automate parts of the recruitment process.

FIGURE 2.1 The many drivers of change

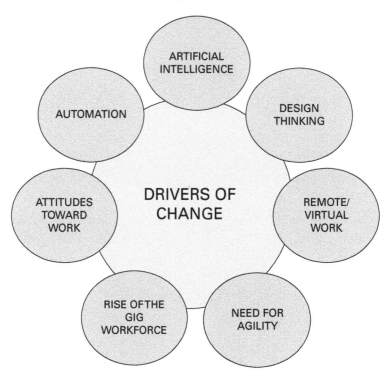

SOURCE Kevin Wheeler

By augment I mean tools that still require human involvement and judgement but improve speed, provide better quality candidates and reduce the workload of recruiters, while automated tools take over the complete job.

It is now possible to use algorithms to find potential candidates, assess their capabilities and skills, determine the appropriate salary and conduct background checks, to list just some of the emerging capabilities. Large amounts of storage, fast processors and affordable access have given us the ability to tap into the data that comes from career sites and that is stored in application tracking systems and human resources information systems. This provides data for algorithms to assess candidates' capabilities, skills, culture fit and the probability that they will be productive employees.

Data

Data is the key to the ability to make predictions, correlations and develop probabilities. Data is the raw material of our time just as iron and other minerals were for the industrial era and land was for the agricultural era.

Data can be everything that can be coded and stored in a computer. Data encompasses facts, numbers, images and photographs that are stored on computer servers or in the Cloud. Data is being accumulated in vast amounts as we use the internet to shop, talk with friends, send emails, post to social media sites, look up information and post photos. The term Big Data is used not just to describe lots of data, but also a high velocity of data and a large diversity in data. Big data is also about having data from different, often unrelated sources which often have different identifiers, making it hard to link the sources and one or more sources with a high velocity of renewal of this data. Mastering the analyses of Big Data led to the remarkable progress in AI we've witnessed over the past years.

Facebook uses the social interactions of its users to identify patterns that can then be used to advertise products. For example, if a user frequently comments on a type of music or a particular performer, they will see more content and advertisements that include that performer or their music. This type of pattern identification has led to billions of dollars in advertising revenue.

Over the past decade especially, the number of people who have a presence on the internet or in the Cloud has increased exponentially. Virtually everyone in a modern economy with a smart phone, tablet or computer has an identifiable presence. It has become impossible to hide or not be visible to those with the tools to search the data. Recruiters are now able to find people with specific skills, experience or education using sophisticated algorithms and search capabilities.

Analytics

The selection and hiring of people is fraught with bias and subjectivity. Psychologists have assembled long lists of these biases which include our tendency to reject new evidence that contradicts something we believe to be true. This is called selective perception bias. Or the tendency to search for and remember information in a way that confirms our preconceptions, called the confirmation bias.

For example, if we believe that people with high GPAs, for example, are better workers, then we will seek evidence to prove that and dismiss any that contradicts it. If we believe an academic degree from a certain university is preferential, we'll remember the failures from another university, and consider the mis-hires from that university 'outliers' that need to be ignored, just like the great hires from a different university are 'lucky shots'.

Recruiters also often rely too heavily on one trait or piece of information when making decisions – often the first piece of information acquired or the information obtained from a trusted source. If someone recommends a candidate, for example, that recommendation may outweigh any facts that contradict or suggest that the person is not so good.

Many recruiters and hiring managers also suffer from what is called the 'hot hand effect' which is the fallacious belief that a person who has experienced success doing something has a greater chance of further success in additional attempts.

Analytics can help dispel many of these by simply looking at the data. Of course one needs to realize that internal data is by definition biased because of past biases. A law firm from Amsterdam that historically only recruited from the universities of Amsterdam or Leiden will have data that will reflect that their best candidates come from these universities. Perhaps also, because of this bias, their view that that no good recruits would ever come from Maastricht or Tilburg will have limited the career development of the few they did hire from those universities.

In recruiting, data can be gathered from hundreds of sources including the applicant tracking system, the career site, the HR information system, internal emails and data gathered incidentally while signing up for a newsletter, responding to an email or filling out an application. This data can be analysed to determine why some employees are better performers than others. Successful employees most likely have traits, abilities, skills or personalities that make them more successful than other employees. Because of the huge volume and complexity of data, a recruiter could never access or make sense of all the data that might be available about top performing employees. Machine learning can analyse this data and use it to recommend candidates with the highest probability of superior performance by matching their competencies and traits to ones previously discovered to indicate high performance.

Algorithms

Every human has a set of values, beliefs, biases and expectations that we use, consciously or not, to make decisions about everything, whether it is the food we prefer, the brands we buy or the people we like. These are human algorithms, and they are formed from our experiences, education and family background. Recruiters use their human algorithms to subconsciously evaluate candidates during an interview on a wide variety of factors from appearance to a judgement of their capability and personality. We all have biases that affect our decisions.

One of the advantages of algorithms is that they promise to be unbiased and only use data to weigh their recommendations. For example, an algorithm might assign different weights (amounts) to various factors or traits (ingredients) to reach a conclusion (cake, for example). An algorithm, to use a very simplistic example, might recommend a candidate to a recruiter based on weighting 10 per cent to education, 30 per cent to experience, 50 per cent to a specific competency or skill and 10 per cent to personality. Each candidate would be ranked according to how well they matched these criteria. The algorithms would not know what the person looked like, what race or gender they represented, nor how they were dressed.

However, most algorithms learn from past data. If that data was biased, then the algorithm will also be biased. An example of how this can happen was an experience at Amazon. An algorithm was asked to recommend people for a certain engineering position. The result was that everyone it recommended was male. No females were included. In examining the algorithm Amazon discovered that most past hires for that position were male and the computer learned that males were preferred and excluded all female candidates. Even if gender wasn't a piece of data in the dataset, the algorithm would look at gender related data like 'chair of women's chess club' or 'fraternity vs sorority'. And of course some job titles, like waiter and waitress, on a CV are gendered too and as those differ per language, it's really hard to exclude all of those factors. Also, although never confirmed, rumour has it that some companies used salaries as a determinant for quality of the individual. However, your salary and your salary increases are as much influenced by your negotiating ability as it is by your performance; so, for example, some companies that were looking for engineers may have defined the best negotiating engineers as the best engineers. Whether true or not, having an accurate datapoint on quality of hire is very hard.

We have learned a lot from this experience and are much more careful about examining the data used to develop algorithms and to carefully examine the output for bias. In Australia the University of Technology Sydney (UTS) has developed the world's first independently audited ethical talent AI process[1] and can certify an algorithm as fair and unbiased. We will see more algorithms certified this way as the United Nations, as well as the World Economic Forum, are embracing certification.

Recruitment (robotic) process automation (RPA)

Process automation has been part of manufacturing and other corporate processes for a long time. It is now beginning to impact recruitment.

Automation in recruiting began with the CV storage and retrieval, CV search and the automation of some types of reporting. Applicant tracking tools, which first appeared in the early 1990s, were the pioneers in this area and have been joined by customer relationship management (CRM) tools and more recently by tools that can help find candidates on the internet, and screen and assess their skills.

Artificial intelligence and machine learning hold the promise to further automate the process, making it both more efficient and better, while making it more equitable. Large language models for example have led to the development of conversational chatbots – tools that intelligently query candidates and lead them through the process of job matching, assessing their skills and recommending they apply for a specific position. Machine learning on psychometric data sets have led to job recommendations from a candidate's casual gaming history to game-based assessments that select on potential and also point candidates to jobs better suiting than the one they applied for.

The reality, however, is that the adoption of tools that use AI automation in a piecemeal fashion have, at best, augmented only a tiny percentage of their processes. There are many reasons for this. First, these tools are difficult to integrate into the normal, manual recruitment process. There are not many recruitment functions with the staff or expertise to do this. The tools often work best when the process is also adjusted, but changing the way a company works is a hard change. The staff also needs to be trained on how to use the tools and last but not least, many recruiters and hiring managers believe they can do a better job than any technology can. It is difficult to get the recruiting team to accept these tools and many are afraid that their jobs will be at risk if these tools gain traction.

There will be certain recruiting functions that will be affected by automation. Scheduling interviews is a task that can, and probably should, be fully automated. There may also be a need for fewer recruiters who focus on screening candidates for basic skills and for interviewing. Much of the initial sourcing of candidates can also be automated, even though it will require human judgement to make a final decision. But perhaps one senior level sourcing expert using automated search tools could replace three or more less skilled sourcing recruiters. Other areas where recruiters might find less need for their skills are in data input and doing administrative tasks such as report generation or in onboarding new hires.

Figure 2.2 indicates areas where algorithms and machine learning can either completely automate a process or augment it. Over the next decade machine learning will have advanced to such a degree that most of the normal recruiting functions could be augmented or automated.

Sourcing using algorithms

As mentioned earlier, it is becoming easier to find people online as more people have internet profiles, use social media accounts, write blogs, create podcasts and videos, and participate in online chats. Here is an example of how an automated algorithm might go about finding a Ruby on Rails programmer.

The algorithm will search a wide variety of sources and will most likely have a ranking of how effective or reliable each source is. It will look for press releases or conference proceedings where an employee has been named. It will scrape corporate websites and newspapers or technical journals for articles or stories about Ruby on Rails and look for names of people who might have written the code. The algorithms can access Stack Overflow, GitHub, LinkedIn or other social media sites for profiles of people who list Ruby on Rails as a skill. As more Ruby on Rails programmers are hired, the algorithm will learn which sources are best or expand its searches to new areas. The algorithms are continuously learning and getting more efficient. Algorithms can be tuned to look for specific capabilities, traits or skills for any profession and over time can learn which sources are most indicative of proficiency or quality.

Privacy and creative rights

Artificial intelligence gives us the ability to search through all sorts of data, without the permission or even knowledge of the person involved. This

FIGURE 2.2 The automation/augmentation of machine learning and algorithms

BRAND	SOURCE	SCREEN	ASSESS	ENGAGE
PROGRAMMATIC ADS	AUTO SEARCH	CHATBOTS	CHATBOTS	CRM
SOCIAL MEDIA	CROWD-SOURCING TOOLS	SIMULATIONS	SIMULATIONS	FACIAL RECOGNITION
BANNER ADS	RESUME PARSING	GAMES	GAMES	SOCIAL MEDIA
CAREER SITE	MATCHING SYSTEMS	PASSIVE ASSESSMENT	ONLINE TESTS	CHATBOTS
TEXT RECRUIT	JOB DISTRIBUTION	EMOTION RECOGNITION	BEHAVIORAL ASSESSMENT	NEWSLETTERS
JOB-DESCRIPTION ANALYSIS	JOB BOARDS	CULTURE MATCH	SKILL ASSESSMENT	PODCASTS
TARGETED MARKETING	REFERRAL TOOLS	REFERENCE CHECKS	PASSIVE ASSESSMENT	VIDEOS
JOB-POSTING OPTIMIZATION	SHARED TALENT NETWORKS		JOB PREVIEWS	EMAIL
VIRTUAL HIRING TOOLS			VIRTUAL TRYOUTS	EMPLOYER REVIEW SITES
			VIDEO INTERVIEWS	ENGAGEMENT SURVEYS

FRONT END

BACK END

ADMIN	OFFER/CLOSE	ONBOARD	MEASURE	PLAN
REQUISITION CREATION	SALARY RECOMMENDATION	CRM	DESCRIPTIVE ANALYTICS	DESCRIPTIVE ANALYTICS
INTERVIEW MANAGEMENT	AI LAWYER	INTERACTIVE SITE	PREDICTIVE ANALYTICS	PRESCRIPTIVE ANALYTICS
SELF-SCHEDULING	OFFER-LETTER GENERATION	VIRTUAL ONBOARDING	BIG DATA	LABOR MARKET DATA
RESUME PARSING	EMPLOYMENT AGREEMENT	ONBOARDING VIDEOS		GRADUATION RATES
REFERENCE CHECKING		BENEFITS SELECTION		
BACKGROUND SCREENING		PROOF OF CITIZENSHIP		

■ 95–100% *automated* □ *heavily augmented*

ability raises legal questions and creates ethical issues. It also raises questions about who owns data.

With generative AI there is a big debate on who owns the data the AI is trained on. Asking ChatGPT for example to write an essay in the style of Stephen King or Donald Trump gives back great results. But an artist like Stephen King never gave his permission for this. So are his creative rights and privacy being violated here? And what about generative AI that can produce pictures in the style of Picasso or Banksy? Although one might ask if this is about privacy or creative rights, the line between the two is very thin when it comes to AI.

Would you, for example, feel your privacy is violated if we could ask the company chatbot to respond in your communication style? Or if everybody could ask the sourcing outreach tool to compile outreach messages in your message style? As that would mean these tools have analysed all your writings without your knowledge.

The same, of course, goes for candidates, where many feel that employers checking their social media, apart from perhaps LinkedIn, is considered a privacy breach. Using an AI tool to analyse someone's personality based on their LinkedIn profile, for many, would also be considered a privacy breach, which raises the question of whether this is actually possible – something that will be discussed in Chapter 5.

Azeem Azhar talks about this in his Exponential View podcast and newsletter[2] as being a Copernicus moment. Copernicus, of course, discovered the earth revolved around the sun and not the other way around which led to many changes in all kind of paradigms. Everything that seemed true wasn't all of a sudden and in the decades that followed, the fundamental structure of society had to be rewritten. Or maybe a Gutenberg moment is more in order, as the printing press had a similar effect on the questions that need to be asked now regarding privacy and more, over creative rights.

Governments, especially in Europe but also increasingly elsewhere, are limiting access to information without the explicit permission of the person involved. This makes it more difficult for recruiters to use analytics and machine learning to evaluate candidates unless the candidate is asked for permission. Privacy laws, however, should be seen as the lowest bar on what is allowed, not the bar to strive for. More and more organizations are putting in place ethical guidelines that exceed the privacy laws to contain what they see as common decency. Asking for permission to access data, being transparent on the use of that data and allowing candidates and employees to remove that data if it's not business critical are parts of those guidelines.

AI can be used to collect and analyse large amounts of data. Organizations must ensure that they are following applicable privacy laws and regulations when collecting data from candidates and employees. They also need to ensure that the data is kept secure and is used for legitimate purposes.

As Azeem Azhar points out, the rise of large language models like ChatGPT and all sorts of AI models will give society, and with that politics, a Copernican or rather Gutenberg press moment, just on steroids. In the same way that it took the printing press decades to be fully embraced, within months ChatGPT already has people asking for new laws and the application of, for example, copyright. The US copyright office has already formally stated that purely AI-generated images cannot be copyrighted.[3] Of course, the question is how AI-generated images adjusted by a human can be, and to what extent they need to be, changed and how this can be measured. This means the entire law on privacy and creative rights needs to be rewritten with AI in mind. Let's not forget copyright law didn't exist before the printing press either and many have challenged creative rights as being unsuited for the digital age. With AI this debate will be impossible to ignore and new laws will have to come in place. It's important for talent acquisition to make sure whatever AI you are using stays within the local laws. And as we've seen with GDPR, it's not just about where you operate, but also who you reach. American companies that reach out to EU citizens will need to keep to EU law, just like with GDPR.

We cannot speculate where this new world of AI will take privacy law and the laws on creative rights. Will the developers of the models need to compensate the artists? Or will the users that prompt 'write an essay in the style of Stephan King' need to pay a fee to Stephan King? Will you need to keep compensating your former employee if you keep the AI write outreach messages in their style with the AI? Or will we do away with copyright and creative rights completely? Or will there be some middle ground? There is no answer to this as of yet, but in the next years or decade we will see the world change when it comes to privacy and creative rights and if you are using any form of AI, and you will be, it's important to follow these developments.

Black box vs explainable AI

One of the key ethical considerations when it comes to AI is the concept of a 'black box' and explainable AI.

A black box is a system where it is difficult or impossible to gain an understanding of how it works or how decisions are being made. This lack of understanding could lead to a lack of trust in the AI system, as well as a lack of accountability if something goes wrong. For example, if an autonomous car is involved in an accident, but the reasoning behind the decision to make a certain turn or braking action is unknown, it can be difficult to determine who is at fault.

On the other hand, explainable AI is a type of AI that is designed to be understandable and explainable. This means that the decision-making process and the reasoning behind decisions can be determined. This can help to increase trust in the AI system, as well as increase accountability should something go wrong.

Ethics

*The advancement of AI technology is rapidly changing the way humans interact with the world. AI technology is being used in a variety of applications, from facial recognition to autonomous vehicles. With this increasing presence of AI in our lives, it is important to consider the ethical implications of these technologies. In this part of the book, we will explore the ethical considerations surrounding AI technology, including its potential for discrimination, privacy concerns and potential for misuse. We will also examine some of the potential solutions to these ethical issues especially for talent acquisition.

Discrimination

*One of the primary ethical issues surrounding AI technology is the potential for discrimination. AI algorithms are trained on data that reflects existing societal biases and prejudices, which can lead to the perpetuation of these biases in AI-driven decisions. For example, facial recognition technology has been shown to have a higher rate of false positives for certain racial and ethnic groups, leading to potential issues of racial profiling. Additionally, AI-based recruitment algorithms have been found to be biased against certain genders and minority groups.

AI can be used to automate the recruitment process, but this automation can carry the potential for bias. AI algorithms can be trained on data sets that are biased in certain ways, which can result in biased outcomes. For example, if an AI system is trained on a data set of CVs that are majority male, it may be more likely to select male applicants over female applicants. Organizations need to be aware of potential bias and take steps to mitigate it.

The above sections on ethics and discrimination (with an asterisk at the beginning of the paragraph) were written by ChatGPT. We used three slightly different prompts asking it to write a chapter about ethics and AI and pasted the different paragraphs from these three prompts together with minimal editing.

The main reason for using an AI writing tool to write this is to show the potential of the tooling and the advancements made in recent times, to emphasize that making decisions on the ethics and the auditing of these ethics is no longer optional for organizations. An interesting side benefit from using the AI tool to write these paragraphs is it actually helped shape the thinking of the authors and helped bring up points they wouldn't have thought about otherwise. So using AI isn't just helpful for content creation, it can also serve as a tool for ideation.

Bias in AI

The European AI act has deemed using AI for selection in recruitment a high-risk category, meaning using AI in talent acquisition, especially in selection, will get extra scrutiny and needs above average auditing when EU citizens can be affected.

One of the reasons using AI for talent acquisition has a high risk of bias is because historical data sets are biased. Societal bias plays a big role in today's labour market in all parts of the world. Societal bias is something that grows over generations and hence is still present for people with different ethnicities and women. Just to emphasize how long equal rights have been granted in several western countries, it wasn't until 1960 in Canada and 1962 in Australia that Indigenous people received full voting rights. The United States only allowed African American women full voting rights in all states in 1965 and Switzerland allowed women to vote on a national level in 1971 and actually on all levels of government only in 1990. In several European countries, like Belgium (1948), France (1944), Greece (1952), Hungary (1945), Italy (1945) and Portugal (1976) full and unconditional voting for women was granted only after the Second World War, meaning at the time of writing there are still women alive that were born without the right to vote, as second class citizens by law.[4] But other societal aspects play a role as well. In a progressive country like the Netherlands, for example, until 1958 it was still mandatory to fire a woman when she married, as a married women was legally incapacitated. She also wasn't able to open a bank account without her husband's approval, along with other things. As freedom of education gave primary schools based on religious grounds their own rights to set policy, this was still common practice until the 1970s, with the last record of a female schoolteacher being fired for getting married in 1978.[5,6] Although the laws have changed a lot and the number of female teachers far outnumber the number of male teachers, the history of women being treated as second-class workers is still present in their salaries for example. Other forms of systemic bias still exist, like for example the 'women are bad at maths' and 'Asians are good at maths' bias. This effect is actually so strong that Asian women that are primed as women before a match test score lower than Asian women that are primed as being Asian before the same match test[7]; on replication of the study it turns out this only works if the person is aware of these general biases.[8] So systemic bias is not just in the mind of those evaluating, knowing what the world expects of your type in general actually affects your performance.

Next to societal bias, organizations will have added their own biases. From bias in hiring to bias in promotions, if we look at the composition of our workforce and compare this to the society at large, it's hard to deny an additional bias has been added.

As AI builds on existing data, understanding that HR data is by definition biased is important to make sure there are guardrails and regular audits. As audits can only be done on explainable AI, no HR system should be using black box technology. This means the system must always be able to explain the correlations it sees and how those are weighted in the decision-making process.

AI ethics in different steps of the TA process

Although when it comes to using AI in talent acquisition we tend to primarily think about using it in the selection process, it is or can be used in different steps of the talent acquisition process and an organization should have ethical guidelines or guardrails for each one of these steps.

AI can be used to write job descriptions as we've demonstrated in this book. However, as AI learns from all the job descriptions out there, which were originally written by humans, bias can creep in the language. Using an AI tool to write job descriptions can be useful, but a guardrail might be using a different AI tool to check those job descriptions for biased language.

It's possible to have another algorithm check the first one, if the first algorithm has the task to optimize the result and the second has the task to check for exclusion.

AI is often used for job advertising and this is can be where, unknowingly, bias creeps in. Although social networks like Facebook do not allow targeting of job ads on things like age or gender, their algorithm is made to optimize for results and that leads by definition to bias. As different groups have different preferences and no ad can emphasize all, every AI that uses programmatic advertising, basically optimizing the most applicants for your investment, will eventually focus on the group most attracted to your ad. But your ad cannot be unbiased, as you always emphasize certain aspects of the job. The way to counteract this is by creating multiple ads for multiple audiences. Writing an ad specially for men and women and perhaps different age groups and emphasizing why this job is interesting for that specific group, accompanied by a photo of someone from that group, makes an advertising AI optimize for that specific group. By having the AI optimize for multiple groups, the bias in optimizing is counteracted.

When using AI in selection it's important to not just make sure that only relevant criteria are used, but also to have a regular audit of the AI as bias can creep in easily. Relevant criteria should be actually tested and not be the beliefs of the hiring manager. Scientific research has shown time and time again that, for example, experience measured in years has no relevance in performance. It's not that experience doesn't matter, it's the quality, not the quantity of the experience that matters. Think back on how often you've had to work with people that were terrible at their job, and you didn't understand how they had ever got that job to begin with. Well, because someone once gave it to them and they were then selected time and time again on the experience they listed in their CV. Next to using only relevant criteria these should be measured in scientifically validated ways. Every test that is used would be scientifically validated and validated for its purpose and the audience it's used for. A test validated for people with a university degree isn't validated for use on high school graduates, just like a psychometric test used for clinical purposes isn't valid to use for hiring purposes. A test validated for academic hires isn't by definition suitable for high school graduates, let alone people with lesser education. You might now think that's logical, but this is actually the number one reason many questionnaire-based tests show racial bias, especially against first generation immigrants who may not be proficient in that country's language, and may not understand all the words or the deeper meaning of some words.

Many facial recognition tests have been shown to be biased against darker skin colours, but not all. If you are going to use these, pay very close attention to their scientific validation reports and possibly hire an expert to look at the studies done.

On the other hand, in recent years, from private sources we found that 'scientifically validated and very trustworthy tests' turned out to be biased against groups we never knew about. For example, it turns out that there is a difference between people from Chinese and Arabic heritage that grew up learning to read and write in a Latin alphabet compared to people from Chinese and Arabic heritage that grew up with only their native (non-Latin) alphabet. Logical reasoning tests, for example, using letters and numbers are a little harder for those that didn't grow up with a Latin alphabet. These tests have been validated for different ethnicities but all of them grew up in Western countries. It turns out the easy solution is using colours and shapes.

Another group that has been historically overlooked when it comes to fair assessment tests are neurodiverse candidates. Here facial recognition, or rather eye tracking, combined with keyboard tracking, can also actually help by being less biased against people on the neurodiversity spectrum, as research by Professor Craig Chapman reveals.[9] Eye tracking and keyboard tracking can help understand how a decision is made rather than just the answer and so helps people on the neurodiversity spectrum be better understood in assessments.

It's important to know the limitations of all the tests, especially if you are building an AI-based selection process on this. Since even when you have a human in the loop, technology bias could creep in, meaning we trust the machine more than we should.

Every organization should have an ethics policy and potential guardrails when using AI for the different steps of talent acquisition. That's not to say you should not use AI or technology in your talent acquisition process, as not using technology and having inherently biased humans making all the decisions is as risky as using the wrong technology.

Limits of automation

Big Data is what feeds the algorithms. Therefore, access to large amounts of data is vital but the quality and variety of that data is crucial to their accuracy and objectivity.

Unfortunately, we have witnessed many cases when the data used was too narrow, previously biased or the sample was not large enough to provide unbiased results. Almost every time you read about an algorithm discriminating against a certain group, this is usually the reason.

One of the many things that differentiate humans from computers is our ability to use emotion, subconscious behaviours and even irrational actions to make decisions. Of course, with these come bias, prejudice and many other undesirable traits. But along with it also comes our unique ability to take a chance on someone, offer someone an opportunity although the data says not to be swayed by our emotions.

Computers cannot and will most likely never be able to do this. None of the tools can replace human judgement or decision making. Instead, they augment our decisions by analysing data better than we can and not deviating from rules. They offer us probabilities and point out things we might never have seen.

But it is doubtful that they will ever be human enough to jump to a conclusion, feel something is right, laugh, cry, empathize or take a chance on some maverick candidate that might invent the next killer product.

The six stages of technology implementation

The process of making technology a real partner to success requires understanding how the workload flows, where data is coming from and where it is going, a seamless integration between each, and a well-designed user interface. There are six stages that recruitment must pass through to eventually achieve a seamless and user-friendly candidate and hiring manager experience. Each stage is a step toward full automation. Each of these stages is explained in detail below.

Stage 1 – No significant technology

This is where many recruiting functions are. They most likely have an applicant tracking system (ATS) used to store and retrieve resumes and generate reports. It does little to speed up the recruiting process and may slow it down because of data entry and other administrative tasks. It is useful for creating reports to meet government requirements.

Recruiters often use spreadsheets to track requisitions, and there is a lot of email and paperwork. Data is not gathered in any systematic way, and collecting data takes time just to get the simple metrics that are reported monthly or quarterly. Nothing is in real-time or readily available.

FIGURE 2.3 Six stages of evolution of the recruitment process

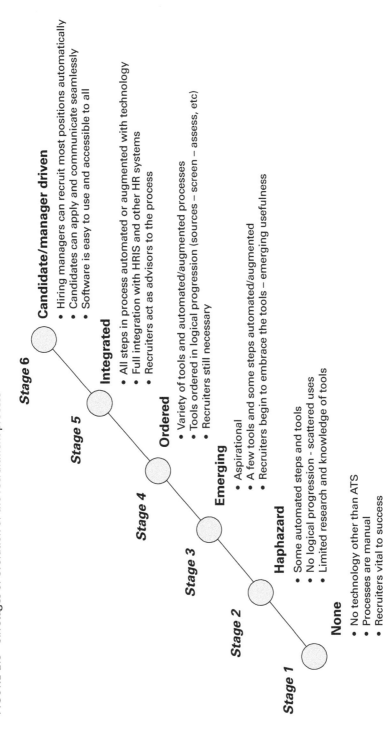

Stage 1

None
- No technology other than ATS
- Processes are manual
- Recruiters vital to success

Stage 2

Haphazard
- Some automated steps and tools
- No logical progression - scattered uses
- Limited research and knowledge of tools

Stage 3

Emerging
- Aspirational
- A few tools and some steps automated/augmented
- Recruiters begin to embrace the tools – emerging usefulness

Stage 4

Ordered
- Variety of tools and automated/augmented processes
- Tools ordered in logical progression (sources – screen – assess, etc)
- Recruiters still necessary

Stage 5

Integrated
- All steps in process automated or augmented with technology
- Full integration with HRIS and other HR systems
- Recruiters act as advisors to the process

Stage 6

Candidate/manager driven
- Hiring managers can recruit most positions automatically
- Candidates can apply and communicate seamlessly
- Software is easy to use and accessible to all

Recruiters spend time searching for candidates using the internet, the career site or job boards manually, schedule and conduct interviews in person, and interface with the hiring managers and perhaps HR and compensation. Each hire is time-consuming and highly administrative.

Stage 2 – Haphazard use of technology

These recruiting functions have a few tools that help them automate some processes. But the choice of tools is haphazard, with no real plan or overall vision. There has been very little research into what tools are available, their capabilities or how they integrate with other tools. And there is little budget or time available for research or testing.

Typically, these functions may have a sourcing tool, perhaps some technology to pre-screen candidates, and a candidate relationship management (CRM) tool to communicate with candidates. The career site may have some interactivity to screen candidates. The function may have invested in a video interviewing tool and may have a way for candidates to schedule interviews online.

Technology is often more of a time sink than a help, and recruiters do most things manually. But there is no integration between the output of the tools and the next steps in the process. This requires recruiters to jump from tools to manual processes over and over.

Stage 3 – Emerging

At this stage, the function has a vision for where it wants to go with technology and may have a timeline and an implementation plan. But only a small amount of effort has been put into streamlining or redesigning the recruiting process to accommodate technology.

Recruiters are slowly adopting new tools but are not well-trained on how to use them. And the tools may not always be the right ones or used appropriately. Recruiters do not trust the tools and often revert to manual processes. There may be a screening tool, for example, but recruiters still do manual screening.

At this stage, there is interest and desire to achieve more with technology, but the knowledge, skills, budgets and time are not available.

Stage 4 – Ordered

The recruiting process is making significant progress in becoming simplified and in eliminating unnecessary steps. Which tools to be used has now been decided and they have been sequenced for effectiveness. There is a logical progression of tools, with the output of one feeding into the next one, as appropriate. For example, screening leads to candidate rejection or to passing the candidate on to an assessment tool or to another opportunity that better matches their skills. Assessment leads to an automatic interview and so on. The tools augment the recruiters who only occasionally need to provide input.

Recruiters are trained and comfortable using the technology and regard it as a helpful adjunct to what they do. The tools improve their productivity and reduce workload, but many steps are still manual. Many areas remain manual and require recruiter time and effort.

Stage 5 – Integrated

The function is mainly automated. Each step in the recruitment process is automated, processes are well thought out, and the work flows smoothly from tool to tool with very little need for a recruiter's involvement. The tools are completely integrated with the HRIS system, and data is collected and analysed in real-time.

Candidates and hiring managers have infrequent contact with a live recruiter because the process and tools provide feedback and answer questions. If the technology cannot handle a question or an issue arises, a recruiter helps. The recruiters become advisors and consultants to the candidates and hiring managers.

Stage 6 – Candidate-/manager-driven

This is an entirely automated and seamless stage. Completely automating the recruiting process may seem pie in the sky, and I admit that we may never see it achieved (and may not even desire such a thing). But it is helpful to imagine what it could look like. Without a vision, it is hard to achieve any progress.

In Stage 6 the user interface has been carefully designed to give hiring managers and candidates a positive and easy-to-use experience. A hiring manager can access the tools they need quickly from a computer, tablet or phone. They can easily indicate the skills and other requirements needed and choose (or be guided to choose) what type of worker would best fit this need. The workers could be full time, part time, a contractor with a fixed timeframe or a consultant.

They would be presented with a slate of potential hires from a global talent ecosystem, and could then get in touch with any selected candidate by email, text, social media or phone. The position can be presented to the candidate in a variety of ways designed to match his/her most probable preferred style. Interviews and skills assessments could be automated or eliminated, as the hiring manager desires. They would be guided through salary and other negotiations by a chatbot, or could speak directly with a candidate. The process would allow great flexibility and provide whatever assistance either the hiring manager or the candidate needed.

Likewise, a candidate could express interest in a project or a position. They could vet the hiring managers and the company by asking for the data on previous hires at this company and by this manager, their satisfaction and tenure.

The software would provide an engaging, easy-to-use and flexible interface for both the hiring manager and the candidate.

What's left for recruiters?

The few remaining recruiters would have new roles and skills. They would use analytics to improve the software and the interface, advise and consult with candidates and hiring managers, conduct exit interviews, work with new university graduates and manage RPO (recruitment process outsourcing) or vendor partners. There would still be a need for consultation with senior leaders and perhaps even the occasional need to recruit someone in person.

Whether or not an organization achieves Stage 6, the evolution and learning on the path toward it would be revolutionary. Technology will play a significant role in the future of all processes and if implemented well would make the experience of finding work far easier and more pleasant than it is with today's archaic systems.

TAKEAWAYS

- Technology is becoming central to successful talent acquisition.

- Artificial intelligence, LLMs like ChatGPT have changed how recruiters work and will change it even more in the time to come.

- Increasingly, data and analytics are critical in marketing to candidates, finding them and engaging them.

- Algorithms are the backbone of all automated tools and understanding them is essential for TA leadership.

- Algorithms must be carefully designed to prevent conscious and unconscious bias.

- New ethical standards are being developed for using AI and algorithms.

- Integrating technology into the recruiting process must proceed in careful stages, but with a clear North Star as your guide.

THE STORY OF FRANKLIN WRIGHT*

Franklin Wright was founded on the idea that a small regional aircraft could be powered by solar power. Its mission was to revolutionize mobility, with plans to make carbon-neutral, private travel possible. From the start it was very open and clear about its roadmap. First it would build a solar-powered plane for the wealthy and from there the development would move towards providing more access to these vehicles for the middle class. It had no intention of competing with the large aircraft manufacturers, as those large planes would not be able to be fully solar-powered for a long time.

After a slow start, with many engineering difficulties and regulatory approvals, it was able to launch its first aircraft and then developments went crazy. Despite the motto of focusing on one product as a relatively small player in the industry, within two years it had launched a solar-powered aeroplane that was also allowed to drive on the road, basically creating a flying car. And very soon after they launched a solar-powered helicopter which was also allowed to drive on the road for shorter distances, making a flying car even more accessible for the public. Business boomed after that and when self-driving cars became the norm, their flying cars and helicopter cars became even more popular. Although more affluent individuals would buy their products, the main clients for Franklin Wright were major transportation-as-a-service companies, the Ubers and Waymos of the world.

Franklin Wright's talent strategy

Franklin Wright realized early on that it needed the best and the brightest in every part of the business in order to succeed in this mission, which meant two things.

First, no matter how big you are, there will always be more talent not working for you than there is working for you.

Second, in order to align all the interests, it's best to align them by giving them a stake in the future success of the company.

Hence Franklin Wright decided to build a shamrock organization (there are variations but this is usually an organization that has three parts, known to outsource some of their functions[10]). It had a core of people working for the company, but would bring in talent of all sorts from all parts of the world to work together on specific challenges. This talent would come and go and many of them would be employed at other organizations/institutions, like universities. It would also put other companies, such as suppliers, in the leaves of the shamrock as they called it.

In the centre of the shamrock was the very small and lean organization that would coordinate the entire process. It would set very strict boundaries on, for example, weight limits for the body of the plane and different components. It would set very high targets for the solar panel output. And it would invite all that felt these were achievable goals to join a leaf and make it happen. There were different schemes for different stages. Early-stage development would be done by competition with large prizes. So the team that was first to be able to achieve the goals set for the project would win serious prize money as well as a large amount of digital tokens. For later-stage developments it would also be a combination of cash and token rewards, where the project would be defined and the team was able to self-select, with a fixed amount of money and tokens being divided among the team members. Suppliers that had joined the early stages had a basic guarantee of becoming the supplier when production started and, as they had a stake in the future success of the company because of the tokens they had been rewarded in the early stage development, they had an incentive not to overcharge.

Franklin Wright had committed early on that at least 35 per cent of the profits each year, when it started making a profit, would be spent on token buy backs. This meant the price of the tokens was directly related to the profit of the company. As a result, early-stage designers and developers who had earned a lot of tokens for their work when they were still worthless became happy campers when the profits went through the roof. This also gave suppliers, who earned tokens for their development work, a reason not to overprice their materials, especially when Franklin Wright was trying to develop the market. By basically printing their own money in the form of tokens, this limited the upfront costs of development, without diluting the ownership.

The early years

As Franklin Wright was mainly still in development, the early talent strategy focused on coordinating talent from everywhere, both geographically as well as legally. So when Xue joined she was given the title of Community Manager, as she was managing the talent community existing of workers, freelancers and those working for potential suppliers. At this time the biggest contingent of the talent was freelancers who believed in the idea and were willing to donate their time and knowledge. When the first phase was done and million-dollar prizes were awarded to the winning teams and Franklin Wright knew their dream was possible, they moved on to the second phase: combining all the knowledge and information from the winners into a prototype.

As reaching the goals triggered a massive new investment round, it was now possible to start paying a lot more people. The model of having non-exclusive partners work so well together and using the specific knowledge of different people that would be almost impossible to hire worked extremely well, and they continued with the shamrock model. Different projects were formulated and all the central organization did was coordinate and set the framework. As it is necessary when designing a plane that the wings actually fit the hull.

Xue quickly became aware that there were several sorts of freelancers in the world with different needs. There were professors at universities who contributed with their knowledge on lightweight materials, aeronautics, aerodynamics, propulsion, solar power and much more. They loved to help and were happy with mainly future payments in the form of tokens. Others were brilliant students who had to choose between a job serving drinks or stacking shelves and this project, so with a small cash payment combined with tokens they had much more time to give. But there was also a group of excellent engineers who loved the project, but in order for them to spend serious amounts of time on it, they needed compensation in order to pay their rent or mortgage. And of course this differed a lot between social economic backgrounds in the world as well. So Xue came up with the simple idea of having people set their own salaries, within limits. The more upfront payment, the less tokens, but at no point would they pay 'market rate' as they had a strong desire to attract people believing in the future of the company at this stage.

She also realized that there were many different communities that would benefit a lot from different community managers. So she was promoted to Community Management Manager and hired a cohort of community managers from different nationalities. This would allow them to tap into different pools of talent as well as be very attentive to cultural norms within groups. The new community management team consisted of Moon from South Korea, Jaina from India, Amin from Iran, Anastasia from Ukraine, Kunto from Ghana, Pierre from France, Juan from Argentina and Pete from the USA. All of them had the task of finding new talent on a project, if needed, and coordinate the work and keep people active and focused, even though working for Franklin Wright wasn't many freelancers' only job.

Because the pay for the freelancers was set so that all westerners would have at least some financial incentive to participate, it was much easier attracting talent from countries within Africa, South America, India and Ukraine. Of course this talent needed to have the right skills, but when they did, they were able to contribute a lot more time and especially with the guidance of some of the brilliant professors who worked on the project as a side gig, which worked really well. It also helped with testing prototypes. Some countries were much more lenient in rules for testing, but also different circumstances, such as the temperature differences between a cold Canadian winter and a hot Kenyan summer, were immaterially worked into the design.

Taking flight

When the first plane took flight and the company started to make money, the value of the tokens quickly increased. Many of the first-generation freelancers that had left the project came back as they saw not only that their dream had become reality but their tokens were becoming valuable. This led to an explosion of new projects and instead of focusing on one product, Franklin Wright decided that using the shamrock model made it possible to start several new product lines simultaneously. Manufacturing was outsourced as well, so a viable new product could be brought to market at minimal risk.

The company hired a lot more coordinators to manage projects and some additional community managers, but it remained a small and lean company. Although by now many freelancers were making more than living wages from freelancing for Franking Wright, the company never hired a single R&D person other than those internally that coordinated the projects. It kept on paying for results and giving the teams the power to self-select other team members and setting rewards for each role. With the profits from the solar plane soaring and many stories in the press on early freelance millionaires there was no short supply of talent that wanted to join. And many more leaves were added to the shamrock: new projects like a flying car, or technically a plane that was allowed to drive on the streets, and a helicopter car, and of course improvements to the existing solar plane as well as new, bigger and smaller, models of this plane.

Franklin Wright was already developing its own solar panels, but it was now even able to develop solar foil that was so thin it was almost solar paint, making the entire vehicle one big solar panel. This technology wasn't just used on their own products, but also sold to car and large aeroplane manufacturers, adding yet another business unit to the shamrock.

Xue loved her work as a manager of the community managers, but more structure was needed on the people front. So Amir stepped up from his community manager's role and took the role of People Tech Coordinator. Because of the unique organizational model of the company, it wasn't possible to use existing tooling for the many issues they faced. So Amir took it upon himself to have a new leaf that designed a VR environment where communities could work together on their projects. But he also realized that this environment would be perfect to assess new talent coming in. So in an exact copy of the VR environment used to develop the product and meet with team members, they set up an assessment for new talent.

Anastasia took on the role of Talent Attraction Coordinator. Although their brand attracted a lot of good engineers, the team knew they had to approach these unique talents themselves. Since these very talented people were used to being hunted and courted and would never consider a new job without being asked for it, she started a project, another leaf on the shamrock, that was able to identify very specific talent based on scientific papers published on specific themes. A second project was able not just to identify these talents, but also to approach them in a very personal way. The sourcing bot used personality data gathered from publications and social media and was able to use this to personalize their message, using scientific persuasion tactics. If there was a response a community manager would take over the contact from the bot.

Moon stared a project to build an AI-team-based coaching bot to signal friction in the team before it started. The second version of the bot was also able to help the community manager to not just signal friction, but also suggest a line of action to mitigate it. Franklin Wright decided not to automate this mitigation part, although many other organizations were doing that, because the teams were not on the payroll. Franklin Wright had grown to where it was because of the community managers. It would augment these community managers as much as they could, but not replace them.

With the success of the company growing, so did the lawsuits and the theft of intellectual property. This was one job that Franklin Wright decided to hire full-time staff for and it wasn't too long before the legal department became the biggest department of the firm. Of course, working with law firms in all different countries in order to deal with the litigation, the legal department had become a significant part of the company. Thankfully as many people had a stake in the company, and because the value of their tokens was based on the company profits, they had a lot of eyes and ears in the world. The legal department actually had several community managers working with them gathering information from the community to help identify and gather information on misuse of IP.

Using the power of community and shared long-term goals, Franklin Wright had changed the world of transportation in a decade, with solar planes, solar-powered flying cars and helicopter cars that were now seen all over the world. With the self-driving, and flying, revolution about to revolutionize the world, the future looked very bright.

This is a fictional scenario on talent acquisition in the near future.

Endnotes

1 UTS (2020) A world first for ethical AI, 8 December, www.uts.edu.au/about/faculty-engineering-and-information-technology/news/world-first-ethical-ai (archived at https://perma.cc/56CQ-TNSX)

2 Azhar, A (2023) Exponential LLMs and the Copernican moment, 15 April, www.exponentialview.co/p/exponential-llms-and-the-copernican (archived at https://perma.cc/FF95-58H7)

3 Escalante-De Mattei, S (2023) US Copyright Office: AI generated works are not eligible for copyright, ARTnews, 21 March, www.artnews.com/art-news/news/ai-generator-art-text-us-copyright-policy-1234661683/ (archived at https://perma.cc/ND2J-FMMJ)

4 Wikipedia (2023) Women's Suffrage, en.wikipedia.org/wiki/Women%27s_ suffrage (archived at https://perma.cc/G7F4-T829)

5 Wikipedia (2023) Employment ban for married women, nl.wikipedia.org/wiki/ Arbeidsverbod_voor_gehuwde_vrouwen (archived at https://perma.cc/C7AM-JBY2)

6 The Trail Back (1996) 1996: Miss, are you getting married? 2, 12 December, www.vpro.nl/speel~POMS_VPRO_489014~juf-gaat-u-trouwen-2-het-spoor-terug~.html (archived at https://perma.cc/WA7U-NSPF)

7 Shih, M, Pittinsky, TL and Ambady, N (1999) Stereotype susceptibility: Identity salience and shifts in quantitative performance, *Psychological Science*, 10(1), 80–83, doi.org/10.1111/1467-9280.00111 (archived at https://perma.cc/F43Z-XAPK)

8 Gibson, CE, Losee, J and Vitiello, C (2014) A replication attempt of stereotype susceptibility (identity salience and shifts in quantitative performance), *Social Psychology*, 45(3), 194–198, doi.org/10.1027/1864-9335/a000184 (archived at https://perma.cc/NK5U-X4H7)

9 Chapman, CS (2023) ResearchGate, www.researchgate.net/profile/Craig-Chapman-4 (archived at https://perma.cc/V2PP-WNM9)

10 London Business School (2015) The Shamrock Organization, 14 January, www.london.edu/think/the-shamrock-organisation (archived at https://perma.cc/9D8Y-DWKF)

3

Talent supply chain thinking

Recruiters rarely think about recruiting as a supply chain, yet it is one, and it is as critical as any other. The talent shortage is as much a result of the lack of a well-thought-out talent supply strategy as it is a shortage of skills.

Every manufacturing organization has a supply chain management team responsible for making sure the parts they need to make their products are available when required, at the quality that is needed and at the lowest possible cost. They use data to determine the supply level they can access and estimate demand for their products. This allows them to find additional suppliers if the supply is constrained, renegotiate prices if supply is large and recommend changes in production efficiency or marketing to increase demand.

Supply chain management is the key to the success of Apple and many other firms, as they need to ensure that they have enough products to meet demand. Of course since the Covid-19 pandemic many organizations have been reevaluating their supply chain, as perhaps too much focus had been on costs and not enough on availability and risks of disruption and cascading effects. Something that has also been true for many people operations. In the coming years we will see specific LPHIE (Low Probability, High Impact Events) assessments for talent to identify HIP (High Impact People). These are employees who would cause a loss of sales, productivity or creativity if they left. Along with this identification there would be a contingency plan in place on how to keep them or replace them. This is, for example, already common practice at some low-cost airlines, where one of these high impact jobs is the person hedging the fuel costs. As that is such a business-critical job, three months without a good person filling this position could bankrupt the company, so there is always a contingency plan to fill this position.

Service functions such as recruiting have supply chains that are slightly different from those for manufacturing. They must ensure they have a supply of the skills and experience necessary to help their customers at an affordable price whenever needed. To do this they need an awareness of business trends and to anticipate client needs. They must have data about the economy, their client's business outlook, and the talent market.

The difficulty currently experienced in finding talent and meeting deadlines clearly shows that existing talent supply chain processes are not working. Recruiters complain about the lack of talent but have not been able to anticipate the demand for specific skills and have little market intelligence on the available talent supply. They have not done contingency planning or created potential scenarios of what could happen to the talent supply and develop mitigating strategies.

While this has not necessarily been requested by senior management or even supported, talent leaders should take the initiative themselves and begin to think more like supply chain managers. If the talent supply chain is weak, there will always be a shortage of skills and the potential to miss deadlines or the inability to meet a customer's needs.

Supply chain elements

There are several steps in any supply chain, as illustrated in Figure 3.1. We have compared each step to a generic model that is used from manufacturing to recruitment. It clearly shows that recruiting can be approached as a supply chain. A recruitment function can make significant improvements in

FIGURE 3.1 Recruitment vs generic chain

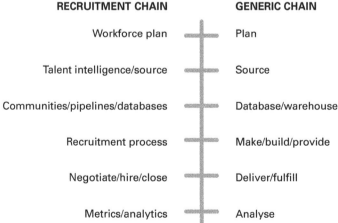

RECRUITMENT CHAIN	GENERIC CHAIN
Workforce plan	Plan
Talent intelligence/source	Source
Communities/pipelines/databases	Database/warehouse
Recruitment process	Make/build/provide
Negotiate/hire/close	Deliver/fulfill
Metrics/analytics	Analyse

time to fill by ensuring that each step in the supply chain has a well-defined process and performance standards.

Let's look at each of these from the perspective of recruiting.

Workforce planning/forecasting demand

Almost all talent functions lack foresight and information about the skills the organization currently needs and what skills may be needed as technology and customer needs change. They lack insight into how many people will be required in the short term and are usually blindsided by sudden demands for new talent.

Workforce planners must be aware of business, economic, political, demographic, social changes and trends. They need to anticipate and predict the necessary skills and be agile enough to find this talent quickly. Demand and supply forecasting are fundamental elements of any supply chain, including recruiting. While it is impossible to anticipate all potential needs, it is possible to use analytics and trend research to narrow down possibilities and develop sourcing strategies.

It is also useful to continuously scan the business environment for emerging trends and new technologies that may impact the business, regularly talk with hiring managers about their needs and build an informant network to provide early warning of emerging new needs.

> In order to tackle short-term forecasting a company like L'Oréal insists that HR and IT are present from the first project meetings, to evaluate the impact on their respective parts of the business. In the case of HR this means they can influence decisions on internal mobility from other business lines and recruitment needs earlier on. By being involved from the start they have the data to build a workforce plan.

Keeping tabs on who has potentially needed critical skills and where they are located can be a differentiator in your recruiting success. Mapping available talent and fully understanding how difficult it will be to recruit this talent will provide the inputs to calculate whether a development programme would be more cost-effective than a recruiting approach or what combination would be most economical and practical.

Therefore, data science has become a core requirement. Predictive analytics can help determine the number of retirements and the amount of turnover that is expected. And analytics can help forecast growth in specific skills. Talent intelligence and market data can give a good indication of how many people with needed skills are available locally and globally, how many are graduating from college and how many could be developed internally.

Even more important is to look at demand by function. For example, there may be a growing need for software engineers and a declining market for network administrators. Comparing the projected or expected demand with the talent supply is important. This includes knowledge of how many are employed by a competitor in the local, national and global markets.

If demand is shrinking, can the current staff be redeployed or retrained for growing roles? Understanding demand and supply at a macro level as well as narrowly is important to respond quickly to changes in needed skills and develop a pipeline of internal and external talent.

Talent intelligence and sourcing

According to Toby Culshaw, author of the book *Talent Intelligence: Use business and people data to drive organizational performance*, talent intelligence 'is the augmentation of internal and external people data with the application of technology, science, insights, and intelligence relating to people, skills, jobs, functions, competitors, and geographies to drive business decisions'.

It is always a challenge for recruiters to find talent. Even after years of sourcing the same skills, recruiters still struggle to locate the people they need. An integrated systems approach involves merging employee development, internal mobility, candidate relationship building, talent marketing, recruiting, retention activities, talent analytics and succession planning.

Broadening sourcing from being the sole responsibility of recruiting to include other functions allows more comprehensive thinking and better planning. For example, when a need for a position or a new skill set arises, rather than immediately opening a requisition, the hiring manager, along with a talent manager, would go through a process of looking at available internal talent, modelling the costs and time involved in training someone for the position, predicting the available external supply and the time to recruit and train someone. They would also determine if a gig worker might be better than a full-time employee.

One way of looking at internal skills is setting up an internal gig platform and giving employees the opportunity to work one day a week, for example, for a different unit within the company. One company doing this is Schneider Electric. Gigs are posted on the internal platform which can range from a few hours a month to a day a week for a predetermined time period. Every employee has the right to apply for such a temporary position. An algorithm based on transferable skills suggests gigs to employees that want that, based on the skills they probably would have acquired based on their previous work experience. This way the company doesn't just give their employees new challenges, it also gives them development opportunities while profiting from internal knowledge and growing bonds between departments and even geographic locations.

The Talent Intelligence dashboard should indicate where people with the required skills are located, what they are looking for and whether they are willing to relocate. With talent intelligence human resources could also advise on opening up new locations in order to have access to the talent. It should map internal talent for possible promotion or a move to another role where their skills would be appropriate. Talent intelligence data can also show what skills are growing in demand and declining. Numerous tools are available to help gather this data, but it also takes a deep understanding of current and future talent needs to make this truly useful.

Scenario planning

Scenario planning and contingency planning are also useful tools. Scenario planning allows recruiters to imagine future talent issues and prepare contingency plans if those situations arise.

Scenarios are carefully crafted stories about the future. They incorporate trends and ideas about the role of technology, people, structure and process in certain situations. They are not predictions but more like hypotheses about different possible futures and their risks and opportunities.

For example, a typical scenario could pose a question about the impact of a novel pandemic on the world economy. The stories could range from it having a minimal impact with a low mortality and rapid decline to the opposite. Included in this scenario would be potential ways to react, communicate and control the impact.

For example, a typical scenario could pose a question on the impact of AI and the blockchain on accounting work and the required skills in the organization. These stories could range from minimal impact where some administrative tasks disappear to the massive impact where much of the administrative staff isn't necessary anymore, but there is an increase in auditing roles with deep understanding of smart contracts and the algorithms underpinning them. These scenarios should be ranked on likelihood and impact, and based on that rating the organization can take measures to prepare for these possible futures. Most effort will probably go to the most likely scenario, but a potentially low probability, high impact scenario cannot be ignored either.

The main purpose of scenario planning is to facilitate decision making and to get prepared mentally with action plans for several plausible potential occurrences or scenarios.

How can scenarios be used for talent acquisition?

To start, you might ask, what are the likely scenarios for recruiting over the next 10 years? Or what is likely to happen in our industry that will impact recruitment over the next 5–10 years? Any big question is good as long as it is future-focused and will lead to some specific contingency plans.

Then you would typically create four unique scenarios based on an analysis of the trends and issues you see happening. Three of these should be what you think is most likely to potentially happen and one should be what is highly unlikely, maybe not even possible, in your thinking. This is called the Wild Card.

Shell, the organization that invented scenario planning, created four scenarios before the oil crisis in the 1970s. Their wild card was that oil would not remain plentiful and that an entity like OPEC would be created and control prices by reducing production. Even though, at the time, this was considered highly unlikely, it is exactly what happened. Shell was prepared because of the contingency planning they had done and within two years went from the eighth to the second largest oil company.

Targeted marketing

It is very hard to attract people with scarce skills to any firm. But in a time of talent shortages and demographic challenges, it is even harder. Candidates have many choices and to have any hope of recruiting them you must get them interested in your organization and in the work you have for them. You must find ways to get their attention and once you have that attention you need to make sure they are engaged and interested. It is completely inadequate to rely, as we have, on posting jobs, using employee referrals and searching the internet.

Using data and information gathered from talent intelligence, it is possible to develop targeted marketing strategies.

For example, if the data you have gathered indicates that there are several qualified candidates in a specific city or at a certain company, you can create messaging directed only to those people in those places. This can include various activities ranging from public advertising to targeted social media ads. For example, construction workers have been targeted with billboards near construction sites. It is also possible to target certain companies on LinkedIn and Facebook or to ask your network for referrals to specific people.

Some providers can match people to either your company or your jobs based on their preferences, like CompanyMatch which lets candidates fill out their desired working styles and matches that to companies. There are several assessment providers that allow candidates to do aptitude tests and suggest jobs based on those qualities.

It is also possible to recruit on potential like the Dutch airline Transavia. In cooperation with a specialized training agency, they tested a lot of people on their potential for IT as well as their learning agility. They were given basic training and for one year and then had four days on the job, with coaching and one day of specific training. The former jobs of these trainees were anything from ballet dancer to a caretaker of dolphins.

You can also set up 'triggers' so that if someone with a particular skill comes to your career site or appears on your LinkedIn page with a comment or a post that is relevant, you are alerted and can immediately reach out to that person with a personalized message.

One additional trigger is when someone updates their LinkedIn profile. This is seen as a sign indicating they might be open for a new job.

> The University of Groningen used advanced data analytics to locate hotspots in certain specific niche fields based on academic publications. They were able to identify several high-quality associate professors who, based on their publications, were very qualified to take on the full professor role that was opening up in Groningen. As academics don't generally talk to recruiters they looked for a link from one of their own staff who had co-authored on a publication with someone that had co-authored a publication with the person they wanted to recruit in order to get a second degree introduction. They recruited several full professors this way.

Talent networks and pipelines

Most organizations have a just-in-time procurement policy to ensure that materials are ready when needed. Recruiting needs to adopt a similar policy by building talent networks and pipelines that allow recruiters to present qualified candidates immediately, especially if the needed skills are well-known and if recruiters have previously recruited for similar roles. No hiring manager should expect to wait weeks for suitable candidates to be presented.

Valuable, robust networks need to meet at least four criteria:

1 They need to be made up of people with similar interests and motivations.
2 They need an instigator, a rebel, a community manager who rouses passions and gets people engaged.
3 They need a large enough number of community managers so that some-one is always 'there' to respond, comment and keep the ball rolling.
4 They need to save time and energy in the screening and interview processes. All in all it needs to add value to the individual that's thinking about joining the organization beyond just joining the organization.

Many networks fail to become significant factors in recruitment because they lack one or more of these criteria. Take a typical recruiter's version of LinkedIn. It probably contains between 400 and 1,000 contacts if the recruiter is slightly above average and has spent some time building their contact list. Most contacts are not personally known to the recruiter and contain a broad spectrum of skills and backgrounds. The recruiter rarely engages the candidates in discussion and learns little about them no matter how long the person has been in their network. Recruiters often pride themselves on the number of LinkedIn connections they have because they focus on quantity, not on how useful those connections are. LinkedIn can be a good source to find talent, but it cannot be described as a talent pool.

Focus is usually necessary and is the first rule for the successful use of networks. An eclectic bunch of disparate people is not a formula for success. No one should be in a network that is not a potential candidate. Therefore, a recruiting network should consist of people with similar or complementary skills. To create such a network, a recruiter needs to know exactly what type of people they are looking for and then spend the time attracting and admitting only them to their community.

A good community adds value to both the individuals joining, who are usually not candidates yet, as well as the organization. A great example of this is the optician chain Specsavers and their Green club. By joining the community, the individuals, usually employees of their major competitors, get access to the e-learning modules for opticians and optometrists that Specsavers already developed for their own employees. This allowed them to not just brand themselves as an employer that cared about their workers' education, but also helped them gather data on their potential candidates. By tracking their behaviours Specsavers was also able to see who might be looking for a new job, as looking at the work culture videos and job openings, which were also on the platform, were good indicators of that. This leads to a win-win situation. The individuals got free training and Specsavers got a great talent pool that not just shortened the time to hire, but also increased the number of hires per recruiter as the time spent on candidates that had no interest in moving dropped significantly.

There also needs to be high levels of interaction and useful conversation. To make sure this happens, a network requires a community manager to foster discussion and engage people in issues that shed light on their interests and skills. If no one comments on posts, agrees or disagrees with a point of view, or adds personal thoughts, most of the value is gone. Creating content, providing information and insider tips, and keeping the community informed of open positions and skills needs are vitally important. Doing this serves two purposes: it encourages candidates with the needed skills to apply and educates others on what skills are being sought.

But a more diverse talent network might be more appropriate depending on the challenges an organization faces. Supply chain models must be adapted to the circumstances and skill needs of the organization.

Succession planning is part of the overall talent management practices in most large American firms and was common in many European businesses in the last century. Succession planning has several advantages and a few disadvantages.

By having several people identified for every key position, the organization is able to fill these roles when vacant with a suitable internal candidate. This helps to ensure that the corporate strategy and culture are maintained and provides a career path that helps with retention. Individuals who are included in the succession plans are usually given additional training and development opportunities to enhance their skills.

There are several disadvantages to succession planning. First of all, whether or not you are chosen as a potential successor is often based on perceived potential, internal politics and personality rather than on skills. The second disadvantage is that it limits the pool of internal candidates to a small number and often discriminates against minorities and women who may not have the visibility, connections or background of those that are chosen. The third disadvantage is that it assumes that the skill needed in the future will be similar or the same as the current skills. With a rapidly changing business environment, it is very hard to identify a skill today that will still be current in three, five or more years. Those chosen often turn out not to be the best choice when a vacancy occurs. A final disadvantage is that development opportunities may not be available to other employees further reducing the pool of skilled workers available for internal promotion.

A great modern example of succession planning is found at the Dutch football club AZ. They are well-known for having lots of great homegrown talents in their first team. They usually rank in the three teams in Europe with the most minutes played in their first team by homegrown players. It's important to note here that football teams train their own talents, unlike in the USA where this happens in colleges and there is a draft, so many of these talents have been with the team since they were in high school. In the case of AZ they have a succession plan for every key position, and of course that includes all 11 players on the field, next to the coach, general manager, trainers and so on. In the case of the players, the youth players know if they are being considered for a spot in the first team and what they have to do to get it. This helps them retain very highly coveted talents as both their possibilities within the club as well as their performance metrics are perfectly clear. It also helps AZ prepare for sudden events from injuries as well as players or critical staff members being bought by competitors, all very common in professional sports.

Recruiting strategy and process

Knowing what talent the organization needs to hire to meet critical business needs is the first step in developing a recruiting strategy. High-volume recruitment requires a different approach than a low-volume one and searching for hard-to-find skills also means a different strategy. There are four separate supply chain models described below that are designed to meet a variety of different needs.

Supply chains models

Supply chains can exist in many different forms. Not every firm needs the same type of supply chain, as some firms hire high volumes of unskilled or semi-skilled people while other firms are looking for a handful of highly skilled experts. In either case, a different model is needed. Many forms will need more than one of these models in place, but each needs a separate focus and approach. It is a mistake to mix these types as that leads to confusion, duplicate effort and less success.

AGILE MODEL – HIRING SCARCE SKILLS

Forecasting demand and supply is useful, when possible, but often the market takes a sudden turn, shifting priorities or requiring skills that were not predicted. This may mean looking for people who are not in your talent network and whose skills have not been anticipated. This would, for example, apply to startups or scale-ups.

In this case an agile talent supply model might be best. The agile supply chain refers to the responsiveness, competency, flexibility and speed in managing the uncertain hiring needs of scarce skills. In this model, only minimal forecasting is possible as the skills needed and demand change rapidly. Talent intelligence and robust search capabilities are critical, as are a wide range of relationships with potential candidates.

Creating and nurturing a highly diverse talent community designed to provide talent and recommend and refer talent can help identify talent, but it also requires a highly developed and sophisticated talent intelligence capability and highly skilled talent sourcing experts. They should have access to artificial intelligence-based software capable of complex global searches.

HR and compensation policies must also be agile and adapt as needs change. Offers must be made quickly and must be customized to individual needs as these skilled people have many other offers and employment opportunities.

FLEXIBLE MODEL – ROUTINE HIRING

Flexible supply chains adapt to relatively predictable customer demands. When organizations plan expansions or introduce new products requiring additional staff, this model allows for quick identification and selection of the needed skills. Forecasting is possible as the skills needed are well-known and it is possible to pre-identify potential talent. The recruiting function needs to be fully aware of corporate plans to expand or shrink the workforce and some idea of the timing of needs. This model would, for example, be fit for manufacturing or customer services firms.

This model relies on multi-skilled recruiters and efficient processes with automated or streamlined assessment and quick offers. A talent community can augment this model and expand its ability to respond quickly. HR policies and compensation can be standardized.

CONTINUOUS-FLOW MODEL – HIGH VOLUME, HIGH TURNOVER

This model is for companies focused on securing employees at the lowest possible cost and high speed. It is also used for high-volume roles such as for call centre personnel or sales associates. Demand is typically seasonal and predictable. Turnover is often high. An example is the Christmas hiring of sales associates for a department store or warehouse staff.

The continuous-flow model aims to deliver a consistent flow of candidates and hires in real-time. The talent network is tuned to supply the needed candidates with minimal search or time. This requires strong marketing, a large and continuously growing talent community, and efficient and highly automated recruitment processes. Screening and assessment can be automated entirely using AI embedded in chatbots and communication tools. In this model, the time to hire should be short. Offers can be made without any interviews or face to face with a recruiter or hiring manager. This model is in use at companies that hire many workers such as Amazon for its warehouses. HR policies and compensation are standardized, and no negotiation is allowed.

GROW YOUR OWN – INTERNAL DEVELOPMENT AND PROMOTION

Historically, a handful of firms – IBM, General Electric, General Motors, McKinsey and others – primarily hired new college graduates or high school graduates and trained them to fit into roles that were needed. They continuously nurtured, trained and mentored these employees while employing them often in a variety of roles.

Managers were encouraged to look for employees with potential or motivation and send them to training. When they completed the training, they were placed in new jobs using those skills and usually also given a pay increase. Over time, almost all positions were filled with internal candidates and external hiring was focused on new graduates and those with interest, motivation and potential.

But to make this model work there needs to be a commitment from senior leadership to this model. There needs to be a culture where internal movement is rewarded and encouraged with managers and human resources aligned and working together to make sure it happens. And there needs to be training programmes and development opportunities that are available and easily accessed.

Recruiting is focused on entry level and university recruitment and on internal mobility.

The role of automation

But for any of these, the backbone of a modern recruiting function is technology. In each step of the recruitment process, there are tools that can improve and augment what we do as humans. Automating parts of the recruiting process benefits job seekers by offering them a more data-based and objective assessment of their capabilities and skills and helps recruiters by lessening their workload and giving them time to focus on finding and engaging candidates.

Figure 3.2 shows where technology can supplement or replace the skills of a recruiter.

Any recruitment process should utilize a variety of tools. If implemented well, they can make the process more efficient and faster while reducing bias and improving diversity in the process. As with all technology, if implemented badly it can make it less efficient and increase bias and reduce diversity. Algorithms can perceive patterns that would be hard for a human to discern and they can make reasonable and data-based decisions or recommendations from hundreds of candidates. Of course, this is only true if the job requirements are clear, accurate and data-based. Many current job descriptions are inaccurate, vague and are filled with wishes more than objective needs. No algorithm will be successful unless their goal is clearly defined and objective.

FIGURE 3.2 Recruitment process

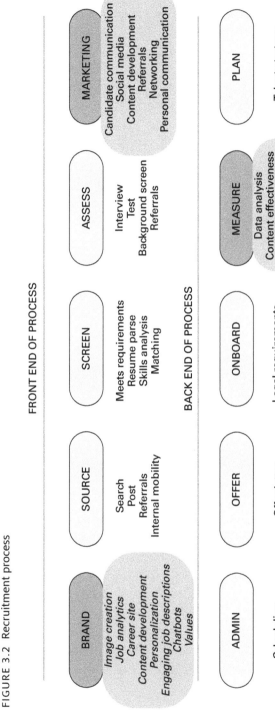

FRONT END OF PROCESS

BRAND
Image creation
Job analytics
Career site
Content development
Personalization
Engaging job descriptions
Chatbots
Values

SOURCE
Search
Post
Referrals
Internal mobility

SCREEN
Meets requirements
Resume parse
Skills analysis
Matching

ASSESS
Interview
Test
Background screen
Referrals

MARKETING
Candidate communication
Social media
Content development
Referrals
Networking
Personal communication

BACK END OF PROCESS

ADMIN
Scheduling
Application
Data input
Legal compliance
Reporting

OFFER
Offer letter
Phone/email confirmation
Start date

ONBOARD
Legal requirements
Introductions

MEASURE
Data analysis
Content effectiveness
Engagement
Metrics reporting
Data anlaysis

PLAN
Talent strategy
Market knowledge
Growth/turnover data

Choosing the right technology for your organization and implementing it well is the key to executing a successful recruitment strategy.

The first rule of automation is that you cannot automate the manual systems you are currently using by duplicating them or replacing them with technology. Implementing technology intelligently combines process mapping and redesign with AI and data analytics.

Some recruiters think that candidates resent not speaking directly with a recruiter, but there is no research that suggests that candidates prefer talking to a recruiter. In fact, some studies suggest candidates prefer chatbots to humans as they are immediately available and responsive; the reality is that most candidates would be fine with interacting with an intelligent and responsive chatbot and algorithm as long as the results were objective and prompt.

Negotiating and hiring

Making an offer is often challenging. Everyone has different expectations, so 'purchasing' talent requires understanding why they want to work for your firm and what they expect to receive. When we face inflationary pressures on wages, the best counter is to stress other benefits, such as ongoing training education, opportunities to work on special projects or travel. The talent community can be an excellent place to influence candidates on the benefits of working for your firm beyond salary.

While people are not 'shipped' in the same way that goods are, they are located in diverse places and not all are willing to relocate. Yet most organizations remain in the mindset that everyone must be located nearby the headquarters or workplace. In this post-pandemic era, it is essential to have a flexible working policy to ensure that talent, wherever it is, can be hired. This will require educating management and changing HR policy to accommodate a more diverse and potentially global workforce.

Negotiations are of course easier if there has been a longer period of 'courtship', like one has in a network or community with frequent meetings. This ensures a higher level of trust as well as a higher understanding of the entire compensation philosophy from the candidate's side.

Data analytics – measuring the success of the recruitment function

Data is the currency of this era and when it is collected and analysed wisely it dispels assumptions and improves efficiency. For recruiters, data analysis can provide insights on who is the best fit for a position and the quality of a hire. But good analysis is hard to do and requires accurate data and the ability to analyse it correctly.

To help understand the potential power of good analysis, the data classification outlined by Tom Davenport, Jeanne Harris and Jeremy Shapiro in an HBR[1] article is useful. It has been adapted for recruiting. It divides talent analytics into six types.

Not many recruiting functions are able to do sophisticated analysis. That will require better data than most functions now have and the employment of a data scientist. The categories here will give you a sense of what is possible and spur more organizations on to invest in improving, collecting and analysing the people data they now have.

1 **Human capital facts:** This includes the basic data that is collected by most talent functions: the number of hires, time to hire, cost per hire and so on. Getting valid data requires good collection techniques, data integrity and integrated systems, which are not the norm for most TA functions. And when this data is lumped together and reported for all recruiters and hiring managers, as it often is, it is almost valueless for good decision making. To be valid the data should be presented for each recruiter and hiring manager and should also include trend data. Even then it would only show what has happened in the past and would not interpret the data. But all other forms of analysis depend on the accuracy of this basic data.

2 **Analytical HR:** This is data collected to gain insights into specific functions or people. For example, each hiring manager's time spent recruiting for a position could be compared to how many people (s)he hired and then further compared to how many of the people hired stayed with the company or got promoted in a period of time. It could include an analysis of the specific skills a recruiter has compared to the time taken to find and assess a candidate. It could include the cost per hire or time to fill for each recruiter compared to the hiring manager involved. This requires a clear understanding of what is going to be measured, over what time period, as well as being sure the data collected is correct. It is also important that correlation is not confused with causation, which might require further analysis and testing.

3 **Human capital investment analytics:** This data indicates which actions have the greatest impact on the business. For example, what action improves employee engagement, what is the impact of onboarding on retention or what effect do the coaching skills of a manager have on performance? This is often referred to as predictive analytics and helps decide where to invest and where improvements should be made. The only talent functions that do this with any rigour are Google and Unilever.

4 **Workforce forecasts:** Data that helps the talent function analyse and forecast future talent needs. This is really a form of strategic workforce planning and requires access to the firm's strategic plans, good data on the supply of specific skills, data on turnover, internal mobility and promotions, the impact of training programmes and much more. This is a complex task and one often frustrated by sudden changes in the business or economy. Probably very few talent functions will ever be able to do a good job of analysis in this area.

5 **Talent value model:** This data helps understand why employees choose to stay with a company. What specific practice, manager or programme, for example, influences an employee to leave or stay? It helps to decide whether to make a counteroffer to an employee who is leaving or to proactively intervene to prevent a resignation.

6 **Talent supply chain:** Highly complex data analysis is required for this level. This data helps determine which positions should be permanent and which ones could be filled with a contractor, temporary or outsourced staff. The data indicates which positions deliver the most value to the organization. This requires objective definitions of value and raises ethical concerns. However, its impact on profits and productivity could be large. No one can do this level of analytics yet.

Analytics will be the most important aspect of recruiting after automation. Just finding and hiring people is not enough if you cannot objectively show value. If you are only gathering and using the basic level of reporting human capital facts, you will need to up your game to remain effective.

Over the past few decades, there has been a growing focus on quantification and measurement. Every academic and commercial entity attempts to measure even those things that are perhaps better left to judgement or that need nuanced thinking and contextual understanding.

There is a belief that numbers are objective, easy to understand and provide 'hard' evidence. We believe we can hold people accountable more readily to a set of numbers than to good judgement or opinion. But unfortunately, just because we can measure something does not mean it is useful. Similar to what Jerry Muller says in his book *The Tyranny of Metrics*, there is often an unexamined assumption when gathering data that sharing that data widely will result in improvements of some sort...[2]

Recruiters gnash their teeth over how hard it is to gather the data they need to generate reports and create metrics dashboards. And there are discussions on what metrics should be reported and which should be reported to senior leadership.

Benchmark reports abound and questions are asked about the number of interviews that should be conducted, or the number of people there should be on a recruitment interview panel. Other questions focus on time or costs or quality.

All this is done with the belief that these metrics matter and that someone cares about them. We assume that these metrics are valid, useful and necessary. But are they? They are reported because everyone else does and rarely do any recruitment leaders question them or challenge the assumptions they are based on. Recruiting metrics reports are often only glanced at or never looked at all, and it is even rarer when there is significant feedback.

Part of the reason for this may be that the metrics are not seen as relevant, or they do not give a credible picture of the effectiveness of the talent acquisition function.

We believe that if metrics were more focused, relevant and offered the information leaders care about, they would then be examined and used to improve the recruitment process.

But measuring the effectiveness of people as opposed to things like sales, production throughput or widgets produced is difficult and subject to biases, manipulation and potential misuse. Is it right to measure the effectiveness of recruiting by counting numbers and time? The semi-standard primary set of metrics that recruiters use – cost per hire, time to fill and quality of hire – seem valid and important at first glance. But we will argue that these are neither useful nor effective metrics. Nor do they hold much interest to leaders. We will then suggest some metrics that may be more useful.

The basics

Organizations have become fixated on metrics. From performance management systems to recruitment, we believe that numbers are more objective and fairer than human judgement, experience or even common sense. In some cases, this may be true, but we often report on things that cannot or should not be measured. The fewer and more focused the metrics are, the better. To report lots of numbers for the sake of reporting is a waste of time.

Five requirements

There are five requirements that valid, valuable and useful metrics should meet. First, they need to be as objective as possible. It is easy to pick only the numbers that support the arguments you want to make or to omit the annoying data points that disrupt what you wish to report. Truly meaningful metrics must be generated from data that cannot easily be manipulated and are not merely the opinions of people.

Secondly, it is common practice to report metrics that are readily available or easy to compute but may not be informative or useful. A good metric must tell us something useful about things that can be improved to increase performance or output. Just because a set of numbers is available does not mean it should be reported. If they simply report on things that we cannot impact or provide factual data that is nonactionable, they are of little use.

Thirdly, metrics must be presented as trend data showing how we are doing over time. A single data point tells nothing but showing data about how we are doing over weeks or months can be useful.

Fourthly, they must be measures we can control and significantly or totally influence. Recruiters are frequently reporting metrics, such as time to fill, that are mainly in the control of the candidate or hiring manager.

And fifthly and most importantly, whatever metrics are reported must be meaningful to those who ask for them. They must tell leaders something vital to their success and that of the organization.

Let's examine three commonly reported metrics – cost per hire, time to fill and quality of hire – and see if they meet the requirements set out above for good metrics, or if they show how well recruiters are finding, attracting and influencing potential candidates.

COST PER HIRE

Cost per hire, as usually reported, is a metric that we find particularly questionable for several reasons.

First of all, whatever it costs us in time or money to influence and ultimately hire a person that invents a new product, procures a patent, fixes a major problem or comes up with the great idea is well-spent.

Using an old analogy, whatever it cost to hire Magic Johnson for the Lakers was trivial compared to his overall contribution to the team and the sport. This is often true of many other people as well.

The cost to find, attract and influence a candidate is irrelevant if the hiring manager is satisfied.

To report cost per hire regularly serves no useful purpose and hinders focus on the more significant need of finding the best person possible for the role.

In addition, we have found that the cost per hire for a particular role rarely varies very much (other than accounting for inflation). The costs hover around a mean, making the exact figure virtually meaningless. As a rule, junior people cost less to hire than more senior people.

And finally, this figure is often used as a benchmark to compare performance between organizations. However, the variables included in definitions of cost per hire are different in every organization. There is no standard, and this makes comparisons inaccurate and misleading.

Measuring cost is an example of the Band Wagon Fallacy – everyone measures cost, so it must be useful, and we are expected to report it. It is also relatively easy to measure, which may partially account for its popularity. But is it actionable? What can you do to reduce that cost significantly? In most cases, very little because a significant portion of the costs are fixed, including salaries, general overhead, equipment and licences. Does senior leadership care more about cost or about the contributions a new employee makes?

SPEED OR TIME TO FILL

Speed is important when you are in competition for talent. The recruiters who can find and attract top candidates and make offers quickly often win. But speed needs to be qualified with added words like 'speed to present', 'speed to find', 'speed to screen' or 'speed to offer'.

Choosing the measure of speed that recruiters can control is critical and should not be overly complicated or get bogged down in trivial details. Focus on what elements of speed pays the highest dividends.

Finding the best or the right person may not be easy and take time, but an effective recruiter would have a pool of potential candidates before the need to recruit.

Proactive sourcing is the best way to ensure that you can quickly meet a hiring manager's need. Your focus should be on metrics that track how quickly you are prepared to present candidates.

Time to fill is not a good measure because it violates one of our five conditions: it is not entirely in the control of recruiters. Candidates take time to respond; managers take time to provide feedback; administrative issues cloud the issue. Recruiters only control one element of this: the time to present a candidate to the hiring manager.

QUALITY OF HIRE

So, this brings us to the quality of hire. Out of all the metrics, is this the most important?

Not really, and not because we don't think quality is important. The challenge is defining what we mean when we say that one candidate is 'better' than another.

Who determines quality, and how can it be measured?   Quality of hire cannot be measured with numbers in the same way as we measure manufactured products that have exact specifications. In manufacturing, quality is not about perfection or opinion; it is about reducing variations from one product or another. In the context of recruiting, this would mean reducing the variations/differences in skills between candidates as much as possible for a similar position. Taken to the extreme, this means hiring people who are virtual clones of each other.

This is the inherent danger of using artificial intelligence to determine who is the best candidate. AI can only match people to jobs based on specific data such as degree, skills or previous experience. We assume these are the best indicators of quality or performance, but research suggests that they are not. It is not possible to define human quality in a way that can be objective, consistent or meaningfully connected to the recruitment process.

Trying to find candidates who are very similar to each other works against reducing diversity and potentially leads to groupthink, and less innovation. If the job we are hiring someone to do is easily defined and quantifiable, perhaps a robot or automated software would be a better choice than a human.

The hiring manager decides the ultimate quality of a candidate, and his criteria are often intangible and determined months or even years after someone is hired. Every hire is judged by a different standard according to the manager and the circumstances of the job.

So, without a defined, consistent and objective measure correlated to quality, we are left with subjective judgement. We all have been in situations when one manager thinks an employee is great, and another manager feels the opposite.

Many intangible factors such as general ability, personality and motivation may be more important. But these are hard to measure.

Some of the other measures that purport to measure quality also have significant flaws.

PRODUCTIVITY

One of the flaws is to attempt to measure how quickly a new hire is productive. The first challenge is to decide that productivity is more important than judgement or innovation or learning. The second challenge is to define what productive means.

This is very hard to do for managerial positions where the output is not tangible. On top of this, how do you tie how productive someone is to the hiring process? The variables that influence productivity include his or her manager, training, the work environment, the new employee's teammates and the corporate culture. There are too many variables to say that the recruiting process alone causes or even has any real impact on performance.

And why is the speed to productivity so important? Perhaps an in-depth understanding of the work by observing and learning and getting a thorough grasp of details that take time to master might be more critical. Good decision making or judgement might trump speed.

PERFORMANCE

Some recruiters measure quality by looking at a new hire's performance rating (assuming your firm still has performance ratings). Once more, this is a *post hoc, ergo propter hoc* fallacy. It does not follow that recruitment leads to poor or good performance.

There are too many other variables that affect performance far more than recruitment. Performance ratings are subjective and depend as much on personality, and the relationship the new hire and the manager have with each other than on actual performance. Many organizations have recently abandoned performance ratings because they are not objective, increase employee dissatisfaction and do not help improve performance.

TURNOVER

And finally, we often see turnover rates used as a measure of quality. Whether someone leaves is much more likely to be caused by the manager, economics, the corporate culture or some other factor than because of the type of person recruited.

Even assuming recruitment makes some difference, the real question is, how much difference? Is the difference enough to justify the extremes we go through to determine someone's capabilities? We believe that the ultimate responsibility for quality of hire lies with the hiring manager and not with recruitment and is a subjective judgement.

As mentioned in our first condition of a good metric, each one should be as free from judgement, opinion and bias as is possible.

SO WHAT CAN WE MEASURE?

Here are several suggestions that give a better picture of the effectiveness of recruiting.

Senior leadership metrics

- How effective is TA in attracting needed talent?
- Number of active applicants
- Number hired from competition
- Job posting effectiveness (# of qualified vs unqualified candidates who apply)
- Capability to hire critical skills
- Size and variety of talent pool
- Breadth and depth of our talent map
- Ratio of offers to accept
- Time to present candidates with critical skills and abilities

Hiring manager metrics

- Hours/days to provide feedback to recruiters on candidates presented
- How many of the job criteria in the job description did the new hire meet? (criteria asked for/criteria hired)
- Candidates per hire (# interviewed/offers extended)
- Number of diverse candidates interviewed/offers (internal and external)

Candidate-centric metrics

- Time spent matching to/searching for a position
- Time (minutes) needed to apply for a position

- Number who do not complete the application process and why
- Candidate rating/feedback on ease of applying
- Candidate rating/feedback on overall recruiting experience
- How many hours/days until the candidate gets a response to their CV with feedback?
- How many days does it take until the candidate gets a decision about the next steps?

Recruiter/sourcing metrics

- Number of qualified candidates available when a requisition is received
- Cost of per acquisition
- Completeness of talent map of competition by critical role
- Percentage of candidates presented to the manager within a given timeframe of receiving the requisition
- Ratio of candidates presented/offers extended
- Number of connections and relationships with external people who have the skills required for specific positions
- Number of people with relevant skills and capability in the talent pool
- Number of diverse candidates attracted to the career site
- Number of diverse candidates in talent pool/pipeline

The metrics we have suggested focus on numbers, ratios, time and purpose. These are elements recruiters and hiring managers can control and can be held accountable for. They are only suggestions and certainly need to be vetted, examined and tested. Cost tells you very little about value or quality. Quality is the byproduct of good manager decision-making.

Supply chain thinking

Thinking like a supply chain manager rather than a recruiter can dramatically change the success of a recruitment function. Supply chain thinking in talent acquisition would start with better planning and forecasting, anticipating the future talent needs of the organization. It would allow the TA department to partner with external talent providers instead of buying ad hoc or develop the talent themselves if talent providers are too limited for the expected demand. It would change recruitment from being in the rejection business to being in the community business and keeping in touch with all potential talent, even those that are not selected the first time around. Supply chain thinking would make TA a long-term focused strategic department instead of the now short-term focused operational department.

TAKEAWAYS

- It is useful to think about recruiting as a supply chain, there are steps in the supply chain and each is critical to success.

- Just as with physical objects, recruiters need a plan, a way to source candidates, a warehouse of continuous supply source, a hiring process that is effective, a negotiation and closing process that is efficient and a way to measure success.

- These steps each require expertise and practices that produce the desired results.

- There are several models of supply chains: agile, flexible, continuous-flow and grow your own.

- Thinking about recruiting as a supply chain can broaden and improve the effectiveness of a recruiting function.

THE STORY OF PURE FOODS*

Pure Foods was a supermarket chain that started from the growing consumer demand for healthy natural foods that was accelerated by the EU's healthy habitat programme, which made more Europeans think about their food and environment. Pure Foods gained a lot of traction after the polluted chicken scandal just a year after they started, as it grew consumer consciousness on healthy and sustainable food even more. They combined a cheap online delivery service for bigger orders with massive shops that had excellent service but slightly higher prices offline. The service they offered on site was beyond anything that any supermarket had ever offered before. People behind the fish counters knew the fish, their taste and what wine went best with it. There was always one person at the vegetable section with the same knowledge as a greengrocer had in the old days. The butcher could tell you about every piece of meat he had and the cheese department was stacked with a really rich assortment of cheeses and of course a cheese expert to assist you if needed.

Their brick and mortar strategy was extremely successful and their local sourcing of many of their perishable goods gave them a unique position among the growing group of environmentally aware customers and also freed them from the farmer protests that emerged all over Europe in their early days. While they started out in the USA they quickly set up mega stores in the UK, France, Spain, Portugal, Germany and slowly moved all over Europe. Their mega stores served as both stores and as regional online distribution centres. While they started with human drivers, they were early to adopt self-driving cars and drone technology to deliver groceries in wide regions around the stores. They realized their unique concept of mega stores serving as distribution centres would require unique transportation, so they co-developed unique small vehicles that not only optimized their logistics, but also their brand awareness.

Martin started as the Head of Talent Acquisition for France as soon as they set foot in that country. Having done such an amazing job in his first years he was appointed to the newly created position of Global Head of TA only a few years after. By appointing a Frenchman as their first global head of TA, Pure Foods showed they truly believed in being a global brand, not an American brand gone global. Because in France the permanent contract is still the norm and Martin wanted Pure Foods to have a positive employer brand, he hired mainly workers on permanent contracts. Because Pure Foods needed to train many of their hires themselves, as there was no surplus supply of knowledgeable greengrocers, fish experts and so on in every location, he needed to make sure he selected the right people from the start.

The Pure Foods talent strategy

Pure Foods' talent strategy was a simple one: hire on talent, teach skills. Talent for Pure Foods meant the potential to become something, based on both cognitive skills as well as attitude. Pure Foods didn't believe there was a shortage of talent in the world, only talent with the right credentials. So in order to solve this they decided to train their staff themselves and create an internal talent pool.

Soon Pure Foods was known as the place to start your career. They recruited as much internally as possible, using their stores as a recruitment tool. Their internal academy was unparalleled, especially in the world of retail and a 'Pure Career' had become a globally recognized employer brand. Pure Foods was known for developing talent and hiring from within, while not paying top dollar. Some competitors called them the 'Pure University', as their employees were hunted regularly, but Pure Foods saw this as a strength, rather than a problem.

Their alumni network was immensely strong and opened many doors for all kinds of collaborations. In addition, every employee was required to work a certain number of months for every course or study they received. Of course they could leave, but if they did they were required to repay part of the education. Often when they were headhunted they would receive a signing bonus for that amount. This way the Pure University was partly paid for by other organizations. As this strategy also meant they had relatively low attrition compared to their peers and recruitment and onboarding can easily go up to 25 per cent of the salary, the total costs for recruitment and L&D combined were not higher than their competitors. Their service levels, customer satisfaction and hence the money spent by customers was much higher than that of other supermarkets.

The early years

Martin came from the world of volume recruitment and knew that in France attrition was high as wages were low in stores. France had been going though many labour market renewals in recent years, but unions were blocking most of the necessary reforms. The generation of Baby Boomers was retiring, but there just wasn't enough talent to replace them. Or was there? The first thing Martin did was something that was hardly seen in France at that time, but something he had seen presented at international conferences. He was going to hire all retail staff based on aptitude testing alone. He knew he could start using the data they already collected in the US, but might need to adjust it to regional preferences. He started using pre-selection tests and instead of relying on one test, he worked with two simultaneously. Using both situational judgement tests as well as a basic chatbot with linguistics he created a wealth of data pre-hire. He made sure from the get-go that the system had a feedback loop and a deep learning algorithm making sure it would get smarter with each decision made, no matter if the hire or training worked out or not. The algorithm would learn from both.

Although this was initially created for hiring retail staff based on attitude, this early decision turned out to be the best foundation for the career strategy Pure developed later on. The general idea in the beginning was to select people best suited for fish advice, wine advice or general logistics, for example, and to see if potential assistant manager and shop manager profiles could be detected early on. This helped Pure Foods not just recruit for the job someone was applying for, but straight away show them their potential within the organization.

For each new country added, the model was reused, starting with the data of the country culturally closest to it, but quickly adapting to new data collected with each hire and sometimes the model was trained not just on a country level but a regional level.

Non-retail staff were hired the more traditional way at first, but as much of the procurement was done locally as well, using local farmers and producers for as many perishable goods as possible, the training and growth model soon started expanding and so an internal talent marketplace was launched. The uniqueness of this marketplace was that each employee profile contained the personality data of that person, next to their experience and ambitions. So when the Lyon centre was looking for a new head of procurement which wasn't available, it would first look at the internal talent marketplace and see that in the Paris or Bordeaux centre there was someone with the potential to become head of procurement, the experience as a procurement officer and the desire to move to Lyon, and then simply hire internally. The success of this marketplace quickly reached the main office in the US and became the company standard.

The later years

Pure Foods became a household name in much of Europe and expanded rapidly. Although their number of stores was very limited compared to their major competitors, their market share was not. With self-driving cars, drone technology and the likes changing the world of grocery deliveries the time had finally come for Pure Foods. The technology was now there to deliver on their dream and their promise, but they also realized no off-the-shelf solution would ever be as good as they wanted it. This meant they needed to develop their own unique delivery technology.

Martin had been promoted to Global Head of Talent, as his system in France had delivered low attrition, high mobility and wages that were on par with industry average. The system for high-volume recruitment had been working well, but Martin's dream had always been to turn their shops into recruitment channels for not just the operations part but the back office also.

They already had a major IT department that had developed their logistics and planning software, but now it needed to add an engineering department. Of course they were not going to develop every bit of technology from scratch, but as they needed to have their own unique delivery system in order to be competitive and not get pushed down to the lowest price, an engineering department was set up. Pure Foods decided on the 'aeroplane development model'. The general design, requirements and limitation are set by Pure Foods.

Different suppliers can develop parts and co-create better solutions, as long as it fits the general framework. All suppliers keep their own intellectual property, but the IP of the final product lies with Pure Foods, keeping their competitive advantage.

The IT department had been fully distributed from the start, as IT talent wasn't scarce as long as you didn't care about the passport of the person. If you offer decent US wages, not even top-level Silicon Valley wages, to Russians, Indians or Romanians living in their own countries you had no issue finding excellent staff and that is what Pure Foods did. Of course cultural integration had been an issue and so rigorous testing on corporate values and continuous monitoring of these values had been a part of the process that had been in place for some time. Martin decided that the new engineering team would follow the same principles and be fully distributed, with rigorous testing on both technical skills as well as alignment with the values of the company.

But with so many new jobs opening up, worldwide labour market shortages with the right engineering skills, he decided it was time to try and realize his dream and make the stores the recruiting grounds for the entire company. This started with asking youngsters to register their studies and graduation dates, so they could be approached for other jobs nearing graduation. Pure Foods always considered it a benefit to have hands-on experience on the frontline of their business. As Martin was an avid gamer himself, he knew game skills showed great correlation with job potential and just adding your gaming profiles was an easy first step. Based on either the game skills, acquired in normal games played for fun, Pure Foods was able to predict job potential. Because not all employees had the opportunity to attend university, Martin decided to create the Pure University offering courses on the most in-demand internal skills. This quickly grew and became a world-leading learning and development system, which had direct links to the talent acquisition. As the data from employees successfully finishing courses was looped back into the system, the hiring algorithm improved over time on assessing candidates on their potential skills.

Because not all applicants and employees were gamers, Martin also used next generation cognitive testing that would test for the same results as using game data. An employee would be able to use these aptitude tests to get access to the training modules as well, but Pure Foods was strict in allowing access. There was no use letting people do training if they didn't have the cognitive traits. At Pure Foods you shouldn't be able to just do a job, you should be able to be good at that job. Pure Foods' L&D motto was: Everybody has talent, but not for every job. Because of the strict policies Pure Foods had on training only those with enough talent to be good at the job, a Pure University accreditation, although not officially recognized by any government, quickly became something many competitors considered very desirable. So Pure Foods created a system that would allow all employees to take the training they qualified for, but receiving accreditation would require them to stay at the company for a certain amount of time, depending on the sort of training they received. If they handed in their notice before this time, which was usually between one and five years, they would need to pay a significant exit fee. This lead to many staff demanding serious sign-on bonuses, creating less attrition, but also funding for the university programme.

Pure Foods also launched an AI coaching tool that helped employees with their career perspectives as well as temporary issues they might face, both personally and work related. This ensured their staff kept a healthy balance and stayed mentally sane. As Pure Careers was the goal, they needed to make sure people would reach retirement in a healthy manner. Although every employee knew the bot was an AI, many treated it like a co-worker and felt that the bot checking in was a great thing, especially since much of the teams were fully distributed. Since the AI got to know the employee over time, it felt more human than most and eventually Pure opened it up for retirees as they felt they lost a friend after they retired.

As the demand for Pure Foods employees grew, management was putting more pressure on restricting access to the Pure University, but Martin was data-driven and showed how the cost benefit analyses worked out. He even offered a skills passport for every employee, making it easy to show the skills and credentials built up during their time at Pure Foods. It didn't take long before employees that moved to other organizations started updating these passports and demanding other employers to credit them for skills gained elsewhere. Since Martin was smart enough to make it really easy to link this skills passport to the alumni community, his recruiters knew which alumni was developing which skills and were able to source skills gained with other employers. Because this was a relatively structured community with structured skills, it was also the perfect place to start working with an AI virtual assistant for sourcing. Whenever a job opened that was hard to fill internally, and of course there were still plenty of those, the AI virtual assistant would look at the alumni community for the relevant skills, considering the reason and the time since this person left and would suggest an alumni to the recruiter. Not long after the initial launch the AI virtual assistant was so good at identifying the perfect alumni it was allowed to approach them even without a human in the loop. Training the AI to do the same with public profiles took a lot longer and had many unfortunate mistakes, some of which made headlines in newspapers. Eventually it did have a high success rate though. Over 85 per cent of the candidates the AI approached understood why the virtual assistant suggested this job for them and was triggered by the personalized approach. This was the moment when talent acquisition at Pure Foods became all about persuading the candidate this was the perfect move for them, rather than finding the candidate and getting this person to talk to you as a recruiter.

This is a fictional scenario on talent acquisition in the near future.

Endnotes

1   *Harvard Business Review* (2010) Competing on talent analytics, October, hbr. org/2010/10/competing-on-talent-analytics (archived at https://perma.cc/32A7-Y3E6)

2   Muller, JZ (2018) *The Tyranny of Metrics*, Princeton University, New Jersey

4

Talent attraction

In this chapter, we'll dive deeply into what most people see as 'core recruiting': talent attraction. Of course, talent acquisition is much broader than the attraction piece. Still, it is the sexiest part, the best visible part and the part that TA professionals usually have the most influence over.

Sourcing

In general, there are two primary ways to engage with candidates: one-on-one and one-to-many. In recruitment we call these sourcing and advertising. Within these two main categories there are different flavours. Sourcing can be done by a specialist, called a sourcer, who focuses only on finding people with the required skills, or we can find people via referrals from employees, our social networks and through advertising.

Employer branding has had a rocky place in recruitment. Many firms rely on the corporate brand to attract candidates while other firms use specialized recruitment marketing experts. As firms scramble to find and hire the talent they need, there has been more emphasis on developing targeted messaging to let potential candidates know that their skills are relevant and needed. Many candidates do not realize that their skills might be attractive to an employer who has not traditionally hired people with those skills. For example, an oil pipelines company may now need employees who can build and install leak detection equipment or detect if the software that regulates flow through the pipeline is being hacked. This requires them to hire people with skills not historically needed. A bank like ING actually rebranded itself on the job market as an IT company in banking in order to become more attractive to IT engineers; just as Tesla says it builds computers that happen to drive on the road.

All of these aspects of talent attraction have been influenced by technology over the past decade and will radically change over the next decade through developments in AI.

Identifying candidates

The internet changed the way firms find candidates. LinkedIn was the first and now one of the largest and most used sources to find professional candidates. Although LinkedIn has become the winner on the global stage, regional players still exist like Xing in Germany, Viadeo in France and Goldenline in Poland.

Before LinkedIn, using specialists to go out and directly find talent was something only done for executive functions. These specialists, sometimes called headhunters, mainly used their proprietary databases and contacts. Sourcing people for technical, professional and specialist roles has now become the norm and isn't undertaken only by external agencies. Companies like Facebook, Apple and Google have their own sourcing teams and many corporations have a few sourcers and expect recruiters to also do some sourcing.

Sourcers use many diverse data sources. If everybody is hunting on LinkedIn, you might as well go hunting somewhere else. Savvy sourcers leverage databases from coding communities like Github and Stack Overflow, comb through event attendance lists, examine design credits and search scientific publications for the names of people they might be interested in. Well-trained sourcers can use all types of channels. They use sophisticated Boolean searches and other techniques. But technology has emerged that is even better at this.

Artificial intelligence-powered technology can augment searches by using algorithms to comb the internet and other sources quickly, and then rank those it finds according to their skills, experience and other factors. This allows almost anyone who can use this software – a recruiter, HR business partner or even a hiring manager – to become a good hunter of talent. Casting a wider net also helps find more potentially suitable candidates.

These tools can search a wide number of networks quickly. Knowing exactly how to query every network and what terms are best used to query is what tools such as Amazing Hiring, Seekout, HireEZ and Talentwunder have mastered. Amazing Hiring, for example, focuses on IT candidates. Hence it knows how to search all sorts of sites where IT people hang out, while Talentwunder specializes in scientists and can search scientific publication databases. Technology can help the sourcer find candidates by developing and applying expert knowledge. Very few recruiters are subject matter experts in the field they are recruiting for, nor do they know how to query the websites where the candidates hang out.

AI is also able to learn as it goes by refining its search criteria based on the candidates that are accepted and rejected. It learns what a recruiter or a hiring manager is looking for without making it explicit. AI tools can also search at much greater speed. Recruit Robin, for example, isn't a tool that has in-depth knowledge of any specific market and isn't a tool to search for the hardest to find candidates, but it helps recruiters who often look for the same profile, whether it is for nurses or electronic technicians. Saving specific search criteria and algorithms helps a recruiter not to repeat the same search over and over again. It also allows for a decrease of the time needed to contact a potential candidate by showing the recruiter the new candidates much faster.

Finding a candidate is only useful if the search results include contact details such as their email or phone. Technology is also extremely helpful because by searching multiple sources it can provide greater accuracy.

The ability for AI to find talent and identify specific skills will only get better over time. Every interaction is a learning point and the more interactions and feedback it has the greater its accuracy and value.

Reaching out to candidates

When it comes to the outreach, technology can play different roles depending on the type of position and the 'power structure' between the candidate and the organization – candidates with unique and in-demand skill sets have a different relationship with recruiters than those that have more general skills. From the organizational perspective we call this high-volume vs specialist recruitment.

High-volume recruiting

In high-volume recruiting where there lots of candidates, chatbots using conversational AI are already at a level where they can initiate a conversation, answer questions and determine basic qualifications. And they can also schedule a call with a human recruiter or an interview.

Amazon has fully automated the screening process for its warehouse staff and hires people without any human contact or intervention. In a tighter labour market like the Netherlands, staffing firm Young Capital early in the pandemic when searching for track and tracers had AI technology called Scotty do the initial phone screen, ask qualification questions to determine if a person was interested in the job, if they were able to join when needed and were in possession of a laptop. If the person answered yes, the system would schedule a call with a human recruiter. Because the recruiter in the phone screen didn't have to spend time checking if the candidate was available, interested and technically qualified, they were able to spend more time focusing on whether the candidate had the relevant social skills, resulting in a much higher quality of hire.

Specialist recruiting

When candidates are scarce and when they have several options because of their skills, it will take more to persuade them to even start a conversation. Generative AI such as ChatGPT might be useful in these situations. Generative AI might start a conversation and provide information and marketing messaging to attract the potential candidate to move forward and connect with a human.

Although generative AI can write outreach messages as well as an average recruiter, no AI can write as well as an exceptional one and it probably never will. In the near future the outreach messages will become even more personalized by using AI to tailor the message to the candidate by using personality assessment based on social media profiles like Crystal Knows. A risk-averse person, for example, could get a reference about the stability of the company while a more status-driven candidate would get messages about how prestigious the company is. Creating personalized landing pages and offers is of course also possible, taking information from a candidate's LinkedIn page and adding that to the landing page created specifically for that one candidate.

Currently technology already assists sourcers with follow-up messages and drip campaigns, making sure it's not just a single outreach, but an entire campaign for that one candidate. These campaigns are predesigned by the sourcer, but in the future AI will adjust the time between messages, perhaps even the media of the messages, combining LinkedIn messages, emails and text messages, according to what it has learned from other similar candidates.

Referrals

Referrals are people recommended by employees. Many firms offer employees cash or other incentives to recommend potential hires with needed skills for a specific role. These are called active referrals. In some organizations there is a big debate about offering cash rewards and there is no one right way to go about this. The reward should fit the organizational culture. In most organizations this is cash, but some offer a donation to a charity of the employee's choice, while others offer a weekend trip, including half a day off, a fancy dinner or a day to a major theme park.

In most cases, the employee has spoken with the person they recommend and know that the person is interested in talking to a recruiter or a hiring manager about the open position.

AI can help employees make referrals by listing the specific skills needed. It can also help with writing an initial message to the potential referral, making it easier for an employee to reach out, but the final decision will need to be human made.

A passive referral is when an employee shares content and jobs on a social network such as LinkedIn. This can potentially attract a candidate to the job. This is an interesting way to leverage employee networks and get free exposure.

AI can help employees by showing the open positions that best fit their background and providing relevant content that an employee can share to attract people. These types of referrals can also be tracked and rewarded.

Branding and marketing

In the world of talent acquisition, the employer brand has never been more critical, yet it's also never been more out of the control of the organization. Social media has given candidates unlimited powers to get bad experiences out. Employer branding has never been owned by talent acquisition or the employer brand manager, but in the modern world it's even more out of their hands. Employer brand managers can, as James Ellis, the author of *Talent Chooses You, Hire Better with Employer Branding*, puts it, 'influence, direct and guide, but never decide' on the employer brand. Every manager, the CEO, mayor or minister makes decisions that influence the perception that others have of your company. That's your employer brand, what other people think it's like to work at your company. And make no mistake, every organization has one. It could be based on perceptions in the media, it could be based on interactions people had with people in your organization, like your customer service staff or truck drivers, or it could be based on something as simple as your company name and sometimes the sector you are in is enough. What are the first thoughts that pop into your mind when I ask you what it's like to work at a bank? At a government agency? At a startup? That's the baseline of your employer brand and it's different for everybody reading this – some people love a steady government job while others love the fast-paced, high-risk startup companies. Your employer brand is different for different people and you don't want to attract everybody, just the people that fit best.

Jeff Bezos said that your brand is what people say about you when you've left the room. That's why monitoring of review pages and social media is important and provides you data about your true employer brand. You cannot control social media, or media in general. It is helpful to know the true perception of your brand. There are several data providers that are, for the larger brands, able to identify your brand and brand attractiveness for different groups. That data can be very useful as well.

So although your employer brand is out of your control, you can influence it. It's important to identify what sets you apart from your peers, both your direct competitors and your labour market competitors, and consciously work on getting those messages out there. Employer branding isn't a campaign, an ad or great videos or photos. It's the foundation of all of that. It's the fundamental message that underpins it all. And if the employer brand is genuinely in line with the company values, all management decisions on what behaviours to accept and who to fire, for example, are in line with this brand. As an employer brand professional you might not control the brand, but you can influence and guide it. Especially in the stages where people are actively looking at your company as a potential employer. You can make sure all the messages are coherent, aligned and consistent. So when a candidate starts looking at your organization, he or she will understand what its core values are.

The employer brand has never been more important than in the current day and age. With so much automation at our fingertips and money being so cheap, it's easier to create a business than ever in the history of mankind. That means people, talent, unique individuals working well together in a team are the only things that can separate a struggling company from a successful one. Talented people will want to work for companies with strong employer brands. Talented people want to work with other talented people that adhere to their values. Every employer brand should attract and repel candidates.

Brand DNA

The employer brand starts with your brand DNA. What are the core values of your organization? This should be three or a maximum of four values that are truly lived within the organization. True values are those that are rewarded, so it helps to look at the reward and promotion policies to determine these values.

For example, an organization that has family values or values work-life balance should have a very generous family leave policy and flexible working arrangements. If an organization has innovation as its core value, but rewards risk-averse behaviour and only meeting financial targets, there is a misalignment.

Although brand DNA is usually based on very broad and ambiguous values, a modern brand DNA comes with behaviours that fit those values. Tangible behaviours on how to deal with a critical incident based on the core value makes it tangible and measurable in order to recruit by value fit.

Of course it's possible that the same value has different behaviours in different markets or even business units. For example, a core value of innovation could mean 'experiment and fail fast' in the marketing department, but 'set up frameworks before it becomes a law' for the legal department.

The essence of your brand DNA is of course that it needs to be lived by the current organization. A true brand value isn't something to aspire to, but something that is part of the organization. One way to get to these values is to have someone, usually an external person as people tend to be more honest with them, ask employees what stories they tell their friends and family about their employer. These employees should be selected based on the fact that their behaviour reflects the type of behaviour that the organization likes to see in their employees. From these stories values can be extracted by looking at common denominators.

Your brand DNA is the building block that your employer brand is built with, and it should always be in line with the brand values of your consumer brand. Your brand DNA is like a human's DNA – the building blocks you have to work with. Your employee value proposition are the elements of that DNA you choose to emphasize and that separate you from others; in humans we call this your talents and your character. Your employer brand is how others perceive those talents and the character.

Employee value proposition

The employee value proposition (EVP) is the differentiator between you and your competitors. These can be your direct competitors or your labour market competitors. It's important to remember that you don't just compete with your competitors for talent, you also compete heavily with organizations outside your direct competitors. Sales, marketing, IT and finance people work in pretty much every organization and hence can work for every organization. So when defining differentiating factors it's not just against your direct competitors.

Your EVP can be best described as your promise to future employees. There are four criteria that an EVP will need to be in order to be successful:

1   **True and believable**

    Of course, you need to make true promises, but not everything that is true is also believable. Hence making it very specific is often necessary in order to make it believable.

2   **Sustainable**

    We don't mean sustainable in the environmental sense of the word, we mean it needs to last for a long time. An EVP doesn't change overnight and it can't change every couple of years. You cannot change your promise too often or it will automatically become unbelievable. It works best if these values are linked to your brand DNA values. And they can't be contradictory.

3   **Attractive**

    Of course, they need to be attractive, but what is attractive to one group might not be as attractive to another. For some people hard well-paid work is very attractive; others like a good work-life balance. Attractiveness is in the eye of the beholder. That doesn't mean you cannot use the values, but in the execution of your marketing you need to differentiate between target audiences. Your brand DNA is the same for all employees, but the values from your EVP you communicate to different audiences can differ.

4   **Differentiating**

    Your value proposition needs to set you apart from other companies that your prospective talent might be thinking of joining. So they need to be differentiating. Of course again in the execution you can choose what value differentiates you from specific competitors.

Your EVP is the total of the values you offer employees to give their time and knowledge to your organization. These are the long-term sustainable values that perks will be built upon. Not every value needs to have a significance for every target audience; it's the toolkit that helps you build perks and communicate them.

Candidate attraction

Your brand is the foundation on which your marketing strategy is built. Your strategy needs to be in line with your brand DNA and in the execution of this strategy you can use your EVP.

There are many tactical choices when it comes to recruitment marketing. One thing that is essential for every recruitment marketing campaign is a great job ad. There are three types of marketing related to talent acquisition.

There is the **employer branding** which is an ongoing process, whether you invest in it or not. Employer branding is what people think of your organization. Your brand isn't totally under the control of the head of employer branding; it isn't even fully under the control of the organization. Banking sector brands were hit hard by the financial crisis in 2009, unrelated to the actual actions of the bank. Banks that had no subprime mortgages still felt the impact. From a TA perspective employer brand can be influenced by continuous consistent communication. Making sure every communication is in line with the EVP.

The second type is **recruitment marketing**. These are the campaigns to attract candidates to the company. This can be to just get the name out there for lesser-known brands, tell potential candidates about jobs they might not think to associate with your company or any other reason to do campaigns that emphasize the company and several jobs.

When it comes to recruitment marketing data can play a big role in choosing the message. Using external data to validate your brand and perceived brand values can help you design recruitment marketing content and messages. KLM, for example, using external data, found challenging work was the number one driver for young IT professionals to choose an employer, but college grads did not associate KLM with challenging work or embracing new technologies, while their internal IT population said it's one of the reasons they loved working there. So they focused their recruitment marketing campaigns on the projects, the challenging work and the technologies they were working with in order to make the perception get more in line with reality, increasing the number of graduate applicants.

The third type is **job marketing**. This is about making that one specific job as attractive as possible. Sometimes that's done by a campaign, but more often it's just writing a really good job ad and buying job slots or social media ads to support it.

Although the EVP is the foundation of all your marketing efforts, the job ad is actually the most important element of your marketing. As that is for many candidates both the starting point and the conversion point. Research from the Talent Board[1] shows that most candidates will only start looking at your company once they find a job that is attractive and a well-written job ad is extremely important in that. So it's not that all the employer branding content isn't important, but it's only important after a candidate finds a job they like.

So it's a starting point, but it's also the conversion point for a candidate, as the job is what they actually apply for. Hence the job ad is the most important aspect of all recruitment marketing and employer branding efforts. And that job ad needs to be aligned with the EVP, the foundation of these efforts.

Career sites

A career site is a window into your organization. It is the primary way that potential candidates get information about what you do, your culture, your working style, what kind of work you have for them and your approach to innovation.

They are where many career journeys begin. A potential candidate comes to the website, either through their own curiosity or because they have seen a promotion about opportunities in your firm. What they experience here is critical.

Most career sites, however, are poorly designed and do not engage candidates. Many people spend less than two minutes on the typical career site before leaving because they did not find what they were looking for or had to read pages of corporate jargon. It's also important to note that around 80–90 per cent of all candidates don't look beyond the job description. As research from the talent board shows 90 per cent of the candidates first look if there is an attractive job opening before even looking at the employer branding content on the site. So the job ads need to sell, both the job and the company. They need to be well designed and offer relevant information. Most careers websites have job descriptions that are legal documents with the standard design the ATS provides. They read like the manual of a TV, but you don't buy a TV on Amazon based on the manual, you buy it based on a well-designed page that looks attractive and offers relevant information. Job ads, which are usually the starting point of the career site journey, need to be more like product pages on Amazon than the user manuals they are now to keep candidates engaged. They need visuals, relevant information and a design that's easy to read.

Good career sites are designed to attract and intrigue a potential candidate with useful information, insider tips and videos of employees or the company's work. They combine visual and written information and offer valuable insights. They can offer a way to give potential candidates updated information or let them join a talent community. Used well, they can help build a pipeline of potential candidates. It's actually interesting to see many organizations claiming to want to build a talent pipeline, and yet just over 50 per cent of all major companies offer the simplest version of this, a job alert, on their careers website.

Of course the application process also needs to be seamless. Research from Attrax[2] has shown that removing a register to apply process, meaning a candidate needs to enter their email address and a password and then confirm that email address, sees between a 55 per cent and 76 per cent increase of candidates finishing the apply process. Research from Digitaal-Werven and Talent Table show that in the Netherlands less than 5 per cent of all major companies still have such a process in 2022 while in Australia this is 24 per cent. There's no data on other countries available yet.

With over 50 per cent of all website traffic coming from mobile phones, career websites need to be mobile accessible, of course, especially, again, the job ads. And of course it pays to have a mobile accessible application process as well, remembering most applicants do not have their CV on their phone. Adjusting the process to accommodate this helps companies attract good candidates.

Your career site is the most critical component in attracting and engaging potential candidates. Careers sites need to be built on solid data, be resourced appropriately and provided with a dedicated person to develop and maintain content and engage candidates. And of course your careers website needs to be in line with your EVP. Your careers website should live your EVP. A 'people-first' company should have plenty of people on their site and an 'innovative' company should have some innovative solutions.

Augmented and generative AI for talent attraction

In mid-2020 the OpenAI foundation launched GPT-3, a language model that can write almost indistinguishably from humans. The English newspaper *The Guardian* actually published an article written by the GPT-3 on AI being harmless to human beings. It was fed some basic ideas and it produced eight different essays that were combined by a human editor to one article, indistinguishable from a human's. Based on this model, programming tools have been developed that allow you to write the desired outcome and the AI will translate it into code. We now see chatbots that are almost perfect in understanding the question, something everybody that has ever had a chat with a service department knows not every human is good at either. In 2022 they launched ChatGPT, a next version that was able to write entire essays so that high schools were now wondering how to evaluate homework, and it actually passed a level 3 coding test. Soon after they upgraded ChatGPT to GPT-4 and error rates dropped dramatically. It scored 84 per cent accuracy on a neurosurgeon board exam[3] compared to 62.5 per cent for GPT3.5.

With the exponential growth of these models it's only a matter of time before much of the standardized writing, something one might argue job adverts are, can be outsourced to AI. Currently there are several tools on the market that will suggest changes to your job ads to improve their quality like Textio and Textmetrics. Some take your desired tone of voice, based on your EVP, into consideration, while others use candidate application data to suggest what candidates find attractive and repulsive. The current tools use data to suggest items, like benefits, that applicants want to know and the layout of a job ad.

The first generation of AI writing tools will be based on human input and generate different job advertisements for the same jobs at different companies based on such inputs as writing styles and company culture. They will use input from job intakes done by humans, usually talent acquisition professionals, and produce ads that will initially need human oversight for potential mistakes. The first thing to be automated will be the job intake, giving the hiring manager some questions to answer as an intake. It will automatically gather the HR data on salary and other benefits from the HRIS and supplement it with EVP-based content on why it's great to work at your company. The AI will quickly learn based on the human feedback on specific items in the job ad and human oversight will probably be very limited only months after deployment.

These tools will evolve into AI not just writing job adverts, but also creating text ads for social media campaigns based on them. This will happen in conjunction with next generation programmatic job tools that are able to predict the context of the prospective applicant, adjusting the text to the recipient. This will start on a basic level using personas. For example, women with children will get an ad that emphasizes childcare while recent graduates might get ads that put the emphasis on career opportunities with matching photos of course.

The second generation of AI writing tools will be able to incorporate desired tone based on the personality profiles the programmatic tools are able to compose of an individual. The ads will be tailored not just in content but also in style. The type of words and the tone of voice an ad displays will be tailored to the individual receiving it within the boundaries of the company culture and the EVP. These ads will be part of every candidate journey, for example, emphasizing the financial security of the company to the more risk-averse candidate and the sustainability of the product to the more environmentally friendly candidate. In case this sounds somewhat futuristic and impossible, this is exactly what Cambridge Analytica did for both the Trump and the Brexit campaign. Although less sophisticated a company like Crystal Knows is able to do something similar based on your LinkedIn profile.

Based on the candidate profiles that click on these ads the corporate careers website will be dynamically adjusted as well. Again emphasizing the elements that are important for the candidate. Not the enormous amounts of content and information about the culture, the colleagues, the locations, the growth possibilities and so on, but information tailored to the candidate reading it. Photos will also adjust based on the candidate profile and the available materials and the sites will be tailored to the candidate instead of the company, all within company guidelines.

Photos and other images can be easily generated by AI as well – AI-generated images are already replacing game designers in China.[4]

Programmatic marketing

In the age of automation data, analytics and algorithms are more important than ever. In consumer advertising, programmatic advertising has been around for a while and now has real-time bidding based on characteristics. In milliseconds real-time bidding algorithms will decide on behalf of advertisers to serve me an ad on Facebook if I'm looking at a cycling page (characteristic 1), my age (characteristic 2), location (characteristic 3) and device (characteristic 4) for example. This might serve me an ad for a new road bike for a low price, because it's not sure if I was visiting the Facebook cycling page as an active cycler or as a fan of cycling. If I just did a search for a washing machine on Google, I'll get an ad from an online retailer selling washing machines for a much higher ad fee, as it's clear I'm looking for it. And if I also love Metallica and I just searched for a washing machine, the bidding begins between Apple music wanting me to download the new album or the retailer wanting to sell me a washing machine. And as it's pay-per-click based the algorithm will also keep in mind that the chances of clicking on an ad for music is much bigger than a washing machine. Although privacy constraints have been limiting these developments because of privacy laws as well as smartphone producers having increased privacy settings, there is no doubt tech giants will find a workaround.

The first generation of programmatic advertising in recruitment is similar to that of consumer advertising, but with a big difference between the USA and Europe. As in Europe, most job boards, except for Indeed, are still pay-per-post while in the USA pay-per-click bidding, also on job boards, is much more common. So while in Europe much of the programmatic advertising is limited to Indeed, Google, Facebook and Instagram, in the USA there is a much bigger variety in platforms. In much of Europe, programmatic often also refers to 'expected applications' for a job posting on a certain job board. This first generation, which has been gaining ground since the late 2010s, is trying to get as much value for money, but it only looks at the last mile, the candidate that's willing to apply.

Very slowly we're seeing the next generation of programmatic job advertising rise, one that treats candidates not like consumers but like candidates that have a journey to go through before they apply. The candidate journey is a popular term, but most organizations think it starts when they apply. That's the applicant journey. The candidate journey starts way before someone becomes an applicant. The old marketing model AIDA is still valid in modern times. AIDA stands for attention, interested, desire, action. Programmatic advertising currently focuses on action, while the next generation of programmatic tools are already focusing on the entire cycle. From drawing someone's attention to an organization to sparking an interest for that organization to creating a desire to maybe work there to eventually turning a candidate into an applicant.

CASE STUDY

Bluetech Engineering

A great example of next generation programmatic advertising is a small Dutch company called Bluetech engineering which recruits young graduate engineers. Bluetech has little brand awareness, but uses a programme they call the recruitment cycle. About six months before a new traineeship starts it advertises general information about careers in engineering, potential jobs and so on via Facebook, targeting students that should be graduating with the right degree the next year. With those that engage, even with just a click, via remarketing they have one or more points of contact in the following months, creating desire with the candidate. In the two months before the traineeship starts they advertise the actual job and traineeship and with this strategy they are able to recruit way more graduates than would be expected based on their very limited brand awareness.

Modern programmatic job advertising will give different messages to different people at different stages of the process before application. Based on behaviours and clicks it will not just serve the next step based on the funnel – moving from attention to interest – but it will try different messages depending on those that resonate best. This could be focusing on different elements of the benefits or using different photos. Next generation programmatic advertising will adjust to the specific context of the potential candidate.

The Cambridge Analytica scandal has proven the power of adjusting advertising based on profile data. In simple terms this data helped the advertisers, both in the Trump and the Brexit campaigns, tailor messages so recipients would be susceptible to them. One example is that in the USA there are several reasons why someone could be pro-guns. Fathers would get messages saying you don't want them to take your guns away, otherwise you can't protect your children. Hunters would get ads saying if the other side won you couldn't go hunting, and so on. The scandal in this case was the fact the data was obtained illegally and by deceiving both people and Facebook as to their intentions. But the consumer psychology behind this advertising has long been used by many advertisers in consumer marketing. There are several recruitment marketing firms that do this by using personas and building campaigns based on those. The algorithms of Facebook, Instagram and Google will automatically serve them to the people most susceptible to them.

CASE STUDY

Schiphol

After a dramatic spring break in 2018 at Schiphol Amsterdam airport where flights were delayed and missed because of a lack of security staff,[5] the security operator I-Sec decided to go all out on hyper-targeted programmatic advertising. It built 10 personas based on talks with different people already working as security guards, all different in age, ethnicity and gender. They discovered that women in their early 30s have different motives for working the same job than a student, a young Muslim man or an older man with Dutch-Caribbean heritage. Based on these 10 personas campaigns were launched, using photos in ads to match the personas and the reasons the job is attractive in the text, via channels such as Instagram, Facebook, Google AdWords and Twitter. Every persona also had its own landing page containing the job advert, again focusing both visually and textually on the person they were trying to convince. It's one of the most successful campaigns in the Netherlands, hiring 350 people in the first three months, 100 above target and close to 900 in the first year, solving its hiring problem. It won awards for best recruitment advertising campaign.

Next generation programmatic job advertising will not just tailor a message to the point in the process that specific candidate is at, but also the context of the candidate. Consumer psychology has known for decades we, subconsciously, tend to feel we belong with people that look like us. So photos in ads and on career websites should be of people we can identify with. Next generation programmatic advertising will adjust the photos, as well as the motives that make a job attractive to that specific person, based on his or her context.

Talent pipelines and communities

Although technically the process described in this chapter as next generation programmatic advertising could be considered talent pipelines, for this paragraph we define a talent pipeline as 'external people who have actively indicated being interested in possibly joining your organization'. We will, however, differentiate between a traditional talent pipeline and a talent community. Internal mobility, also a talent pipeline, will be discussed in another chapter.

For ages it has been said recruitment is primarily a game of chance. Only if a job opens at the exact moment a candidate is looking for it and it is posted in a newspaper or on a website this candidate is reading will you have the perfect match. Talent communities and talent pipelines have been seen as the Holy Grail to solve this game of chance for decades, but never really took off. But since the mid-2010s we have seen several successful examples.

Talent communities

The interesting thing about the success stories is they are totally different in every way. Some use the strong employer brand to get people to sign up, like Zappos. Others focus on providing learning experiences for the candidates like Specsavers and STRV. The key to building a talent pipeline is to keep the talent engaged by offering them content that makes them feel part of an exclusive community and offering value to them.

CASE STUDIES

Zappos

In 2014 online shoe retailer, and now part of Amazon, Zappos, launched Zappos Insider. The company used their excellent employer brand to set up their talent community. Zappos was getting 30,000 applicants while only hiring 300 a year. Zappos is rather a unique case as their employer brand was so strong those applicants were engaging on only the prospect of a job. Zappos made it clear that they would only hire from within the talent community and those most engaged would be in the front row.

The Zappos case is unique in many aspects and very hard to replicate, as it has a really strong product brand. As that strong product brand translated really easily into a strong Employer Brand it was a lot easier to pull off. Of course they nourished their employer brand well by building their talent community. This community and the way they ran it aligned well with their values. Of course, they had engaging content on what it was really like to work at Zappos, but unlike many average or above-average brands the prospects of working at Zappos engaged a lot of talent.

Specsavers

Specsavers is a retail optician chain in Europe. They built a community called the Green Club that offered a big part of their internal e-learning courses to everybody who signed up. They created a free learning experience for all the staff of their competitors, but also gained access to their contact details and permission to approach them. Specsavers used a brilliant method – sending specific information to individuals based on their previous behaviour. They were able to track the type of content that was consumed and would follow up with related content. As they also knew and rated the consumption of this content they knew who was most active and who had not just consumed the e-training but also looked at a vacancy, for example. They managed to increase the hires per recruiter by 400 per cent because they were now just contacting 'hire-ready' candidates.

STRV

STRV is a Czech technology firm that delivers services to many big Silicon Valley names. Their talent pipeline strategy consists of a public newsletter that gives access to exclusive content – technical content from their own developers, written by ghost writers and editors together with the technical staff. Based on their interaction with the content, people can be put into a bronze, silver or gold category. Candidates in the silver category had some perks, like being invited to larger gatherings and drinks. Candidates in the gold category had even more perks, like being given access to internal training sessions or round tables. They created a learning experience for the candidate, while engaging them with their organization. In order to grow their pipeline, one of the things STRV does is host social events for expats during the summer. As many companies run on skeleton crews, Friday drinks often become boring or are cancelled during the summer. So STRV invites all expats, who often stay in the city when locals leave to be with family in the countryside, to join them for Friday afternoon drinks, BBQs, yoga sessions or game nights. STRV found most of their hires came from this community and they had on average a 13-month 'pre-application' process before a candidate actually expressed interested in a job, either on their own accord or after being asked by a recruiter from STRV. The actual recruiting process took between two and three months, sometimes including relocation.

Both Specsavers and STRV, although focusing on totally different talent markets, use the same principle to build a talent pipeline: create educational content, track behaviour and engage with candidates based on their behaviour. As the jobs at Specsavers are more straightforward, they use their talent pool as a sourcing tool, while STRV has bigger labour market competition so they include more offline activities to persuade the candidate.

Although building a talent community isn't easy and requires persistence it is one of the recruitment marketing activities that will see enormous growth in the near future. Organizations that truly believe talent is their greatest asset will move their model from lucky incidents where the best person is looking for a job when it opens up to a model where the talent is known and courted way before a position opens up. Building talent communities will also be a core differentiator for RPOs in servicing those companies with lesser well-known brands. It might even create a new niche of RPOs or agencies focusing on specific sectors. The modern talent pipeline is the replacement of the old Rolodex, but now in constant, warm connection, augmented with all kinds of data on the candidate to make the perfect match.

Talent pipelines

The difference between a talent pipeline and a talent community is best described as the difference between a database and a chatroom. Several talent communities were described in the previous paragraph. At Zappos candidates could interact with each other and employees of the company, at Specsavers they came to learn and interact with the company and at STRV they could interact with the company digitally and in the physical realm.

Talent pipelines should be considered much more like a database. It's a group of people that have shown an interest in working in your organization, but at a time you couldn't find accommodation for them. It could be silver medallists, people who were fit for the job, interviewed, but there was just someone (that seemed) better at the time. These could be people that applied but didn't even get invited or these could be people that just showed interest and sent you their CV.

Under GDPR it's important that you engage with your talent pipeline at least once a year, renewing permission to keep them in. This might also be a good moment to see if there is an update to their profile to match with your jobs.

When CVs in an ATS count as a talent pool, almost every organization has one. But for as long as there have been ATSs, consultants have been telling organizations to use the talent pools and managers have been frustrated as to why they aren't used. There are three main reasons for this.

The first reason is the technology itself. Often it's not easy to find the right candidate matching the profile, usually because an ATS uses keyword matching and not semantic search where the search doesn't just look for exact matches, but looks at synonyms and related skills as well. Although technology to fix this, Textkernel is one of the suppliers offering this, has been around for some time, it's not standard in an ATS and needs to be purchased separately.

The second reason is that the process doesn't make it easy. A database search is often a totally different part of the ATS to the entry of a new job opening. This is easily fixable, but organizations need to want to. It would be very helpful if for every job opening that's entered into the ATS the system would auto suggest candidates already in the ATS matching the required skills. If it's the hiring manager who's entering the job in the ATS, she or he can automatically check already existing candidates.

The third reason is the human factor when it comes to reaching out to candidates. Sourcing is a special skill within recruitment that some people are better at than others. This has to do in part with the same skill: some people are better hunters in sales and others are better farmers, it has to do with the fear of rejection. Many TA professionals question if someone is still open for a job and make assumptions rather than reach out. This reason can be partially mitigated with technology that reaches out to candidates more often and asks them if they are still open for a job and the sort of job they might be looking for. Chatbots can be very useful for this purpose.

In a world where there is more emphasis on skills, rather than a degree or experience, the future will move more to matching based on assessment data rather than CVs. From cognitive ability to personality traits, applicants will be tested more and based on those results can get more opportunities suggested to them. Of course this also works for suggesting candidates to hiring managers based on these skills. Already we're seeing organizations that fully embrace test results above experience propose positions they didn't apply for to candidates based on their test profiles. With automation this could be scaled up, suggesting positions or roles to candidates based on their profiles and have them show interest in those profiles, or outright reject them, as well as suggest candidates in the pipeline that are a fit based on their skill profile, although might not have the right degree or experience.

Organizations that are able to automate most of the work concerning their talent pipeline will be able to utilize them. Automation is key in keeping the information up to date, keeping a candidate engaged and suggesting candidates to recruiters and hiring managers. Human interaction is key in closing the deal.

Bots

Chatbots have traditionally started as so-called 'decision tree bots', basically programmed to ask a question and continue based on the answer. Although these bots have their use, for example, in navigating complex information about visa procedures for relocation workers, their use was limited and they often couldn't really help candidates with specific questions. The rise of AI and especially ChatGPT, discussed earlier, has given chatbots the foundation to deliver actual value to candidates and become a channel within the TA landscape. Many suppliers have changed their proposition for delivering a chatbot to building conversational AI to emphasize this. This means the bot is an algorithm that is able to have a conversation with a candidate. This could either be on a social platform like Facebook or WhatsApp or on your own corporate careers website. These conversations could be about information that a candidate is looking for to search for open jobs and applying to them.

Although adoption is much slower at first, voicebots will eventually follow as voice-to-text is also evolving at an exponential rate. Although there are differences, such as the moment of use and the interface with which they are being used, with or without a screen, the technology is closely related. So in this paragraph we will talk about bots where it applies to both chatbots as voicebots and only explicitly name one or the other when relevant.

Bot technology for marketing purposes will be used both inbound as well as outbound. It can help answer questions by candidates, like it does for other customer support. Although many organizations have relied too much on bots to handle their customer support and didn't invest enough in them to offer great service, making many people question their ability, there are also plenty of situations that worked out really well. When because of a snowstorm many of the flights from Amsterdam's Schiphol Airport were cancelled, over 80 per cent of KLM customers were able to rebook their flights the same day using a bot, while other airlines took days to reschedule everybody because of a lack of manpower in the contact centre.

Bots can be used to help candidates navigate information about jobs and the organization. Bots are able to solve the old 'library problem'. Should a book on the effect of CEOs and corporations on society be filed under management or society? Do you look for *Harry Potter* under fantasy or teenage lit/young adult lit? Or in the case of a corporate careers website for an organization that hires for relocation, do you have a section on the services you provide as a company talking about assistance with the visa application and housing, or do you have a section on the visa questions, from eligibility to the assistance you provide and put the other services you provide somewhere else? A bot is able to fulfill the job of a librarian for your corporate careers website, helping the candidate navigate information, but also collecting information candidates are searching for that isn't currently available yet.

More advanced bots are able to pre-screen candidates. UK-based elderly care organization Anchor was able to pre-screen candidates that were interested in a 'learn on the job' programme via a chatbot. With a few simple questions they were able to check if a candidate was truly interested and potentially capable to do the job, check for the openings nearest to the candidate, ask the candidate if the travel time was acceptable and directly book in a phone screen with the hiring manager. Several retail organizations use chatbots to check candidates for in-store jobs in terms of availability and some background information and either schedule an interview or sometimes just schedule their first shift, as there is no better way to see if someone is fit for the job than to let that person perform it. The 24/7 availability of the chatbot lowers the bar to talk to someone and apply, making this not just a screening tool, but also a marketing tool.

The true marketing strength from bots, however, is in the outbound marketing. The candidates in the ATS has been the worst utilized company asset for decades and with GDPR in Europe it's currently illegal to keep candidates in the ATS for longer than one year, unless you explicitly ask them if they are ok with that. Bots can do that and even start a conversation with a silver medallist that could be taken over by a human if there is a fit for a currently open role. It could also get candidates to update their experience, if they are still interested in working for your organization. WhatsApp bots are perfect for this and can even act as a job alert if an opening in the vicinity of the applicant opens up.

For certain roles, for example PhD positions at universities, but also traineeships at specific companies, candidates tend to show an interest way before graduation, often a year in advance. One university uses a chatbot to engage with them and help them navigate the PhD possibilities, but also asks about expected graduation dates. It will restart the conversation about three months before this date and ask if the expected graduation is still on track; if not, the conversation is moved and if it is the bot will try to engage the candidate to look for current openings in his or her field.

In Russia several voicebots have been known to call candidates who left their CV, with a phone number, on a job board for some pre-screening questions and to schedule a call with a recruiter in case the pre-screen questions were answered correctly. This of course only works in employer-centric markets, where employers are in control. Hence it's mainly used for either high-volume jobs or for getting in touch with people from countries where unemployment is very high. Blind robot calling becoming an acceptable form of first communication will probably very much depend on the quality of the technology used.

Since in Russia for some positions, like truck drivers, a candidate does not send a résumé but phones in to show interest, voicebots are able to handle large volumes of candidates applying. In Australia voicebot technology is used to lower the bar for applicants from their Asian neighbour countries to apply for call centre jobs, automatically screening for the quality of the applicant's English.

Bots are without a doubt part of the future of talent marketing, for both inbound and outbound activities. Reaching out to candidates on Facebook, WhatsApp or whatever platform the candidate is on will be part of the future of recruitment marketing. Automatically keeping in touch though these bots, in chat or voice, something the candidate should be able to decide, is also a part of the future of recruitment marketing.

TAKEAWAYS

- Your employer brand isn't your latest video; it's the underlying messages in all your communications.

- Depending on your target audience, you should have a different strategy when it comes to the mix between direct sourcing, recruitment marketing and referrals.

- Your corporate careers site is a multiplier, either of your budget or your ROI on other attraction methods.

- Talent communities should not be about attracting the talent; they should be about adding value to the talent.

- AI will change advertising both in the personalization options of content and the targeting of potential candidates.

- AI will change sourcing both in the identification of a candidate as well as in writing and personalizing the outreach on scale.

THE STORY OF PERSUASION FORCE*

Persuasion Force is an IT company building a next generation customer growth platform using the most sophisticated AI tooling together with the most advanced scientific knowledge on consumer psychology. It wanted to go beyond the usual CRM systems and add marketing automation and content creation to its standard portfolio. It was founded by consumer psychologist Linda, video specialist Ola, engineer Siv, data analyst Tom and sales expert Da. As all of these founders already had track records either in a company or as founders, they had a huge seed round to build a unique product. Persuasion Force combined data analytics and consumer psychology to adjust campaigns not just on results but also to auto suggest variations and tests to run on consumer databases. It had its own web and email analytics tools tracking behaviour, but it became an overnight hit with the launch of its deep fake AI video possibilities.

Being able to create a spokesperson for the company that would never leave or get into trouble in real life – as the person was a deep fake AI indistinguishable from a real person – gave it an edge on every other CRM and sales system out there. Using the OpenAI linguistic text generator it was able to generate ads and texts based on simple prompts and was even able to suggest prompts after the initial calibration. As the AI was able to suggest and even automatically create messages tailored to specific clients or prospects based on their personality profiles stored in the system, welcome messages, emails, videos, et cetera would be perfectly aligned in tone, wording and messages.

Because Persuasion Force was founded by such a diverse team in every way, it built a structure that would resemble those strengths from the beginning. Its teams were solution focused rather than discipline focused. There was no IT department, video department, usability department or even recruitment department. Every product line had one or more psychologists, developers, data analysts and, if needed, other specialties. Sales and marketing were centralized as were the finance and people functions. The latter did have a few centralized recruitment support functions, which handled the careers website and the TA technology stack for example, but those were supporting the recruiters in the business units and coordinating efforts between the recruiters in the units.

Unlike many other startups, Persuasion Force opened several major offices and allowed very limited remote work and working from home. Because so many disciplines were working together and diversity in their organization was so high on so many levels, they believed they needed proximity to succeed. Their first office was on the west coast of the USA, and after their massive series B funding round they opened offices in Mumbai and Barcelona. They allowed one day a week to work from home and there were opportunities to work remotely for an extended period of time, while travelling, for example. However, Persuasion Force was an office-first company and proud of it. This had massive implications on their talent acquisition, of course.

The early years

Like most startups, Persuasion Force first recruited within the networks of the founders, but as soon as they started growing they invested in making referral recruitment a strategic part of their talent acquisition strategy. One of their early hires was a recruiter called Helen who, as part of the onboarding process, would sit with the new hire and look at the open jobs and the potential candidates for those jobs. Of course, the new hire was in control of who they would approach, but this meant it wasn't just in the back of the mind of the employee, it was proactively solicited to think about new hires. Later, this became part of the digital pre- and onboarding application. The new hire would be asked to share their LinkedIn network with an app, and despite the fact that 'No' was a perfectly fine answer, most new hires agreed to share it. Based on matching technology they would be shown a maximum of five potential matches and the new hire could say if they would be a fit or not and immaterially send them a message with a tag for a potential referral fee.

Persuasion Force, of course, used all the persuasion tactics in the book to get their people involved as much as possible in recruitment. Hiring was seen as a team effort and everybody contributed. This was supported by the fact the recruiter was part of the business team and not 'someone from that other department'. They also held regular referral drives where they highlighted specific jobs and asked people to share those in their networks. In this case it wasn't just about the jobs in your department, but rather from outside departments, creating a friendly competition between departments to help other departments. In the spirit of this friendly competition and cross-department collaboration, the rewards were usually something like the most helped department had to cook for the most helpful department, paid for by the company.

Persuasion Force also invested heavily in programmatic advertising and because of its own expertise in both psychology and data analytics it ended up taking a minority stake in a programmatic advertising agency. They shared not only their knowledge and expertise, but also parts of their technology to help the programmatic agency grow to a another level. The same technology that helped assess both the position in the funnel as well as the best messages for persuasion of prospective buyers in their core product helped the programmatic agency assess this for candidates. As a launching customer for each new feature they had great successes and big failures with personalizing ad messages to candidates based on both their expected readiness to apply combined with the motivational factors to apply.

Of course, as for most IT companies, direct sourcing was an important part of the talent attraction strategy as well. Persuasion Force's sourcing strategy had two layers to it: first it was direct sourcing for an open position, the traditional sourcing of people ready to join. This included much relocation recruitment as they wanted people in the offices. The second part of the sourcing was for hackathons and games. Persuasion Force would organize online coding challenges with serious prizes twice a year as well as local hackathons in tech-heavy hubs where they had no office. Inviting talent to join a hackathon locally was an indirect way of sourcing and assessing talent. Persuasion Force held hackathons all over the world, supporting local causes while offering serious prizes for the winning teams.

Because of the success of the indirect sourcing strategy using the hackathons and online coding challenges, they almost accidentally built a talent pool. Helen soon realized they needed to expand the central team to manage this and although Persuasion Force did as much locally as possible, Piotr was hired to manage the talent pool. He set up an automated candidate nurturing system. Everybody in the talent pool would receive regular updates all catered to their specific desires. Coders would receive code solutions and technical information. Psychologists would receive the latest information on the tests that were run and the psychological science that was confirmed, debunked or amended. Data analysts would receive information on the data science and the engagement scores of the candidates would be tracked. Piotr even went as far as to build a model where the most engaged candidates, within the group of desired candidates, would receive benefits for their activity in the talent community. Some would be invited, travel and expenses paid, to the yearly developers conference; others would receive small gifts and so on.

Centralizing

As the importance of the talent pool grew, so did the centralized team. With a bigger and stronger centralized team, friction appeared. More and more policy was dictated down to the line and the embedded recruiters in the business units felt they had lost their autonomy. When several of the first generation left, the choice was made to centralize the entire recruitment. Helen was now officially the Global Head of Talent Acquisition.

With a new centralized team, Persuasion Force decided to go all in on employer branding and recruitment marketing. A big campaign was launched, and the brand name became one that resonated with many people and the number of applicants went up.

As the labour market was becoming more and more candidate-driven, even in countries that still had higher labour supply, it became harder and harder to hire for Persuasion Force. The number of referrals went down and three years after centralizing recruitment the percentage of new hires from referrals was down from 45 per cent to 15 per cent, while agency spend more than doubled. Marketing spend was up as well, while offer-acceptance rates were at an all-time low. While Persuasion Force had always prided itself on having an offer-acceptance rate of over 85 per cent, even in the difficult candidate driven markets, it was now just over 50 per cent.

While at first the changing labour market conditions were blamed, many department heads had another view and they expressed this to the C-suite during one offsite event. They used to have embedded recruiters in their team that really understood what they were looking for, now they have to do a request to the centralized department and they get a new recruiter every time that presents them with candidates that just don't fit like they used to. Hence they hire agencies more and more as they seem to have more time to talk to them and present the right candidates.

Although Persuasion Force thought centralizing recruitment would lead to lower cost per hire, counting the agency spend and the lowering of the referral hires, they ended up spending more on recruitment than before. After four years, the decision was made to reverse the centralization and decentralize again.

Back to the roots

Because the new central talent acquisition organization was only there to support the recruiters in the units, Helen left. Florence, who was already in the team, took her position and the role changed to Chief Talent Acquisition Support Manager. Most of the team went to different business lines, some left and a small support team stayed in the central organization. The tasks were also clearly defined. One of the new tasks in the central organization was talent intelligence – looking at the global labour markets to find pockets of specific talent and helping the business units hire from there. Amir joined to lead the talent intelligence initiative.

As Persuasion Force was already using dynamic generated ads in their programmatic advertising, it felt strange that they would land on the same job description. Florence challenged the team to consider whether it could be possible to not just target the messages in the outreach to candidates but also adjust this message on the website. Florence herself coordinated this programme and first developed a dynamic adjusting job description on the careers website. The job description and its presentation would adjust the photography that was used, but also the benefits that were highlighted based on the ad that visitors clicked when they came to the website. Later it would also adjust the linguistics in the text, just like in the ads, based on the personality profiles that would most likely fit this candidate. In the third stage of this process they were also adjusting the job descriptions based on behaviour on the site, even when a candidate wasn't coming in via an ad. The conversion rate went through the roof, although there was initially some pushback from the media. Of course, Persuasion Force never lied or omitted anything; they just highlighted aspects of the job and the offer that were more relevant for that person. People that looked at the video on the work-life balance would see the benefits they offered relating to that and people that looked at the renumeration would see the salary really prominently in the job description – all the rest was still accessible, just not emphasized at first glance.

With the recruiters back in the business units, referral hiring went back to 30 per cent of all hires, as hiring became a team effort again and not just the job for 'those people in the recruiting department'. The success from the referral drives, in particular, went up because of the dynamic generated content on the site, as, of course, sharing the content led to people visiting the careers website and the job ads on that website, which were now dynamically adjusted to the person visiting.

The candidate profiling was unique and helped Persuasion Force considerably in rolling out their fully AI-based sourcing tools. Sourcing had always been a part of the strategy, but even with all the technology to search for candidates, it remained a manual process that was costly and time-consuming and great IT sourcers were in such high demand that it was hard to retain them. As the tools for searching had improved dramatically, Persuasion Force went one step further, having an AI do the first outreach. Either by phone, chatbot or email, depending on the contact information available and, based on the profile, the channels via which the candidate was most likely to respond.

Because of the profile data, the AI was able to adjust the messaging to increase the chances of response and soon had the same response rate a human sourcer had. Because the AI was learning quickly, it of course made terrible mistakes that made HR news headlines, but within a year after launch its response rates were 25 per cent higher than those of the human sourcers before. After the initial contact a human recruiter would take over and add the human touch in testing the quality of the candidate as well as persuading the candidate to join.

Amir was brought into the team to develop a talent intelligence platform. As Persuasion Force was growing it was opening up more locations in the world – both sales offices as well as new development hubs. As Persuasion Force still relied heavily on offices and people being in the office, the location choice was very important. Amir was responsible for delivering the talent intelligence when looking at new locations. Did a city have enough talent? Was it attractive enough to relocate to? How much competition for the talent did the city have? How did the wages compare to other cities but also to the living wages in the city itself? Of course Persuasion Force wasn't opening up offices on a monthly basis, so Amir also did research on pockets of talent. This helped the sourcing and the talent pool development, as local hackathons were still an important part of the strategy. Amir's work helped detect pockets of talent in regions with relative low competition. Using multiple sources of data, from academic papers to code submitted to GitHub, he was able assist Piotr with his talent pool strategy and steer the AI sourcing tool to talents that it would never had found using only existing data. Amir's talent intelligence unit, which never expanded beyond him and Fen, was able to combine internal and external data and use human judgement in a way no AI would ever be able to. Using this information Persuasion Force kept ahead of the competition and kept building its amazing product.

Although many other organizations would look at the waste within Persuasion Force, as the decentralized organization wasn't great in helping candidates that applied to one unit get a job in another unit. Of course, they tried, but in reality they lost some talent that might have been suitable for another unit. For Persuasion Force, however, the decentralized approach, the self-sufficient business units, worked better. Having embedded recruiters helped make recruitment a team effort and that gave them more referrals than any of their competitors, while having a close to zero spend on agency fees.

This is a fictional scenario on talent acquisition in the near future.

Endnotes

1 TalentBoard (2023) The 2022 Global Candidate Experience (CandE) Benchmark Research Reports, www.thetalentboard.org/benchmark-research/cande-research-reports/ (archived at https://perma.cc/SNN3-7VPR)

2 Digitaal-Werven (2022) Tot 75% meer conversie na vervangen van registreren voor sollicitatie, digitaal-werven.nl/tot-75-meer-conversie-na-vervangen-van-registreren-voor-sollicitatie/ (archived at https://perma.cc/N4MC-M7GU)

3 Ali, R, Tang, OY, Connolly, ID, et al. (2023) Performance of ChatGPT, GPT-4, and Google Bard on a Neurosurgery Oral Boards Preparation Question Bank, medRxiv 23288265, doi: 10.1101/2023.04.06.23288265 (archived at https://perma.cc/G2WG-V2D3)

4 Rest of the World (2023) AI is already taking video game illustrators' jobs in China, 11 April, restofworld.org/2023/ai-image-china-video-game-layoffs (archived at https://perma.cc/CDD8-SL4N)

5 NL Times (2018) Some 6,000 travelers depart from Schiphol a day late, 30 April, nltimes.nl/2018/04/30/6000-travelers-depart-schiphol-day-late (archived at https://perma.cc/2HCD-D6D7)

5

Selection

Selection has traditionally been about reducing the great many applicants back to a number a recruiter and hiring manager can handle in order to select the best ones for the job. In some organizations the first selection is made by the recruiter, in other organizations the hiring manager does this and in a few organizations the first selection is done by technology, be it through 'knock-out questions' or more advanced testing algorithms. The typical traditional selection process usually looks a little like Figure 5.1.

Some organizations will have an assessment in there, usually after the pre-screen, but the exact position also depends on the organization. Some will have a phone screen as a pre-screen, others have a phone screen after the pre-screen on a CV.

For almost every organization the CV is still the document used for the very first screening of a candidate, even though there has not been a single scientific study that's been able to find a single predictive value in a CV. One of the most important elements recruiters and hiring managers claim to look for and select on is experience, even though it has been proven many times by many academics that experience measured in time has no predictive value whatsoever.[1] It doesn't matter how long someone has been doing a job; it matters how well the applicant has done the job and under what circumstances this person did that job. Information that just isn't in a CV.

There is, on the other hand, overwhelming evidence that selecting on a CV is a recipe for bias and discrimination. The biggest predictor of getting invited to a job interview was often a person's name. In the USA African American names had much less of a chance while in Europe 'native' names had up to three times the chance of getting invited than Muslim-sounding names.[2] Research actually shows labour market discrimination has been increasing in both Europe and North America against people with a Middle Eastern and North African heritage.[3]

FIGURE 5.1 Traditional selection process

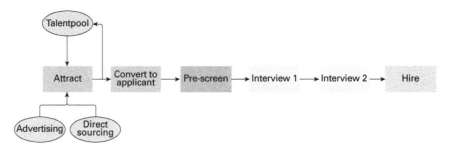

Another problem with starting the selection with a CV isn't just that we're stopping great talent at the gate; it's also that we're letting mediocre talent through. And, moreover, we're letting them through because we believe they are qualified and then our confirmation bias kicks in. This bias makes us look for confirmation of what we already believed, based on the CV that has no predictive value, and hence we often end up with a bad hire.

Bad or mis-hires

Depending on the definition of a mis-hire and the level we hire for, between 40 per cent and 60 per cent of all hires should be described as a mis-hire according to Dr John Sullivan.[4] If these numbers sound high, that might be because of another bias called selective perception. We tend to forget many bad hires either because someone left really quickly (we could not have foreseen that) or because we lower the bar (those targets were way too high in hindsight).

Few parts of an organization would be allowed to perform as badly as selection does and we are seeing more and more people in the industry questioning the common practice of selection, as described in the first paragraph. Organizations are changing the model, especially in startups and scale-ups, where there is a culture of continuous improvement. When Google and Facebook were still scale-ups they designed their own models to make better hiring decisions. In the case of Google this led to the 'rule of 4' where every candidate has four separate interviews that all have veto rights; in the case of Facebook they designed a complete library with every possible question a recruiter or hiring manager is allowed to ask linked to a skill and every possible answer a candidate can give linked to a score. Many others, especially the current scale-ups, are looking to technology to help them improve their quality of hire.

The first wave of technological innovation in selection was focused on programming and testing applicants on their ability to code. As coding is relatively easy to evaluate by algorithms and work sample tests have a very high prediction of someone's ability, this was a great first step. However, there are limitations to these tests. First, a work sample works best if it really reflects the actual work, so if an organization has a pair programming model and gives a candidate a take-home test, this might not be the perfect test. The second limitation is the fact that work samples just look at your ability to do the work, not how you will do the work. It tells the recruiter or hiring manager nothing about the personality or character traits a person has.

During this first wave of innovation there were two other types of jobs – high-volume roles, like those in call centres and retail, and sales jobs – where testing was relatively easy to automate. This has to do with two requirements needed to build a reliable algorithm: a definition of quality and enough data. In high-volume roles, like call centre and frontline retail staff, there was plenty of data (it's called high volume for a reason) and the main measurement of quality, especially at first, was defined as retention. The second type of job was 'quick' sales. With quick sales we mean sales with fast feedback loops like retail sales, hotel event sales, car sales and so on. These jobs are usually less high volume, but still have enough volume, and have a clear definition of quality as few things are as measurable as sales.

Between 2015 and 2020 a second wave of innovation in selection hit the market, trying to emulate the successes of the first wave, but for (mostly white collar) jobs, which are much harder to automatically screen. As for most jobs there just isn't enough data to undertake good data analyses and there is a less well-defined measurement of quality for a hire. This doesn't mean it's impossible, it just takes more time and knowledge to implement and because of slower feedback loops a longer time to see the benefits. The first jobs where the second wave of innovation succeeded were those with relatively clear quality of hire data, like stock market traders and air traffic controllers. As with air traffic controllers those that graduate from the academy are by definition good because let's face it, when was the last time you heard about an aeroplane crashing because the air traffic controller had a bad day at the office? The quality control is in the training programme, so graduating from the training programme is a measurement of quality.

This new wave isn't just led by startups, governments and major corporations are slowly modernizing their selection as well. Interestingly enough the reasons are different, as startups want to reduce the number of mis-hires, governments want to increase fairness in the hiring process to increase diversity and ensure an equitable process and many major corporations want both while often also trying to increase the pool of suited candidates.

Post-Covid the labour market changed in many parts of the world. Some call it the Great Resignation, others the Great Reshuffle or the Great Rethink. Whatever you want to call it, it's become a candidate-driven market and demographics show that there's no reason this will change anytime soon. In many parts of the world this meant organizations needed to shift their selection process from selecting out to selecting in. Instead of selecting the lucky few from many applicants the market is now seeing who is willing and able to do the job. In some cases this has led to open hiring, several warehouses have decided that the only prerequisite you need is to be able to lift a 5 kg box for example and if you want the job, it's yours. But for other jobs it's about having the potential to learn it and so aptitude testing is becoming more and more common in the post-Covid era.

Talent puzzle

One of the main reasons it's so hard to get (pre-) screening right is the fact there are so many factors that contribute to a good hire.

There's the ability to do the job, combined with the training and coaching to use that ability. But there's also the motivation and ambition to use that ability. And that's just on the functional side of the spectrum, as there's also the human side to being a good hire. That has to do with a value fit with the organization, but also a team fit and in some cases a fit with the manager. All of this needs to be combined with the knowledge that diversity of thought brings better results in the long run.

Because there are so many moving parts it's close to impossible to put the talent puzzle together completely, but that doesn't mean we shouldn't try. When doing any type of (pre-) selection testing it's important to understand what part of the talent puzzle you are testing so you can focus the other parts of the selection process on the aspects you didn't test.

The simplified model in Figure 5.2 is useful for considering the ingredients needed for a successful hire. Now to be clear, this model means you need to define what you are looking for on all three elements, for some jobs ambition is important, in others there is little to no need for it. And

FIGURE 5.2   Elements of success

SOURCE Bas van de Haterd

hiring someone with great skills that doesn't fit the organization, as it was called in Silicon Valley, the brilliant jerk, doesn't help in the long run either.

For the purpose of this book we use the following definitions.

Talent: This can be the potential to be good at something or their current skill level. It also has to do with the cognitive and in some cases physical capabilities, or rather potential capabilities, of the person.

Character: This is the values and character traits a person brings to the table. What's truly important for someone? Are they more of a team player? Detail-oriented? Analytical or work on gut feeling?

Ambition: Although it could be argued that ambition is a character trait, for work purposes it's such an important trait we mention this separately. Ambition is the multiplier of someone's potential, but it also interacts with character traits, like being a team player for example.

Interestingly, many qualities don't fit into one of these three boxes. Detail orientation is both a talent and a character trait. Some people are actually physically better at seeing details, and more naturally willing to devote time to them. To put this in perspective, Bas once worked with a professor of electronics who could spot a mistake on a microchip working in nanometers, but seldom wrote an email without a spelling error. He applied his innate talent for detail orientation in a visual setting but never in a linguistic one. He used to say: 'If you understand what I meant to say, that's good enough, but if there's a mistake on the chip, it won't work.' The same is of course true for character and ambition as the ambition to lose weight, for example, can be very real, but without a character trait like tenacity it's close to impossible to accomplish.

In the remainder of this chapter we'll talk about putting this talent puzzle together as well as possible during the selection process.

Pre-selection

Pre-selection for the purpose of this book is defined as the first selection after applying. Depending on the organization and the role there are different pre-selection mechanisms in use and several organizations use more than one from this list:

- CV
- knock-out questions
- phone screen
- digital assessment

Most companies use a CV as the primary pre-screen mechanism, even though as we described earlier it has been shown to have no predictive value in a standalone situations whatsoever. As we said before, it's not that experience doesn't matter, it's just that experience measured in time isn't relevant. So, experience that can be seen on a CV becomes valuable when it's combined with an assessment that is able to show the quality of skills.

The main goal of pre-selection is to assess if an applicant might have the qualifications for the job.

This simple sentence has two implications:

- There needs to be a very clear measurable definitions of minimum qualifications.
- Pre-selection isn't about selecting out the 'less qualified'; it's about selecting out the unqualified.

In some cases it's very clear what the minimum qualifications are:

- You need to be over 18 to serve alcohol in many counties
- You need a driver's licence to be a taxi driver
- You need to be a registered nurse to be a nurse
- You need to be a member of the bar association to be a lawyer

And in some cases these qualifications could be very situation-specific, like being able to work a certain shift or have your own laptop.

At the beginning of the pandemic the Dutch temp agency Young Capital was requested to quickly deliver hundreds of employees to do track and trace activities. They used an AI calling solution to call 7,000 candidates in their ATS (applicant tracking system) for a phone screen in four hours, asking them the basic questions: checking if the age in the ATS was indeed correct and the person was over 18, if the candidate owned a laptop, if the candidate was able to attend the onboarding day and if the candidate was interested. If the answers in the pre-selection phase were all positive, a human would call and do the actual selection on qualities.[5]

In some cases these qualifications might not be clear at first, but by analysing enough data they can become clear. For many jobs over the past couple of years suppliers have been able to identify key skills that every worker needs to be able to do the job at a certain minimal level, mainly in the earlier mentioned high-volume jobs.

When Harver launched in 2010 its solution was revolutionary for its time. It's first client, Bertelsmann, had a 300 per cent attrition rate per year. By getting rid of CVs and actually measuring on the 24 traits a contact centre agent needs, from short-term memory to ear-hand coordination and a large enough vocabulary, they were able to lower this attrition to 20 per cent in two years' time.[6]

Using digital assessment technology can also be very useful when your organization has too many applicants and, although it seems for many those days are behind us, there are still parts of the world where have plenty of applicants from which to choose. Only when your organization is swamped with applicants can you also choose to not just pre-select on minimum standards but on 'nice-to-haves'. For example, the level of English for applicants, in other countries, applying to be a call centre agent could be at a minimal standard, but given enough applicants, this could of course be a deciding factor in pre-selection.

> According to one company, via a confidential source, in the first month of the pandemic, hiring was frozen in many places and in the Philippines many people were fired. So when a job did open up, especially one for a call centre that served American clients, they applied *en masse*. So many people applied that one specific call centre got 450,000 applicants on a single vacancy for 10 agents. If they had not been using pre-selection software that used AI to measure, among other things, the applicant's level of spoken English and their ability to be a great agent, it would have taken months of human labour to check all the applicants based on their résumé and do a phone screen to check for the quality of English.

Although the speed of adoption of digital assessment technology has been very different for different organizations, the adoption of pre-selection tooling is growing tremendously. With stricter anti-discrimination laws in the EU on the horizon, the death of the CV that has been preached for decades might finally arrive, although the AI regulations could put the brakes on developments.

Pre-selection assessments

Digital assessment technology comes in many different forms and shapes, all with benefits and disadvantages.

QUESTIONNAIRE-BASED

Questionnaire-based tests have been around for a long time and are considered to be the standard for psychometric testing. Although there are many different tests with very different qualities, which will be discussed below, the methodology is generally accepted by both the public as well as scientists as very valid.

Weaknesses   They have four general weaknesses. One is they rely on the self-knowledge of the applicant. Although this is generally not a massive problem, there are people who have no idea how they are perceived by their colleagues.

The second weakness of every questionnaire-based test is that the applicants understand what you are asking, so they can be manipulated. Any good test cannot be manipulated to be 'perfect', but that doesn't mean they cannot be manipulated to some extent. Scientific research has shown that the difficulty in manipulating a questionnaire-based test is not the test itself, but the desired result to get the job that many applicants get wrong.

The third weakness in these tests are cultural differences when answering questions. Although every supplier will claim these are 'culturally neutral' these academic validation studies were done in times where countries were much more homogeneous in population. A simple example: an American on a 5-point scale will most often choose a 1 or a 5, while most northern Europeans will choose a 2 or a 4. Americans love to be specialized, while Europeans will not easily say they are 'just one thing'. This is best shown in sport: Europeans love football where you have a task, but even a striker needs to defend from time to time, while in American football there is a specialist for everything and from offence to defence the entire team changes. So using a questionnaire-based test on an American living in Amsterdam or a recently migrated European in New York will give different results for the same personality, simply because of the cultural way they perceive themselves and hence fill out the questions. Of course, this applies to many other cultures as well. Because in most of Europe it's illegal to ask about heritage or race in an application form, it's impossible to correct for this.

The fourth weakness is the language level. Most of these tests have been validated with people with an above-average understanding of the language they are administered in, often college graduate and up. This means they are simply less reliable for anybody with a lesser degree of the language, because they didn't go to college or because the language it's administered in is not their native language, and the candidate simply doesn't fully understand the question.

With the rise of generative AI like ChatGPT it's now also possible to have ChatGPT help you give the answers to be a great fit for a certain job. Although there is great debate still in the scientific community about the extent of this, it seems evident that ChatGPT and AI bots alike are or soon will be able to make these tests with perfect matches for the job at hand.

> In a Dutch healthcare organization they used a Big 5 personality test as part of the application process. Based on the results they automatically gave their new hires a personal development plan for the first year. About a third of all the new hires went to HR after their probation period and asked for a re-sit of the assessment as they manipulated it slightly and now were being given training and coaching on elements they were actually already pretty good at but not on the parts they felt they needed to improve on.

NEVER USE MYERS BRIGGS (MBTI), DISC OR OTHER PERSONALITY-TYPE TESTS

Two models that are very well known are the Myers Briggs, also known as MBTI, and the DISC model. Neither should ever be used in recruitment. Period. They have no scientific validity whatsoever, despite claims of those selling them. They have limited test and retest validity, meaning your mood of the moment influences the result you get, but more importantly humans are far too complex to put into a box. There are more than four (DISC), or even 16 (MBTI), personality types among humans. Just like intelligence, character traits should be measured on a scale. Nobody is fully introverted or extraverted and nobody acts fully intuitively or fully rationally. MBTI, DISC or any other personality-type assessment that puts a candidate into a pre-determined box, from letters to types to colours, should not be used in hiring as there has not been a scientific validation that held up to scrutiny.

BIG FIVE & AND HEXACO

The Big Five model, and the Hexaco model, which is derived from the Big Five, is scientifically validated and can therefore be used in recruitment, although its usefulness is limited for selection.

The five personality dimensions the Big Five model measures on are:

1 **Openness to experience**[7] **(inventive/curious vs consistent/cautious)**
   This means you are more inventive and curious. Openness involves six elements: aesthetic sensitivity (the ability to connect, judge and appreciate art and/or beauty), attentiveness to inner-feelings, adventurousness, intellectual curiosity, psychological liberalism and active imagination. People high in openness are usually motivated to seek new experiences and to engage in self-examination. Structurally, they have a fluid style of consciousness that allows them to make novel associations between remotely connected ideas.

By contrast, being less open means you are more consistent and cautious. Closed people are more comfortable with familiar and traditional experiences. For example, an art director will need to be high on openness to be successful while an auditor will need to be low on openness to be successful.

2 Conscientiousness[8] (efficient/organized vs extravagant/careless)
Conscientiousness is the only trait in the Big Five that science has proven to have a positive effect on pretty much every job, but it does matter more for some jobs.

In this regard being conscientious links to a desire to do work carefully and diligently, and to take others' obligations/requests seriously.

Conscientious sales people that methodically follow up on every lead are known to be very successful. Also, editors benefit greatly from being conscientious while it matters a lot less for writers as much of writing is a creative process rather than a diligent and organized process.

3 Extraversion[9] (outgoing/energetic vs solitary/reserved)
Extraversion tends to relate to energetic, outgoing personalities. Introversion tends to relate to more reserved personalities. Although extraversion and introversion are even on the Big 5 opposites, Carl Gustav Jung, who coined these terms himself, argued everybody has their extraverted and introverted sides. That is why the Big Five model isn't deterministic, but shows a score on the continuum with one side being a little more dominant than the other.

Being somewhat extraverted helps with outbound sales as reaching out to people as an introvert costs a lot of energy. Although in the sales process being too extraverted is a risk too, as salespeople need to be able to listen very carefully. Many great IT developers are more introverted, but here also being too introverted is a risk as it might prevent the person from asking if they are building the right product in time.

4 Agreeableness[10] (friendly/compassionate vs critical/rational)
Agreeableness is a personality trait that manifests as behaviour that is perceived as sympathetic, kind and cooperative. Although agreeableness is often seen as a very positive trait, how often do we hear that those in power were only surrounded by 'Yes men' and hence made all the wrong decisions?

Just as with extraversion and introversion, it's a trait where being on the extremes is probably not good for any job. Especially for good management, it's a balancing act between being agreeable and being rational. We can probably think of enough jobs where being agreeable is a very good trait, from teachers and nurses to customer support. Procurement officers, however, should probably score below average on agreeableness.

5   Neuroticism[11] (sensitive/nervous vs resilient/confident)
Such people are thought to be quite sensitive to stressors and respond more badly to them than the average person. It is believed that they are more likely to interpret ordinary situations, such as minor mishaps, as appearing very difficult. Although this might seem like a trait that is negative in all situations, it's not that simple.

Again scoring too far on the neuroticism scale is never a good thing, but for some jobs a certain level of neuroticism can be very useful. Think spies or other (counter) intelligence officers or security guards or IT security staff. One might even argue that having some members of parliament that score high on neuroticism, together with low agreeableness and high conscientiousness would help uncover many political cover-ups.

Hexaco has added one extra dimension: Honesty-Humility, that basically measures integrity.

The main difference between these tests and the MBTI and DISC test is that the Big Five and Hexaco are not deterministic. A person in these tests isn't an introvert or an extravert, but has a score on a scale of 0 to 100 from introvert to extravert. Everything they measure is on a scale.

The upside of these tests are their scientific scrutiny and validity. The main downside is the fact that administering them well can hamper the candidate experience as it takes a lot of time to do an assessment nobody really likes. Although in the past decade the time to complete it has been lowered a lot without hurting their reliability too much, they are still generally perceived to have a negative impact on the candidate experience. Next to this downside they are always administered via a questionnaire-based assessment, making them susceptible to all the before-mentioned issues from cultural heritage, lack of self-knowledge, lack of perfect language understanding and the possibility to manipulate by those that do have perfect language understanding.

Another downside to Big Five and Hexaco tests for pre-selection is that the traits measured often have very limited predictive value for job performance. For a team it's usually good to have people in it that score differently on these traits. Hence these tests are great to use to complement an existing team, and they are very useful to have as talking points in interviews, but are close to impossible to build an automated pre-selection tool on.

Situational judgement tests

Situational judgement tests (SJT) are, along with questionnaire-based assessments, the longest and most scientifically validated type of assessments in the industry. As a methodology they are very reliable if implemented well. Implementation is key to their success as they are always organization-specific and here lies their biggest risk or weakness.

Their other weakness, although this is a very limited downside, is that in a SJT sometimes a candidate would have a solution or an answer not in the list of potential answers.

One very well established way of building a SJT is using the 'critical incident technique' where you take a critical incident from the past of the organization and give the applicant several potential ways to respond to this, one of which is the best answer, there is often one that is totally unacceptable and then between one and three answers that are acceptable. These questions could refer to a work situation, but also be (potential) incidents concerning company values.

A great benefit of a SJT compared to a questionnaire-based test is the candidate experience. As they are unique, candidates tend to be less annoyed by them and if designed well they have a high face value (value = validity), meaning the candidate understands the relevance of the questions being asked. Although more questions/situations give better results, it's also possible to limited the number of situations tested and still get acceptable results, lowering the time required from a candidate to apply.

Because an SJT is organization-specific, these tests are very well suited as pre-selection tests on personality and especially testing if a candidate's values matches with the organizational ones.

Work sample tests

There is no better way to know if someone can do the job than to have them do the job. So of all the assessments, the work sample test has the highest predictive value for job fit. However, job fit means being able to do the job right now. So this form of assessment doesn't measure the organizational fit or the potential to learn to be great at the job.

The biggest weakness of the work sample test is that for many types of jobs it's very hard to codify the results, making it impossible to fully automate it. For more numeric or technical jobs it's easier to codify the results into good and bad, making it easier to automate. Hence the great number of suppliers for coding tests, work sample tests for coders. For engineering in the physical world, like construction or electrical engineering, it's also doable to develop scenarios with clear good and bad outcomes. In data analyses the way a calculation is done can be automated but the interpretation is almost impossible. In healthcare the previously described SJTs are sometimes used as work sample tests in 'How do you respond to this patient's situation?' questions. However, in sales and marketing, HR or recruitment, teaching, social work and so many other professions dealing with people, there often isn't one correct answer.

Sometimes knowledge tests are used as work sample tests, but their predictive validity is much lower as knowing how something works doesn't mean you can apply that knowledge. The other way around is true, not knowing how it works certainly means you cannot apply the knowledge, but just knowing isn't blissful. Someone might know exactly how to technically write a great boolean string to source a candidate, but that doesn't mean this person is able to understand who they are searching for or how to approach this person. Someone might know all there is to know about the possibilities that Google Adwords offers, but not understand a single thing about actually setting up a great campaign. Knowledge tests aren't work sample tests, although they are often branded as such as their predictive validity is much lower.

Work sample tests are best used for jobs where the new hire needs to be productive quickly, as they usually do not test for potential, although there are exceptions that prove this rule.

The City of Rotterdam uses a work sample test as their pre-selection for a traineeship for social workers. They do not ask for a résumé, invite everybody to apply and have no requirements when it comes to education or experience. The work sample test is a genuine case study that a previous trainee solved years ago and they ask the applicant to write a short essay on the interventions they would try to implement. The evaluation is done manually and is judged on feasibility and creativity, as they are always looking for new lines of thought. Over 80 per cent of all trainees get offered a permanent position after the traineeship.

They are a great pre-selection tool, but for many jobs very hard to automate. In some cases it's possible to test if a person can come up with the right answer, but for many jobs there's more than one right answer. As reviewing work samples usually takes a lot longer than reviewing CVs this form of assessment is in limited use outside of the IT realm.

Will AI solve the grading problem for work sample tests? There are suppliers who believe so and invest heavily in this and with decent results. They have the first batches graded by humans and the AI looks at many data points in future solutions, from linguistics used to the way a candidate behaved in the tool to come to the solution. Whether AI will ever be able to judge these tests well and is also able to adjust to changing demands in a job remains to be seen.

Game-based assessments

For the past decade or so game-based assessments have been in all the media. They have been hyped and given magical powers and they have been trashed and been made the root of all evil. What has usually been lacking is a definition of what a game-based assessment is, and hence this category needs to be made into different sub-categories in order to be able to explain the benefits and risks of every type.

GAMIFIED TESTS

The most common type of game-based assessments are actually just gamified tests that have been around for ages. It's the same cognitive or psychometric test that has been used for ages, just made a little more fun. For example, instead of showing an arrow that points right and the word left in it, it's now a car on a road that turns right, but the sign next to the road says left.

Gamification has also been used with SJTs, where people either were set in a specific office environment to answer the different situations or perhaps do some more cognitive tests within the same platform. Other suppliers have done the opposite and taken their environment as a fantasy world. The latter have had lots of criticism as it had less face validity, candidates didn't understand what this had to do with the job they were applying to, and from an employer brand perspective employers had questions. Most have changed their environment because of this, which doesn't mean the science behind it wasn't solid, but when both applicants and customers question the science because of the design choices, they decided to change the design.

Other gamification elements that can be added to these tests are things like photos of jobs when candidates are expected to choose between two options or a 'score' that increases to give people the confidence they are doing great combined with the impulse to keep doing their best.

The only gain there is in these tests is that it's usually more fun to do, so it improves the candidate experience.

The downside is that there is sometimes less face validity, meaning the candidate doesn't understand why the test is relevant. Although this was sometimes also the case with traditional tests, the pushback on gamified tests has been bigger. It's unsure if this is because of the gamification or because times have changed and we now live in an age where if people don't understand something, it must be wrong or bad, as many seem to be unable to understand the limits of their knowledge. There has been a lot of debate in the scientific community on the importance of face validity. As some tests and especially outcomes have great face validity, like the MBTI, but no scientific evidence, and yet others have great scientific evidence, but as ordinary people, the ones taking the test, just don't understand them or disagree with the outcomes, often because of a lack of self-knowledge, this could hurt the entire belief in assessments as a selection tool.

Specific assessment games

Within the sub-category of specific assessment games there are again more sub-categories, all with their own benefits and downsides.

Some providers have made a game of gamified tests, as described above. These are basically gamified tests with a storyline. This makes for a better user experience and gives more data on certain traits. As some tests are able to measure multiple traits, it's possible to double check and sometimes slightly adjust a candidates score on one test with another one in the game. This can only be done reliably if the tests are done by all the participants in the same order. The downside to this above the single use of gamified tests is that the storyline never fits every organization so it sometimes lowers the face validity and every candidate needs to do every test, even if it's not relevant for the specific job, making the test battery longer than absolutely necessary.

Some providers have developed their own unique tests whereby playing a game all kinds of traits are measured. Some of these games look like actual casual games and are really fun to play, others do have a more testing look to them, but are still fun to play. With these games it's always important to really check the science behind them as some have an amazing scientific validity and others are comparable with the MBTI – they might sound good, but the science doesn't exist. The upside is that they are usually a lot of fun to play and because the game is fully designed only for the purpose of the assessment, they are able to rigorously test the candidates and give amazing data. The downside is that they often have no face validity so candidates, and the media, love to trash them and this can hurt your employer brand.

The great thing about actual game-based assessments is ChatGPT can't solve them for the candidates, as your game play decides the outcome. This makes these tests more 'AI-resistant'.

Data from casual games

Many casual games also have psychological constructs in them, that's why so many games are so addictive. And although the way you play a game can be very revealing about your personality, these games were not build to measure that. So although it's not possible to measure your entire gameplay, two things are measurable and have proven to have at least some predictive value. The games you play for fun are actually already telling about your strengths, as we tend to play games we are good at. At least, outside of the direct social setting, as there might be social pressures applicable. Hence these assessments look at the games you play online, alone or with an online community for fun. The other element that's telling about your personality is the achievements you have, measurable in the badges you earn, as a player. The first research into this was actually in 2010 and 2012 when Stanford published a paper[12] on the fact guilt leaders in *World of Warcraft* seem to be better managers. As in *World of Warcraft* the leaders are chosen from within the group and there is no incentive to want to be one, except the fact you think you are a great manager. This created a natural experiment worth researching. Later research[13] shows guilt leaders are in fact better managers.

Since the research on using casual gaming data is still limited and not everybody has access to games, these types of assessments in pre-selection should be limited on selecting in rather than selecting out.

The Dutch military uses casual game data to inform candidates about potential jobs within their organization. By giving the algorithm access to their game account, it suggests potential jobs for them. According to their own research the Dutch military says 85 per cent of all candidates agree the suggested jobs fit their skills. When a candidate applies to one of the jobs based on their game profile, they are automatically bypassing the CV check and moving to step 2 of the selection process, as the military says the game data has a higher predictive validity than a CV.

Linguistic assessments

Does what you say and how you say it reflect your personality? There is a good chance it does. Although the scientific research goes as far back as the 1970s, only since social media started providing enough data and machine learning was able to process this data has the research really taken off. The words you use and the sentences you create might be able to show different character traits, but as of this moment there are as many questions about this unanswered as there are actual answers.

The potential upside of this technology is huge in several ways. As writing is something applicants are used to in their applications, the candidate experience is very good. It could also make assessments of people based on their social media, which in most cases reflect a person's most natural behaviour, if privacy laws allow for it. It could also partially help analyse work sample tests, and the technology is already being used by some providers for this, as many of those are written solutions.

However, there are still many questions and potential downsides to linguistic assessments. The science is still limited and mainly focused on the English language and although many providers make robust claims about other languages, independent research remains very limited and hence poses a risk. As the research between native and non-native speakers is also still limited, this too poses a risk for potential bias, and let's remember that American English, British English and Australian English aren't equal either – a British person might not be native in English according to some algorithms as more research on this technology is done in the USA and Australia than the UK. Another risk is that the types of language being assessed might not be equal. As some people that write professionally, from authors and journalists to scientists and public servants who write a lot of policy, tend to use different language in articles than they do in conversation it's important to make sure the way your organization collects this data is equal to the way the tool is optimized.

Linguistic assessment technology has great potential, but isn't as mature when it comes to scientific reliability as other forms of assessment. That doesn't mean it's impossible to use; there are use cases, especially in high volume, that have been proven very effective. It does require even more diligence in the selection of a provider than with other types of assessments in order to limit the risk of bias and discrimination.

Automated video interviews

Video interviews are one of the most debated topics in the talent acquisition industry. Some TA leaders believe it's a candidate experience killer, others believe they are very helpful and that candidates don't mind them. Unfortunately there is no independent research to support either statement and the data that is available supports both statements, as some candidates hate them and others don't mind them, just as with every form of (pre-) selection.

The benefit of having an automated, or one-way, video interview is that the interview in itself is highly structured. All the questions will be asked by the same person, in the same voice, with the same expression in the same order. As structured interviews are known to have a higher predictive validity than unstructured ones, the benefit is clear. Another benefit is the scale of automated video interviews, as it doesn't take a human to conduct them. The question of whether it should take a human to evaluate them is less clear. Many attempts to automate the evaluation process in pre-employment have failed. In the USA HireVue has abandoned its AI assessment of video interviews[14] after mounting pressure from legislators based on audits that it was biased against people of colour. In Europe, German startup Retorio was found to have, among others, a background bias[15] giving people with a bookcase in the background different Big Five personality scores than the exact same video in front of a wall. In the last case according to Retorio this was based on machine learning by human interpretations, making it replicate existing human bias. However, the rise of new technologies like deep learning and artificial neural networks might be changing this. With AI being able to summarize the content of video interviews and extract important information from it, mapping this to skills and behavioural traits, the need for a human to do this diminishes.

Emirates Airlines is using automated video interviewing to pre-select for customer care agents. They are now able to interview thousands of candidates (they have over 200,000 applicants for these roles per year) to give as many as possible a chance. The automated selection algorithm uses linguistic analyses to either accept or reject the candidate without a human being involved. It can also put a candidate on manual review for a human recruiter to review the applicant and help the algorithm learn.

Automated evaluation of video interviews is risky, but also brings opportunity to eliminate, or at least minimize, human bias in interpretations. Research by the universities of Utrecht and Ghent,[16] for example, shows that well-designed algorithms can correct human bias when it comes to assessing a candidate's motivation for the job. This research interestingly showed that when assessing how motivated a candidate is for the job, recruiters tend to look at the right non-verbal clues, but actually interpret them totally wrongly when it comes to a candidate subconsciously signalling their motivation.

Automated assessment of video interviews based on (micro-) expressions has a big risk of being biased against people of colour and for once this is not because of the training data, but because the darker the skin, the less contrast it has as light and shadows are simply less visible on darker skin. This means that algorithms have a harder time actually identifying (micro-) expressions on darker skin and this problem is close to impossible to solve.

This doesn't mean that it is not possible to automate the assessment of video interviews. It is, for example, possible to use the previously mentioned linguistic assessments and of course the factual answers themselves, but then the question remains what the added value of video is when only the text is used. It's also possible to measure heart rates and hence stress levels and excitement on video based on a vein in the human forehead and the changes of skin colour. Research shows this can be done for every skin colour. Interesting information can be collected on stress and excitement levels during applications and tests. Analysing the content of the interview is also very valuable, and there are several models that are able to build personality profiles, for example on the Big Five or Hexaco model from the answers given to questions in the interview. This new interview tech, which is often able to be used for both video and on-site interviews that are recorded via an app on the phone, is able to build profiles of the candidates based on their answers.

Automated video interviews are mainly popular because interviews are known and accepted selection methods. When humans appraise the videos there is a huge risk of bias, from a candidate's looks to background and video quality, all issues that in most cases have nothing to do with being able to do the job. Algorithms can do a much better job, but come with a risk depending on how they work. The expectations of really good algorithms that are able to accurately assess a candidate are there, but you need to be very aware of how it does that and what data points are being used. From a diversity and inclusion perspective you need to really know what data points the algorithm is measuring in order to be sure it's not a liability.

The selection process

Step two in the selection process is the selection itself, which usually consists of different interviews, sometimes a technical screen and a physical assessment.

As many books, some good and some not so good, have been written on interviews and questions that should or should not be asked, in this book we'll focus on the process itself and the benefits and downsides of different possibilities in this process.

The first item in the process is picking the selection committee. Research tells us few things about a great selection committee, except for two things. More diversity leads to better outcomes, as diversity gives more perspectives and this can be good for both spotting talent as well as spotting risks with a candidate. The other interesting fact comes from former Google manager Laszlo Bock's book *Work Rules: The hiring manager* – as this person is the one feeling the pain of an empty seat, they are often willing to lower the bar or hire lesser qualified candidates. Although it's not possible to not have the hiring manager involved in the interviewing process, if only because the candidate wants to meet the person they are going to be working for, it's important to avoid mis-hires to have a system of checks and balances to overrule the hiring manager's verdict.

Google also tried to research the skills of a great interviewer. It turned out that they could not find them, within all of Google there was only one person with a success rate of hires that was significantly above 50 per cent, meaning no person was able to individually really assess talents well. They did, however, find that the wisdom of a crowd worked really well, meaning the combined opinions of multiple people that are not experts turns out to be a great predictor. But only if those interviewers work fully separated, meaning they do not interact with each other in any way before coming to their conclusion. Google found that a candidate being interviewed by two or more people had little to no added value and was a waste of time for the second interviewer, while having more one-on-one interviews did add value. They also found that more than four separate interviews did add some value, but not enough to cover the time that fifth interview cost.

The result of this is Google's rule of 4. A candidate has four one-on-one interviews and each one of those has a veto on the candidate. As Google also sees the opportunity costs of a missed great candidate, they do reject a CV twice before really rejecting a candidate. So not one, but two different hiring managers or recruiters need to reject the candidate based on the CV before they are really rejected.

Lots of academic research has shown that structured interviews are better than unstructured ones. Despite this knowledge, unstructured ones still seem to prevail, unfortunately. A structured interview means you ask all the candidates the same questions in the same order, so their responses are comparable. The extra benefit of a structured interview is that as you decide on the questions to ask these are usually related to competencies that need to be measured. So in order to have a structured interview, it's important to first define the competencies a candidate needs to possess in order to define questions on how to measure these.

Facebook has taken structured interviews to a new level. For every job there is a list of questions that can be asked by recruiters or hiring managers and only the answers to these questions count. All the possible answers a candidate can give are also structured and ranked. This way the candidate rating is automatically calculated and the best candidate will evolve. As the system already knows the questions a candidate has been asked, the candidate will not get the same question twice from different interviewers. This way Facebook is also able to assess a candidate's level in a job on the same scale all around the world, meaning a senior developer in Japan has the same skills as a senior developer in India and in America.

Although somewhat at odds with the structured interview, pre-selection testing has opened a new possibility for interviewing. More and more pre-selecting test providers offer interview questions based on the traits measured and how they relate to the job. Sometimes a candidate might score lower or higher on a certain characteristic than the ideal profile would suggest, but if this candidate is aware of this they might have found ways to deal with it. For example, a very extraverted person that is aware of their extraversion might have found ways of dealing with more introverted candidates in meetings. Having data upfront and combining this with behavioural interview questions is a new way of checking if the tests are accurate, if the candidate is aware of this trait and if they found ways to deal with this trait in a work environment.

Technical screenings have become common for developers. These work sample tests, often not common for other jobs although they have high predictive validity, are both loved and dreaded. There are different ways of performing a technical screening, from a take-home assignment to an online coding test to a pair programming challenge and a technical interview. Neither of these are by definition good or bad, the most important thing is that they resemble the actual work at your organization. If your organization works with pair or mob programming, a take-home assignment that is done alone doesn't reflect the actual way of working and hence isn't a great test. Important here to note is that there is a lot of candidate tech available to cheat on these tests. ChatGPT has shown to be able to pass a level 3 coding test and there have been demos floating around of candidates using text to speech recognition software, directly feeding it into ChatGPT and getting the correct answers to coding questions. This means that there is a high risk for take-home technical tests or remote interviews to be cheated on.

An interesting debate that surfaces every so many years is whether candidates should be given the questions before the interview so they can prepare or not. Although this feels counter intuitive to many recruiters and hiring managers, there is a solid argument to be made that allowing candidates to prepare actually makes the interview better. Since without preparation you are not just testing a candidate's skills on the subject, but also improvisation skills. If improvisation is a part of the job, like for example with sales people, there is a valid argument to be made that it should be part of the interview as well. But if there is a possibility of preparing well for the actual job, candidates should be given the same opportunity.

EPSO, the European Personnel Selection Office, responsible for the selection of all the staff of the European Commission, decided during the pandemic to publish all its selection criteria and questions. This was because they were afraid people would have an unfair advantage because some digital interviews might be recorded and shared and some people could have access to their questions and others would not. Their analyses after becoming fully transparent showed that candidates didn't regress to the mean, but the candidates were more spread out between good and bad. The distribution of candidate qualities increased. Whether this is because some candidates prepare and others don't or because now people were able to better show their skills is unknown.

Interview augmentation technology is also helping recruiters and hiring managers make better decisions. This technology is based on artificial intelligence and is able to automatically detect the skills, competencies and personality traits of candidates based on the words they use and point to why someone exhibits certain traits with the words used in the interview. This makes it completely transparent for interviewer and interviewee. It's also able to detect linguistic matches between candidates and an interviewer, something to be aware of as a linguistic match might feel like the candidate is a fit, but that's just because the candidate uses words the interviewer would use and vice versa. This can serve as a potential bias alert. This also makes it easier to share interview reports with other people in the selection committee that were not present at the interview, summarize the interview, perhaps highlight important parts of the interview and allow others to listen back to those parts.

Interview technology is also able to detect other biases in the interview process. For example, if certain hiring managers let men talk more than women, interrupt younger people more than older people or have interviews with women start late more often. This technology can help recruiters identify these patterns and make changes to the interview process to avoid them. It can also help coach hiring managers to become better interviewers. Bright Hire in 2023 shared data[17] that shows that with video interviews male interviewers with female candidates started 68 per cent on time while all interviews were 73 per cent on time. It also shows that on average they spend 30 per cent less time interviewing female candidates than male candidates.

The technology can be used with video interviews, but also by recording an on-site interview via an app on your phone.

Open hiring

Open hiring is a concept that started in 1982 at the Greystone Bakery in New York. The concept is very simple: a candidate writes their name on a piece of paper, and when your name is on the top of the list and a job opens, they are hired.

The concept has been copied in many places all over the world, sometimes with a small adjustment like at the Dutch baby product webshop, MammaLoes, where a candidate needs to pick up a 5 kg box, as that's what you need to be able to do.

Of course technically many gig platforms work in a similar way. For Uber all you need is a driver's licence and a car. The fact that open hiring helps with diversity and equity was best described by Belgian politician Gilles Verstraeten in a speech[18] in 2019: 'Jobs at Uber and Deliveroo actually help the young people from my neighborhood, that has many underprivileged people from different ethnicities, get jobs and start a life of honest work instead of a life of crime, nothing has reduced drug dealing as much as Uber and Deliveroo.'

Of course open hiring doesn't work for every job, as there are simply jobs you need qualifications for. But more and more organizations are skipping the selection process altogether. Especially in times of very low unemployment, it turns out open hiring is a way to attract people to the labour market that wouldn't otherwise apply as they have always been rejected.

Dutch drugstore chain Kruidvat decided to implement open hiring for their warehouses in 2022, as they needed to find more staff quickly. As showing up for work was actually the main criteria for being able to do the work, they decided to have 'open hiring days'. Everybody that showed up and was still interested after having a tour of the facility and an explanation about the job was hired. Their ghosting rates, the people that didn't show up for their first day of work, were similar to the rates when they still did interviews.

Virtual internships and apprenticeships

Virtual internships or apprenticeships or job try-outs give candidates not just an opportunity to see what the job is actually like, it also helps them gain skills as well as a chance to showcase their talent, without having to be selected to do so first.

It works by the candidate signing up for a virtual apprenticeship that usually lasts several weeks. Sometimes there is a fixed start date, other times they can start whenever they desire. In these weeks the candidate gets several assignments to complete, usually real-world assignments that the company has successfully completed. The candidate submits their solutions to the task or challenge and gets feedback with the actual solution the company implemented. AI rates the candidate's solution and sometimes a human from the company does as well. Based on these ratings a candidate can earn a badge for certain skills, like analytical thinking or creative problem solving.

The company of course has access to the candidate's profile and solutions and is able to source the best candidates based on their virtual apprenticeship. The candidate gets a better understanding of the job while gaining skills in the process.

TAKEAWAYS

- The biggest effect AI will probably have is in (pre-) selection as that's where the most gain is to be made.

- Nothing beats a structured process.

- There is no academic research ever proving a correlation between anything in a CV and future performance. This is most likely why every AI based on CVs ended up being extremely biased.

- There are several scientifically validated ways of testing candidates. When selecting a methodology for this, make sure it's fit for purpose and it's scientifically validated. The fact that methodology in general terms is scientifically validated doesn't mean every test from ever supplier is.

- There are several technologies on the horizon that are worth watching, but there is uncertainty as to whether they will ever stand up to rigorous scientific scrutiny.

- If showing up is the primary qualification a candidate needs to have, open hiring might be a good idea.

THE STORY OF ROYAL RESORTS GROUP*

Royal Resorts Group was founded in the wake of the bird flu pandemic when the hospitality industry was at its financial low point. As tourism crashed while most hotels and resorts were just recovering from the Covid pandemic, many properties went up for sale and needed bailing out. As travel was picking up, this incredibly well-funded new venture, backed by capital from the Middle East, snapped up many high-end properties all around the world. Its focus was on high-end hospitality. As they did not expect business travel to ever get back to pre-pandemic levels they focused on leisure while not ignoring the business traveller. They quickly built out a globally distributed team to assist all the local operations with finance, HR and marketing.

As Royal Resorts bought up many different properties with all different models for recruitment and HR it decided in order to have consistent quality it needed one global policy on talent. This policy needed to be implemented while many of the resorts were in full swing as economies and global travel were opening up. Because it needed alignment between units that had different histories and different ways of working, they set a people strategy North Star early on and every decision made needed to be aligned with their North Star.

When Houssam came on the scene as the Global head of Talent Acquisition he quickly realized that although all the different purchases had different models of recruitment, they had one thing in common: they had been suffering from lack of investment. Not just during the pandemic, but from way before that. Recruitment had always been seen as a cost centre so he decided to outsource all recruitment except for the executive recruitment. After a careful selection process where local presence in important markets like the Middle East and Asia carried a lot of weight, Robert Page & Associates was selected as an RPO partner to handle every aspect of recruiting, except for the executive recruiting.

The early years

It was in the summer just a few months after Houssam had joined Royal Resorts Group, which had only been founded six months earlier, as their Head of Talent Acquisition. He would be working closely with Anna, their CHRO, who had also only recently joined the company. Houssam reported to Anna, who was a C-level executive, but as it had been Anna that recommended him for the job he knew they were perfectly aligned on the new talent strategy. The first years would be tough, although Royal Resorts might be a newly founded company, it had been buying high-end resorts and hotels all around the world that all had their own ways of doing things. The organization was very well funded by several Middle Eastern wealth funds and had a clear goal: to become the biggest high-end hospitality group in the world. It had already grown like no company had before by buying up properties in the hospitality world that were in dire straits after the second pandemic in a decade. Being the best high-end hospitality group in the world meant that next to having the best locations they needed high-quality staff.

The strategy Anna presented as part of her application process was simple in theory, but hard to execute. Hire on potential, train for skills against the lowest possible cost. The RPO deal with Robert Page & Associates meant that in every country the talent attraction would be done at the same costs and both employees as hourly workers would be supplied via the RPO partner. As standards, for example on friendliness and openness of employees, were set at the global level, the quality of the employees was similar across the globe.

The first thing Houssam insisted on was an assessment of the level of English of very applicant in the world, as English is the one language that needs to be spoken by every applicant. Since most communications in hospitality are verbal, this was done by an automated video or phone interview and reviewed by an AI engine that would qualify the quality of English. If an applicant did not meet the minimal requirements the person would be automatically rejected and they would be told that whey were welcome to apply again if their level of English had improved, together with a report on how their English related to the required quality. In order to minimize the risk of substitute applicants they used a video tool that was able to also check the person's ID card photo with the person behind the camera.

If the application passed the English language test the same data would be used to broadly assess their character based on the actual answers provided in the interview. This too was assessed through an AI matching system that relied on both the answers given and the linguistics of the answers. So it looked both at what the candidate said as well as the words that were used to say it. Because of the extremely high volume of applications that came through the system of Robert Page, not just from Royal Resorts but also all the other hospitality companies they were serving around the world, this technology, which was bought as a startup by Robert Page, quickly matured to a level that was close to perfection.

Because of the huge amount of data Robert Page collected on job descriptions, the number of applicants and the quality of those applicants, they were able to create their own AI writing tool, using OpenAI's APIs, for job descriptions in many local languages. After several years of assisting recruiters with their writing, eventually the tool was able to publish job descriptions written in the tone of the client based on data from the intake. As Robert Page realized that preferences in language change, it had built a tool that would experiment and always try multiple versions of a job description and the ads it generated for them.

The data Robert Page as an RPO working for many different organizations had on advertisement gave them the opportunity to develop their own programmatic advertising tool, keeping cost as low as possible while generating enough candidates to keep Royal Resorts a happy customer.

Houssam kept executive recruitment internal, as these were jobs that the board of directors would know and ask about. Executive recruitment for Royal Resorts consisted of the location managers and all director level jobs at the head office. Many location managers were promoted from within, often deputy location managers or other senior staff at one of the locations, and only a few times a year did Houssam have to look outside for these roles.

One of the things Anna and Houssam insisted on when they first signed their contract with Robert Page was an open API on the ATS that Robert Page used to automatically transport all data gathered on the hire to their HRIS system. This proved to be a very smart move later on as they would use the data gathered by Robert Page at the recruitment stage to spot talent and develop employees according to their strengths.

The break up

Although the relationship between Robert Page as an RPO and Royal Resorts was generally good, friction came when location managers started complaining to Houssam about the quality of hire for more senior staff like team leaders. Too often their knowledge level wasn't beyond that of the staff and the reason they didn't promote from within was of course because they considered the staff not yet ready.

As location managers were complaining and thought they could do a better job themselves, the CFO was pressuring Anna to lower the cost of recruiting and believed it would be cheaper to do it internally. As Robert Page wasn't willing to significantly cut costs, Royal Resorts decided to take matters into their own hands.

As many systems needed to be set up, the costs were mounting quickly. From a localized global ATS to hiring recruiters, setting up careers websites, calibrating assessment and video tools using AI, it took much more than the projected six months they had left on their contract with Robert Page.

It wasn't long after the contract ended that problems started to occur. It started with not being able to hire enough recruiters in every location and spending lots of money on agencies. Cutting corners in hiring, lowering the bar for the level of English for the hospitality staff, as well as less rigorous testing, if any at all, on service orientation for new staff had negative consequences on the customer satisfaction ratings that season. When some high-end locations were not able to open on time for the winter season because of staff shortages, the board of directors were looking for a scapegoat. Although the CEO and CFO wanted to scapegoat Anna, as it was her responsibility as CHRO to ensure the transition went smoothly, she was able to send the notes from the meetings to the board that clearly showed she didn't believe the transition would be possible in six months nor would it save money going internally. The board decided to side with her and appointed a new CEO who decided to undo his predecessor's policy.

Return to the roots

After the worst year in Royal Resorts' history in terms of financial results, customer satisfaction, hiring and retention, they decided to go back to Robert Page and write off all the costs for trying to build their own tech stack and recruiting teams.

Of course the issue of the quality of hire for senior staff was still on the table and so the process was evaluated. A work sample test was added to the selection process. In conjunction with Robert Page, Houssam developed a VR assessment that had several tasks which fitted perfectly with the job at hand. Because it was all in VR an algorithm was able to automatically assess the quality of candidate. Depending on the country, either candidates would be assumed to have access to a VR headset, were sent one on loan or would come into the local office or the location itself to do the VR assessment.

The open API that allowed all the data on a hire to be rooted directly into the HRIS proved to be very useful because this allowed Royal Resorts to have all the personality data in an employee profile. When the predictive analytics tools Royal Resorts had deployed were predicting attrition based on events like being passed over for a promotion it turned out this personality data was a very important factor to predict attrition. It also helped with predicting who had both the ambition as well as the traits to move up to more senior management roles. Although Royal Resorts had some internal development programmes, it decided to scale those up and set targets to have at least 50 per cent of its new location managers promoted from within in three years, and it met those targets. As the system for identifying the hires with the talent and ambition to become location managers improved, they were able to get to 75 per cent promotion within three years within a decade after starting the programme.

For supporting coaching and mentoring Anna had an AI-based personal coaching bot developed. For this bot, too, it was very helpful to know the character traits of a member of staff and the bot would adjust the methods used for motivating the employees in the programme according to the best practices known on motivating people with specific characteristics. The courses for those in the management development programme were in hybrid form, combining e-learning and face-to-face training with coaching by both the AI bot as well as a mentor.

Meanwhile Robert Page had invested heavily in talent intelligence, knowing perfectly from where to recruit certain types of staff. Although as an RPO they have no influence on where Royal Resorts would open up a new hotel or buy a new venue, it was able to predict very accurately in what parts of which country it could recruit certain types of workers the cheapest and since many of Royal Resorts staff were international hires, this significantly reduced their cost of hire and increased their margins. As their collaboration grew so did the ability to predict future performance of the talent hired. Although this was a difficult sell to the board, the business case made sense to give small fees to the RPO for every internal hire that was promoted. They wanted their RPO recruiters to recruit on potential and rewarding retention and growth gave Robert Page a reason to invest in analysing and hiring not just for the 'bum in seat', but also for potential.

This is a fictional scenario on talent acquisition in the near future.

Endnotes

1 Beard, A (2019) Experience doesn't predict a new hire's success, *Harvard Business Review*, September, hbr.org/2019/09/experience-doesnt-predict-a-new-hires-success (archived at https://perma.cc/P4YP-QWQT)

2 Quillian, L et al (2019) Do some countries discriminate more than others? Evidence from 97 field experiments of racial discrimination in hiring, *Sociological Science*, 6, 467–96, www.sociologicalscience.com/download/vol-6/june/SocSci_v6_467to496.pdf (archived at https://perma.cc/DCL2-8WXV)

3 Quillian, L and Lee, JJ (2023) Trends in racial and ethnic discrimination in hiring in six Western countries, *Proceedings of The National Academy of Sciences*, 120 (6), doi.org/10.1073/pnas.2212875120 (archived at https://perma.cc/E7JR-FB7V)

4 Sullivan, J (2017) Ouch, 50% of new hires fail! 6 ugly numbers revealing recruiting's dirty little secret, ERE, 10 April, www.ere.net/ouch-50-of-new-hires-fail-6-ugly-numbers-revealing-recruitings-dirty-little-secret (archived at https://perma.cc/UJE5-7AL4)

5 Werf& (2022) Robot recruiter Scotty screens up to 500,000 candidates per hour (YoungCapital submission), 25 March, www.werf-en.nl/robot-recruiter-scotty-screent-500-000-kandidaten-per-uur-inzending-youngcapital/ (archived at https://perma.cc/9MZZ-Z3FX)

6 How Arvato reduced employee turnover by 63%, Harver, Case study, harver.com/clients/bpo/arvato/ (archived at https://perma.cc/PD3M-SFCW)

7 Wikipedia (2023) Openness to experience, en.wikipedia.org/wiki/Openness_to_experience (archived at https://perma.cc/4VEQ-MAJW)

8 Wikipedia (2023) Conscientiousness, en.wikipedia.org/wiki/Conscientiousness (archived at https://perma.cc/YC4Q-M42S)

9 Wikipedia (2023) Extraversion and introversion, en.wikipedia.org/wiki/Extraversion_and_introversion (archived at https://perma.cc/P5AC-87L6)

10 Wikipedia (2023) Agreeableness, en.wikipedia.org/wiki/Agreeableness (archived at https://perma.cc/7UGM-RRCS)

11 Wikipedia (2023) Neuroticism, https://en.wikipedia.org/wiki/Neuroticism (archived at https://perma.cc/4JCF-E24K)

12 Kraskovsky, M (2012) Why feelings of guilt may signal leadership potential, 13 April, www.gsb.stanford.edu/insights/why-feelings-guilt-may-signal-leadership-potential (archived at https://perma.cc/R42E-2GSE)

13 Adams, S (2012) New study: guilt-prone people make better leaders, Forbes, 31 May, www.forbes.com/sites/susanadams/2012/05/31/new-study-guilt-prone-people-make-better-leaders/ (archived at https://perma.cc/R9F6-MCSQ)

14 Maurer, R (2021) HireVue Discontinues facial analysis screening, 3 February, www.shrm.org/resourcesandtools/hr-topics/talent-acquisition/pages/hirevue-discontinues-facial-analysis-screening.aspx (archived at https://perma.cc/H2X2-NDCA)

15 derStandard (2021) Application AI prefers job seekers with a bookshelves in the background, 19 February, www.derstandard.de/story/2000124300995/bewerbungs-ki-bevorzugt-jobsuchende-mit-buecherregal-im-hintergrund (archived at https://perma.cc/UFE7-X29G)

16 Kappen, M and Naber, M (2021) Objective and bias-free measures of candidate motivation during job applications, *Scientific Reports* 11, 21254, doi.org/101038/s41598-021-00659-y (archived at https://perma.cc/HZJ8-WET3)

17 Hung Lee (2023) LinkedIn, GENDER BIAS AT INTERVIEW – THE DATA (Blog), www.linkedin.com/posts/hunglee_iwd-gender-interviewing-activity-7039165915820670976-iJSX/? (archived at https://perma.cc/Q2UU-26W6)

18 N-VA Brussel (2019), Twitter, 8 October, twitter.com/NVABrussel/status/1181568312507092995 (archived at https://perma.cc/QHJ9-8XFC)

6

RPO or in-house?

Recruitment process outsourcing vs internal recruitment

Recruitment process outsourcing (RPO) is thriving and has been for some time. The industry has seen double-digit growth every year since 2015, driven to some degree by the demand for talent that has put pressure on internal recruitment functions. The demand for RPO is strong in many verticals, including fintech and non-contact payment services such as Square and Stripe. Pharmaceutical firms and medical institutions, manufacturing and defence contractors are also increasing their use of RPO. RPOs have developed global operations and have the capability to source and recruit anywhere. According to Everest Group's recent report on the RPO industry, over 45 per cent of all RPOs are recruiting globally.

Many organizations expect RPOs to take over the entire spectrum of recruitment, including tapping into and hiring the internal and contingent workforce. While large firms have been more likely to engage an RPO, recently, most growth is from the mid-sized and smaller firms, especially in APAC and Asia. RPOs are capable of quickly responding to both startup and large multinational firms' changing needs. They allow corporations a flexible recruitment strategy that can adapt to the ups and downs of markets.

The challenges faced by internal TA

Internal talent acquisition has never been immune to significant downsizing or even elimination during economic turmoil. Leaders often see it as a function that can be turned off and on as needed. An internal function has to be as efficient as or more efficient than an outside provider to remain competitive. This means continually improving operational excellence, adding appropriate technology, accessing detailed market information, coaching hiring managers and building a reputation for adding real value through the quality of talent it provides.

Internal functions often have difficulty developing efficient, streamlined processes and lack a coherent talent strategy for several reasons. First of all, both recruitment leaders and recruiters often see recruiting as a stepping-stone to a broader HR role and not as a career, which leads to short tenures and lack of continuity.

Recruiting leaders also struggle to get the support and budget required to create an efficient and proactive function. There are many costs involved in putting together a recruitment function. Some of those include the costs of technology and licences for a variety of applications such as LinkedIn. There are the costs of posting jobs and creative services for branding and marketing and reporting and analytics. Recruiters need to be trained and incentivized to perform. As new technology becomes available, it needs to be evaluated, purchased and integrated with other HR and organizational software. Most recruitment functions do not have skilled IT professionals to help source and evaluate technologies, and internal IT departments are often busy with higher priorities. The budget burden is high, and very few internal functions can fund all of these needs adequately.

Without technology, internal functions lack the data and data analytics that help them determine where the best talent is located, what attracts them to the firm and what skills are the most likely to lead to success. In effect, they are flying blind with only anecdotal evidence to support their sourcing and assessment of candidates.

On the other hand, RPOs hire IT professionals to purchase or develop technology and spread costs over many clients. Therefore, they can afford to invest heavily in technology and other services. And because of their clients and analytics, they have wide-ranging knowledge of the recruitment landscape, the skills a particular employee needs, the pros and cons of various technical solutions and deep expertise gained through engagement with numerous clients.

Why investing in technology is key

Over the past 10 years recruiting technology has developed to the point that it can augment many recruitment activities with artificial intelligence, machine learning and natural language processing. For example, programmatic advertising can target individuals with specific skills and interactive websites incorporating chatbots engage, inform and even screen candidates without a recruiter involved. A variety of available tools can screen and assess candidates and rank them according to predetermined requirements. Other automated tools can schedule interviews, recommend salaries, prepare offer or rejection letters, send emails, deliver documentation, conduct background screenings, and provide engaging and virtual onboarding. This means that in a function that takes advantage of these technologies, recruiters have more in-depth knowledge of where candidates are located and what skills they need to have. They can spend more time talking to and engaging candidates, discussing job requirements with the hiring managers, building relationships with potential candidates and getting to know internal employees' capabilities.

To their disadvantage, most internal recruiting functions have not implemented technology in a comprehensive or integrated way. Most have only an applicant tracking system (ATS) that provides candidate tracking and reporting. They do not have an integrated series of tools and continue to use people to source, screen, schedule interviews and do all the other tasks associated with recruitment. They have not been able to reduce costs or staff nor increase the number of positions a recruiter can handle. And they have not had the tools to build talent pools or develop robust talent pipelines. For most internal talent functions investment in technology is seen as a cost, while in an RPO it's seen as a benefit. When an internal function becomes more efficient, often their budgets get limited, while an RPO has a better margin.

They are also missing the insights that artificial intelligence can provide about candidates through better assessment capabilities. AI-enabled tools can objectively assess a candidate's skills in an area such as programming and do personality and culture-fit tests. Without this capability, they cannot quickly and objectively assess multiple candidates. After interviewing several candidates, it becomes harder to remember each one's strengths and characteristics. Automated tools can stack rank and tap into far more data than any human can process.

On top of these issues, they have to deal with internal politics, regional conflicts, the different needs of each hiring manager, complex bureaucracies and lack of senior-level support.

The advantages of recruitment process outsourcing

For a long time, internal talent acquisition used RPO functions to offload recruitment for high-volume roles such as retail sales associates or call centre staff. As these roles were considered high turnover and low-skilled, internal TA functions used cost as their primary selection criteria for an RPO. Top-level executive roles were outsourced to executive recruiters or agencies that specialized in executive talent. The internal function focused on primarily recruiting mid-level professionals.

But RPOs have grown in their ability to recruit both the lower volume roles and the more complex ones. Many RPOs can target candidates across various occupations and employment types, while other RPOs focus on vertical markets of specialists such as medical professionals, academics or financial professionals. RPOs have developed complex, customized solutions for clients that are far more sophisticated than in-house recruiting functions can manage.

For example, a global healthcare company with over 21,000 employees has been using RPO to deliver a best-in-class, centralized talent acquisition function focusing on speed, scale and experience. The RPO consolidated over 100 individual recruitment centres into a single centralized structure that delivers a consistent process and experience for hiring managers and candidates. This has also enabled the firm to expand existing centres and add new ones to their network. Rather than continue with the usual reactive recruitment process with an 'evergreen req,' the team utilized historic turnover data for each role and re-engineered the process to hire proactively for each critical role before the need arose. The RPO reduced costs by 10 per cent while improving the time to fill and cost per hire significantly.

RPOs can provide innovative solutions like this because of their expertise in technology. They also have technical experts, highly trained interviewers, candidate engagement specialists, and skilled and experienced recruiters. These employees often come from top-notch corporate recruiting functions or recruitment agencies and have experience and skills that are often better than corporate recruiters. RPOs also invest in training recruiters, which many internal functions do not have the resources or time to do.

Next to their technological advantages, many RPOs also have a dedicated training programme for new recruiters. This gives them an advantage in being able to train new recruiters to be the best in class. Many of these training programmes focus on a specific vertical, for example, sourcing or recruiting tech talent. RPO recruiters are not just equipped with better tooling, they are also better in using that tooling.

The growing benefits of RPO

The Coronavirus pandemic has forced organizations to restructure how employees work and allow greater flexibility in work arrangements. This will continue after the pandemic as organizations employ globally dispersed workers, many of whom may not be permanent employees. Employers are utilizing the skills of more part-time and contract workers, expanding their talent pools and making sourcing more complex. RPOs are well-positioned to source and recruit the virtual and gig workforce through their global networks. Some RPOs can also often additional services such as managing the contingent workforce, doing payroll and other administrative services.

RPOs allow recruiting function to scale their workforce without the worry of overstaffing or layoffs. Using an RPO lets them manage the workforce's size better and tailor it more closely to their needs as market conditions and talent needs change.

RPOs investments in technology can offer far more than the simple source and screen services. RPOs have developed deep databases of potential candidates in many verticals, and they can quickly tap into those databases to find the best candidates. RPOs can provide other services such as video interviewing and virtual job fairs to clients who lack these services or skills. Some RPOs are even offering outplacement and coaching services to laid-off employees.

The high level of data collected and analysed by RPOs gives them the ability to provide clients with a great deal of market intelligence. They can gather data about talent availability, including its location, which skills are most in-demand and the hardest to find, what marketing techniques are the most successful, what salary levels are normal and much more. Internal functions rarely gather and analyse this amount of data.

Many talent leaders consider RPO to be more expensive than internal recruiting, but the RPOs ability to leverage technology and put in place efficient, proven processes is often overlooked. This allows them to offer superior service at a lower cost. Internal functions also carry costs often overlooked when making comparisons with RPOs. They have their staff's continuing salary cost with benefits and other expenses and little flexibility to scale with market demand. There are also costs associated with physical buildings, equipment, leases and licences. RPO can be price-competitive and often less expensive.

How firms are using RPOs

Augmented recruitment

Existing talent acquisition functions use RPOs to take over the recruitment for some roles but not all. The mix of roles taken on by an RPO varies according to industry and employee. Typically, perhaps 40–60 per cent of roles are sourced and recruited by the RPO. The rest are retained by internal TA. RPOs are often chartered at first to recruit the high-volume roles and over time take on recruitment of professionals. They may have responsibility for advertising and branding, sourcing, assessment and even hiring. In other cases, their role may be only to source candidates or source and screen them and then turn them over to an internal recruiter.

In most cases, internal TA retains university, senior-level and executive recruitment. The range of RPO services is large and growing and includes many services not offered by internal functions.

Each situation is customized, and often the RPOs use a combination of internal recruiters and their recruiters. In other cases, they use their recruiters exclusively who act as if they were employees of the organization and, in pre-Covid times, might be physically located at the employee's place of business.

One example of how an RPO can work with an internal function is a large medical institution that needed to hire all staff levels quickly. They entered an RPO partnership and set goals that included strategically enhancing the talent acquisition function, ensuring compliance and governance, improving service levels to hiring leaders and optimizing the candidate experience for internal and external talent. The result was a 40 per cent reduction in the cost per hire and a $3 million saving in the first year.

One of the other advantages of using an RPO is that a client can have the RPO either utilize their existing ATS and technology or allow the RPO to use their own proprietary ATS and technology. Because of their investment in technology, RPOs can usually offer a more comprehensive and integrated solution than that of the firm, allowing greater efficiency and lower costs.

Total recruitment replacement

Many small and mid-sized firms find that letting the RPO take over all of their hourly and professional recruitment is an optimal solution. RPOs can provide a candidate experience that maintains the organization's culture while enhancing or replacing their technology. RPOs generally have more sophisticated technology solutions and a better ability to source candidates than the internal function. If the firm has recruiters, the RPO can usually take them on as employees and supplement them with their staff.

Organizations can reduce their internal staff to a few people with broader and more strategic roles while allowing the RPO to take on the end-to-end recruitment process. This lowers their cost by eliminating the need to purchase, upgrade and maintain recruitment tools and technology as well as the overhead and salary costs of a recruitment team. It allows maximum flexibility of labour costs and enhances the global sourcing of candidates.

Many firms transition to RPO in stages by letting the RPO take over recruiting the lower-level positions and then gradually allowing them to assume responsibility for additional roles. University and executive recruitment often remain with the internal TA function.

It is frequently the case that the RPO uses a client's existing technology as well as their own. For example, if the firm already has an ATS the RPO might continue to use the ATS but augment it with their CRM or other tools.

The head of recruiting at these firms acts as the facilitator of the transition and is responsible for providing feedback and suggesting continuous improvements to the process. The talent acquisition team's role becomes setting strategy, working to define needed skills, anticipating the future talent needs of the firm, and influencing and coaching hiring managers.

The hybrid recruitment model

A hybrid model may emerge from this pandemic, with RPO playing a significant role. The internal TA function will set strategy and act as the liaison between senior leadership and the RPO. They can also serve as coaches for hiring managers and provide employee development opportunities.

When there are particular roles that the organization does not want an RPO to recruit, they could form an ad hoc, cross-functional recruiting team. A hiring manager could become a key member of the team with perhaps a marketing professional to provide targeted messaging and social media advertising. A technical expert could help make sure the selection criteria is appropriate and help in the assessment. This web of allied employees would increase the speed and efficiency of finding and hiring the right person.

The future of recruitment and RPO

Over the next decade, organizations will go through profound changes in their structure and workforce. The pandemic has had the effect of accelerating a trend toward virtual work. Firms will reduce their permanent workforce and leverage more contingent and virtual workers. They will also focus much more on moving people internally and offering more employee development. RPOs are well-positioned to tap into the total workforce, whether internal or external, contingent or permanent, local or global.

Unless organizations invest considerably more in their internal function, it will be increasingly challenging to provide the quality, speed and efficiency of the modern RPO. As a total talent acquisition philosophy becomes normal, firms will need to seek people with the required skills and abilities no matter how they prefer to work. The contingent workforce will continue to grow and become essential to success. Finding people that fit the culture of the firm will also be necessary. RPOs can use their data to analyse the corporate culture and ensure that all matches are compatible with both the overall culture and the hiring managers.

Does your C-suite truly believe that your talent is your competitive advantage and are they willing to invest in the talent acquisition department for the long term?

Stay in-house and possibly scale with embedded solutions in case of peak demand.

Does the C-suite treat you like a cost centre?

You should seriously consider going RPO and decide if there is a certain part of hiring, executive or graduate for example, you want to keep in house.

In whatever way the future evolves, RPO will be an essential part of any successful recruitment strategy. Their superior use of technology and data analytics will help firms uncover hard-to-find talent faster, lower costs and make better matches for hiring managers.

The early 2020s were challenging times for recruiters and lay out a blueprint for what the industry will likely see again. Although these times historically had been normal in the USA, for most of Europe this was a relatively new phenomenon. As American companies have always been built on money from external investors, most European companies stem from either government entities that are privatized or family-owned businesses that have grown over decades or even centuries. Labour law also plays a role here, as it's much harder to fire people in Europe and in some countries, like Sweden – if you fire someone because of economic circumstances and you rehire for that job within six months, by law you are obligated to offer the person you fired the job first.

With the increasing number of venture backed startups and scale-ups the events that were witnessed in the early 2020s will become more common in Europe as well. After a period of massive over-hiring, layoffs occurred and also many among recruiters. With uncertainty over the economy, many organizations fear they hired too many people or people with the wrong skills. Rising interest rates made VCs less willing to shower firms with millions of dollars, so startups were relooking at their employment levels and burn rates and cutting staff. However, many organizations also understood the labour market has forever changed with retirements at all-time highs and labour market shortages in every sector of the economy. So even in the USA most organizations did the layoffs with grace and gave very decent severance packages.

In many cases firms over hired in previous years. When Amazon announced a big reduction in workforce of 10 per cent, this was actually less than the number of people they hired a year before. And the same was true for many other tech firms.

Embedded talent

One trend that has emerged in Europe, where firing is harder and more costly than the USA, is embedded talent solutions. Contrary to RPO this isn't outsourcing the entire department, but rather having recruiters 'on call'. Organizations like Join Talent, Immersive and We Are Keen, for example, deliver TA professionals in a matter of days rather than the months to hire them and these professionals are very quickly productive as they are well trained and often equipped with technology that helps them excel at their task. Most are also specialists in certain areas of talent acquisition like sourcing or even tech sourcing, interviewing or recruitment marketing. Several of these embedded talent solutions organizations also have traineeships for new recruiters so they are able to deliver better quality at scale. Embedded talent offerings are different to RPO in that they don't take over the entire TA department, or parts of it, but they are 'on call' additions to the team. Although some work on site and offer those options, the rise of remote work has also greatly expanded possibilities in offering this on call talent.

With these developments in mind, organizations need to have a clear recruitment strategy. The hiring and firing recruiters on the spot isn't a model that delivers quality results in the long term and it will eventually be more costly if the hiring cost of the TA department as well as severance package are truly calculated. And we are not even mentioning how these hiring and firing cycles hurt your employer brand.

TAKEAWAYS

- When your C-suite treats recruitment like a cost centre, consider RPO.
- When your C-suite considers talent acquisition to add value and provides a reasonable budget, keep recruiting in-house.
- RPOs have in many cases a big advantage over in-house talent acquisition because of their technological advances.
- Even with modern SAAS (software as a service technology), often the technological and data know-how within an HR or TA department is lacking to ensure optimal use of these tools.

THE STORY OF V-FARM*

V-Farm started buying up old office buildings in Amsterdam and, soon after, one in London and Brussels. They refurbished these buildings to vertical farms, building on the fast development from the knowledge that different light influences growth and nutrition of vegetables. With modern technology they were able to grow four crops a year, similar to sub-tropical climates, but with more nutritional value because of the lighting used. This was further improved as the time from harvest to kitchen was reduced by months.

When the European Union decided to increase the tax on carbon emissions and other pollution from transport the business case became solid overnight. Being able to 'hand deliver' vegetables to restaurants by bike as well as have pick-up points for 'healthy vegetable boxes', they were able to cut out the mighty supermarket middleman and keep margins at levels that were necessary for this product. Of course, drone technology for delivery was already on the radar from the beginning, but the technology hadn't matured enough for reliable delivery yet.

V-Farm knew their Dutch heritage was an advantage to start with – building on the knowledge of the world's most renowned agricultural university in Wageningen as well as the heritage on lighting technology and innovation that Philips, now called Signify, installed in the technical universities – but it needed to scale up, fast.

With their healthy margins, unique product and their 'love brand' they had venture capital investors knocking down the door and when the board finally made the deal, it was time to go into hyper-growth.

Sophie, as a head of people and culture, had always been close to the board so she knew what was coming. And even though she had been in companies that were doubling or tripling in size before, this time it was different. This time they needed to scale up in different cities and countries simultaneously. New locations would open in Berlin, Munich, Madrid, Barcelona, Paris, Marseille, Milan, Rome, Naples, Porto and Lisbon within months and this was only the first wave. Many other major cities in Europe had been scouted already and she was told that after 12–18 months they were planning the next round of investments and would set up shop in the USA, expecting to open in 25 major cities at once. And all those locations needed to be staffed with technicians to keep the location up and running, but also general staff to pick the fruits and vegetables, riders to deliver to restaurants and of course they needed localized sales and marketing. To foster this type of growth in the timeframe she had, she decided there was only one route possible – use a recruiting process outsourcing firm (RPO).

As she had always scaled her own teams, she realized she didn't have the experience she needed to do this massive RPO deal all on her own. That's why she decided to hire an expert to help her select the RPO best suited for the job. Although she had plenty of experience buying technology in the past, now she needed to evaluate both the technology this RPO was using, the way they were using it and their vision on collaboration. This was an entirely new ballgame and as she had been very aware of bias in the past, she was afraid the likability of the sales manager handling her account was going to get in the way of a rational decision. To avoid this, she hired an expert that possessed many different traits and complemented her and also liked different types of salespeople. Her expertise in scaling and growth combined with his expertise on RPO deals was seen as annoying to some RPOs pitching for the deal but amazing to others.

The first choice Sophie had to make is what jobs would be outsourced or rather what part of the recruitment her current, small team would keep. Because so many new countries needed to be added at such a high pace, it was decided only corporate staff at headquarters would be done in house and all national and local operations, including the national white-collar workers, would be hired by the RPO. So they needed an RPO with a huge presence all around the world, or at least in Europe, the US and Canada to start with.

When evaluating the different RPOs they looked for a long-term partnership and she convinced the board that they should enter into at least a 10-year agreement with a fixed price per year over that time, unrelated to the hiring needs of any given year. This would give the RPO the incentive to hire for fit and keep attrition as low as it could while building talent tools to fill positions as fast as possible with the right people. The board agreed that a long-term partnership would benefit both V-Farm as well as the RPO. There were three main factors that determined hiring need – country, city and number of farms in a city – which would be the three factors on which the RPO fee would be determined. Since V-Farm knew their current recruitment costs of operating in a country, the extra costs to add an extra city and the additional recruitment costs of operating another vertical farm in a city, they set this as the absolute top limit. They also knew that their current operations had been underfunded, so with investments in technology they knew an RPO should be able to save a lot of money in the long run.

Because the RPOs that were pitching had been investing in technology and optimizing state-of-the-art technology for their use for years before Sophie's request for proposal came, she knew they could ask for everything at once. Instead of buying and implementing technology themselves, the RPOs had figured this out for other clients, so it was mainly a matter of selecting the right one. And of course, no RPO was perfect or had scored an A on every piece, so they made a scorecard.

The scorecard looked at a range of items: the attrition at the RPO itself, as they believed that only if you take care of your own employees are you able to take care of those at V-Farm; cost was also important, as was experience in both countries, and hiring for the type of roles V-Farm needed. Bonus points on the scorecard were given for hiring for other organizations in hyper growth.

The tech stack was another important part of the scorecard. Although it's the RPOs job to provide candidates at a fixed price, knowing they can actually deliver candidates is more important than any potential penalty for not being able to deliver in time. Even more important is the candidate experience these tools deliver – as V-Farm is a customer-facing company the chances of applicants being potential customers is very high. There is a potential loss of millions of dollars for having a bad candidate experience.

Three types of technologies were assessed: the basics, the must-haves and the nice-to-haves. The basics were the ATS and CRM system, the data dashboard, the programmatic technology and the sourcing technology used. As it was important that candidates had a great candidate experience, V-Farm insisted on keeping 'silver medallists' on record while of course fully complying with the privacy laws in every different region. It also insisted on addressing candidates in their local language, which meant, for example, that the application forms behind the career websites should change language as well.

The must-have technology was the assessment and screening technology, the pre- an onboarding tools, the candidate nurturing technology and the bias audit software. V-Farm wasn't hiring just anybody; it needed the staff that handled the consumer side to be extraordinarily friendly; it needed their technicians to have high learning agility as the world of vertical farming was in its infancy, and new technology and better ways of working were discovered every day. These are features you cannot find on just any résumé, so the assessment and screening technology was essential, just like the bias audit software as it had a brand to protect. Much of the onboarding could be done digitally, so fresh hires would know the layout of the building and where everything was before they even started.

The nice-to-have technology entailed the referral tooling, augmented writing technology and VR technology for job previews and/or assessments.

Many RPOs were invited to the selection process, as Sophie wasn't sure their global ambitions could be served by a single player and many big RPOs fell through the cracks when they were pushed on local presence in different nations. Several of the world's biggest RPOs in turn only had real presence in the USA and Canada while some European players had a presence in the USA, but not on the local level that was needed for this business. Eventually one stood out, C-Man, which had been investing in lots of technology and had the local presence in all the major cities V-Farm was planning on expanding to at first.

Since C-Man had everything in place and integrated, V-Farm was able to scale really quickly. With their amazing programmatic technology combined with their automated searching technology, getting candidates in wasn't a big issue. The V-Farm love brand helped a lot of course and having built excellent career websites, based on a global template, but tailored to local preferences, it wasn't long before V-Farm was in hyper growth and was rejecting a lot more people than it was hiring.

Because C-Man wasn't about to let these talented people go, even though there may not have been a job at the company at that time, using candidate-nurturing technology they built a candidate pipeline and made sure these silver medallists were kept in the loop. Of course, the pipeline contained only those that passed the initial tests on customer friendliness for customer-facing jobs and learning agility for the potential on-site engineers. The others were kindly rejected with specific explanations on why they didn't fit with the company. This candidate pipeline soon turned out to be a goldmine for C-Man, as over half of all the hires now came from people that were already interested and just needed to be activated. Cost per hire dropped and with the fixed price on the contract, margins were good. As V-Farm was able to expand as fast as they wanted to with fixed prices for every new location they opened, there was no complaint from them either.

The pre- and onboarding tools were adjusted to each new site, making it a smooth entry for every new hire. As the tool was so engaging, most new hires started with great confidence. They knew what was expected before they started. They knew where to go to change into company clothing or what the rules were on dating a colleague. V-Farm had clear guidelines on politics in the workplace and what was considered intolerable behaviour. In the hiring process these behaviours were tested, but the fact they were intolerable was emphasized again in the pre-boarding process and it was clear where you could go if you felt you weren't treated fairly.

As humans are flawed, it wasn't sunshine all day every day. V-Farm was very aware that its core customers would react badly to any form of bias in the hiring process. So they published all the numbers on ethnicity and gender per role (if local law had allowed them to register that), as well as the average pay in that role for each subset. The system would also have bias alerts. If a certain location or country would be diverging too much from the baseline there would be an analysis on why that was, and if it had to do with bias, it would be corrected. Additionally, V-Farm undertook a yearly 'external bias audit' by having mystery applicants apply and see if the systems treated everybody equally. This audit was done by a third party, as it was in part auditing the RPO as well.

This is a fictional scenario on talent acquisition in the near future.

7

A radical new model
for talent acquisition

As we have mentioned throughout this book, today's recruitment functions act too slowly and often lack knowledge about the business and the skills needed. They have a poor picture of the available talent supply, lack marketing expertise and hinder efficiency with complex administrative systems. They do not meet the expectations of many candidates or hiring managers accustomed to fast service and prompt feedback.

Recruiting functions are organized for an era that is gone. The current model worked well when skill needs were predictable and the positions that needed to be filled were stable. It worked when the talent supply was generally plentiful and primarily local. But it is clear that this model, a relic of the 20th-century manufacturing era organizations, needs to be radically disrupted.

A new model

Figure 7.1 lays out the elements that are required for an effective, modern and agile talent function.

The newly structured function assumes the responsibilities for talent management, recruiting, employee development and internal mobility. It becomes the overall talent arm of the organization. It is responsible for ensuring the organization can meet skill needs as quickly as they arise. This means that it must be agile and attract all types of talent, whether permanent, freelance or consultant. And it needs to do this either through its own processes or by utilizing RPOs (see Chapter 6) or other external resources.

FIGURE 7.1 Revised recruiting model

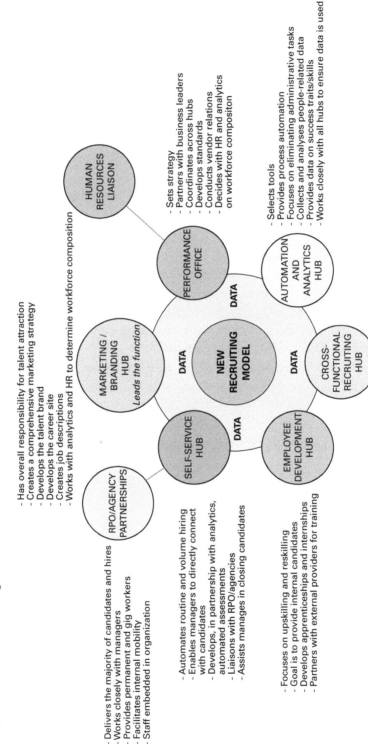

- Has overall responsibility for talent attraction
- Creates a comprehensive marketing strategy
- Develops the talent brand
- Develops the career site
- Creates job descriptions
- Works with analytics and HR to determine workforce composition

- Sets strategy
- Partners with business leaders
- Coordinates across hubs
- Develops standards
- Conducts vendor relations
- Decides with HR and analytics on workforce composition

- Selects tools
- Provides process automation
- Focuses on eliminating administrative tasks
- Collects and analyses people-related data
- Provides data on success traits/skills
- Works closely with all hubs to ensure data is used

- Delivers the majority of candidates and hires
- Works closely with managers
- Provides permanent and gig workers
- Facilitates internal mobility
- Staff embedded in organization

- Automates routine and volume hiring
- Enables managers to directly connect with candidates
- Develops, in partnership with analytics, automated assessments
- Liaisons with RPO/agencies
- Assists manages in closing candidates

- Focuses on upskilling and reskilling
- Goal is to provide internal candidates
- Develops apprenticeships and internships
- Partners with external providers for training

- Acts as talent advisors
- Focuses on low-volume, hard-to-fill position
- Vets referrals
- Ad-hoc team members: managers, HR, technical experts, recruiters
- Heavy focus on internal mobility
- Does university and executive recruitment
- Coaches managers and candidates

HUMAN RESOURCES LIAISON

PERFORMANCE OFFICE

MARKETING / BRANDING HUB
Leads the function

AUTOMATION AND ANALYTICS HUB

NEW RECRUITING MODEL

DATA

DATA

DATA

DATA

CROSS-FUNCTIONAL RECRUITING HUB

SELF-SERVICE HUB

EMPLOYEE DEVELOPMENT HUB

RPO/AGENCY PARTNERSHIPS

It must also be continuously aware of emerging skill needs and provide coaching and learning opportunities for internal employees.

It is broken into six focus areas, each with its own expertise.

Marketing/branding hub

This hub is at the top of the model to reflect its importance in recruiting. Recruiting is primarily a marketing function and needs a high level of expertise to attract candidates in a talent-short and competitive market.

The era of post-and-pray and searching LinkedIn and the internet are no longer adequate. Even a good employment brand is inadequate to attract the best talent.

Organizations need to use the techniques of product marketers to differentiate their jobs, work culture and other factors from their competition. They need more comprehensive and global talent intelligence and need to target specific types of candidates. Very few current talent functions have the expertise to research and create effective marketing campaigns or build a strong brand. This requires the use of data and creative skills to develop and curate content, develop relationships, build communities and do all the things required to generate a flow of qualified candidates.

Talent is harder to acquire without independent and robust marketing functions, and many highly skilled people are never seen.

Performance office

The performance office is the strategy development arm and integrator of the numerous elements needed for a complete talent picture. It is responsible for ensuring the organization has the skills and people to meet any future requirements. It is designed to set standards, negotiate with vendors, use data to decide whether to recruit or develop required skills, work with the automation hub to select tools and integrate them into the various functions, and coordinate activities between the different hubs. It liaises with both the RPO vendors as well as with human resources. The HR liaison is critical to ensure that policies are in alignment.

Automation and analytics hub

Since recruiters are not technologists and should not be, and corporate IT functions have other priorities, creating an automation hub makes sense.

In such a hub, a team of technicians, analysts and recruiters work together to select, implement and continuously improve recruitment tools, the career site, assessment and the application processes. This relieves recruiters from doing what they lack the expertise to do and provides candidates the experience they expect – quick service, feedback and prompt decisions.

This hub simplifies and automates the administrative tasks associated with recruitment. Automated tools, powered by artificial intelligence and machine learning, offer candidates a personalized experience with relevant and engaging content. They can also screen and assess candidates and recommend selected candidates for hire with increasing accuracy as more and more data is accumulated and analysed. These tools can find suitable candidates, communicate with them and do the administrative tasks associated with hiring.

To enhance the automated tools' ability to make good decisions and ensure information is available to the recruiting team, there must be the capability to gather and analyse all sorts of data about people. This includes assessing skills, analysing work patterns, measuring performance, and correlating skills and abilities with the work needed.

Cross-functional recruitment teams

If direct human-to-human contact is necessary, ad hoc recruiting teams formed and disbanded as needed can be charted. They can be focused on hiring a vertical, a unique individual, global hiring or whatever is required that is not routine or high volume. Hiring managers become vital team members and take over some of a recruiter's functions. The team might include a technical expert who would help make sure the selection criteria is appropriate for a position and, of course, a marketing person to create a strategy for attracting the needed talent. This network of allied employees can significantly increase the speed and efficiency of finding and hiring the right people. Only a handful of experienced recruiters are needed as the self-service hub and RPOs handle most volume recruitment.

Removing artificial barriers and fostering cooperation and sharing among those who formerly worked in functional silos allows people to expand beyond narrowly defined roles, take on new roles, learn and bring fresh ideas.

Employee development hub

Being able to develop talent is an integral part of any talent strategy. An organization needs to analyse the skills of existing talent, assess the availability of the skills it needs in the marketplace and develop those skills internally and externally when the supply is constrained. Today this function is often separate from recruiting and may not align with it. By integrating recruitment, data analytics and development, the organization can proactively find ways to accelerate skill development. The organization can offer apprenticeships, internships and rotations to build internal talent, which lessens external recruiting.

Self-service hub

Self-service tools provides the organization with a fast and effective way to hire many employees. Effective marketing will attract candidates and combined with straightforward job and accurate skill criteria, it can assess candidates using variously accredited online tools. Hiring managers can choose from a vetted list of candidates. Other tools can generate offer letters, employment contracts and do all other administrative requirements.

Giving candidates and managers the option to use these tools would be the first step to an automated recruitment capability. There are only a few cases where we need extensive human-to-human direct contact. The majority of open positions can be filled quickly if we have good marketing and data-driven assessment. It is only logical that in an increasingly self-service and automated world, we allow candidates and hiring managers to find each other and communicate without any recruiter involved.

Of course, there are variations on this model that may suit one organization better than another. I understand that this model would only be possible in a large firm, but some of the same ideas can be modified for smaller firms. Automating high-volume recruiting may be a challenge but would almost immediately relieve recruiters of the administrative tasks and volume overload they face. It would allow them to engage with the business in more meaningful and strategic ways.

The key message is that those firms that attract the best talent will enjoy a competitive edge. This will not happen given the current recruiting functions' administrative and tactical structure.

TAKEAWAYS

- Figure 7.1 presents an ideal model, best suited for a large organization, but any recruiting function no matter the size should rethink how they are now structured.

- The key is to identify areas where you are struggling and find solutions to improve them, other than working harder or hiring more people.

- Make or buy decisions, both on technology as on RPO, should be made consciously and methodically.

- It may be possible to partner with the firm's marketing or IT function to improve recruiting marketing and gain insights using analytics.

- Rethinking the metrics you currently use and developing more useful metrics and ways to show your success are important to continuously improve your effectiveness.

- Employee development and internal mobility are now important to augment external recruitment. Every recruiting function should either take responsibly for employee development or partner with that function.

THE STORY OF BIOVAC*

Biovac was founded in the wake of the Covid-19 pandemic. After the pandemic the interest from investors as well as established researchers and young talent into vaccine research and development was booming. Although the major pharmaceutical companies were hiring as well and several scale-ups got their major break with the Covid vaccines, a group of researchers felt they needed to take a different route. So they founded a new company – Biovac. The founders were several researchers that had been researching vaccines into all kind of diseases like HIV for decades. It took years before Biovac had its first product on the market – a Covid-19 vaccine that was resistant to all mutations – but because of the way regulatory bodies had changed their operating procedures, it was way faster than would have been possible before the pandemic. Unlike the other vaccines on the market their vaccine was able to recognize and counter every mutation the virus could throw at them, making it a desired vaccine if a more deadly variant emerged when nobody expected a resurgence. Realizing the potential of this vaccine development platform they decided to start researching a flu vaccine as well as several other diseases.

After the bird flu pandemic a few years later their vaccine development platform turned out to be the key to saving the world from another catastrophe. As the bird flu was spreading among humans and killing a hundred times more people than Covid-19 did in its first months, the US government decided that the vaccine was allowed for emergency use without proper testing for healthcare workers that desired it. It turned out to be both safe as well as extremely effective. Up until that point Biovac had limited production facilities located in the USA and India and because of the pandemic supply chains were hit, hampering the speed of production of this much-needed vaccine. Moreover, the US and Indian governments claimed the first right on all production, increasing the impact of the pandemic on Europe and the rest of Asia. After the bird flu pandemic was contained, many countries demanded and subsidized production facilities of Biovac within their borders. Now, Biovac is the largest vaccine manufacturer in the world developing vaccines for many diseases and they are even funded by the World Health Organisation to research vaccines for the most serious animal diseases that could jump to humans. They have many manufacturing plants on every continent. Their R&D facilities are also distributed and they have several laboratories on every continent, often in close vicinity of a major university.

Lucy started as the Head of TA just before the bird flu pandemic when Biovac was in growth mode but depended on new investment. So, then, it was a struggle for money combined with a little-known brand competing with organizations that had seemingly unlimited funds. She did, however, have direct access to the founders, who had great reputations in academia. One stormy afternoon in autumn she sat down with the founders to talk about their talent strategy. The founders had been talking about how they wanted to be different from other biotech and pharmaceutical companies, yet they were emulating their biggest rivals when it came to their talent strategy. Lucy confronted them that afternoon with their own company heritage. Biovac was established because the founders had been ridiculed for decades for chasing their dream. They believed you could make a vaccine that mutated with the virus and this would make the world a safer place. How would people like them find their way into the company if they did talent acquisition in the same way the others did? After a long uncomfortable silence the board decided that the Head of Talent, a position held by Frank who was the former Head of TA, needed to become a position in the C-suite. Lucy, as the Head of TA, would still reside under the Head of Talent, but would be invited at least every quarter to speak directly with the entire C-suite. Talent wasn't just 'their most important asset' in words only, but now had a permanent position in the C-suite, and talent acquisition wasn't just a department within the talent function. Attracting the right talent had become the centre point of their talent strategy; you cannot develop an Olympic champion horse if you only hire ponies. Truly putting their employees first meant they also didn't see talent acquisition and talent development as cost centres but as essential to the business and funded them accordingly.

Very quickly, several talent-related strategies were established. One of them was that base pay was a little below average compared to other pharmaceutical companies, but every employee had both a profit share as well as payment in shares. Although investors were not happy with their dilution, the founders still had the majority of shares. Every new investor would have to sign off on this strategy. The goal was for the company to be majority owned by (former) employees, something they managed after about a decade.

Another important strategy Frank managed to pass that same year was that Biovac would not require any employee to work full time or exclusively for the company. Several C-suite members already had positions as professors at prestigious universities, but for non-executive employees there wasn't yet a specific policy. Frank managed to put a policy in place that not only was this allowed but it actively promoted staff to have a second job. Furthermore, they opened their employment ranks up for researchers that wanted to start 'a day a week' to see if the commercial world was to their liking.

Biovac's talent strategy

Biovac is now seen as an example of an excellent talent strategy. Because of the nature of its work, Biovac knew it needed centralized locations, as working with deadly pathogens is not something you can do from home. So it needed laboratories. Yet as academics that had collaborated with other academics all over the world on rare diseases, the founders knew talent was distributed equally in the world. So Frank and Lucy devised a model where every location was equal. There was no main office and no boardroom, even the board of directors was scattered across the globe and met virtually most of the time. The board had a quarterly physical meeting and the company had a yearly internal conference where all employees would gather, bond and share knowledge. Their researchers would have two scientific research conferences a year, close to the company-wide meeting, which were also open to external academics. These meetings were of course also attended by the talent team, scouting new talent. Knowing diversity of thought increases chances of success, Biovac actively promoted exchanges between their locations and having done tours abroad it was seen as a big plus when it came to promotions. They also promoted exchanges between the company and universities. They pioneered an open talent strategy where everybody in R&D could leave, do a public research project at a university, sometimes funded by the company, with the security, but not the obligation, of returning to the company.

Biovac has a fully automated system to spot rising talent in the academic fields of healthcare based on academic publications. This was something Frank had pioneered in his days as TA manager at a university, but never got beyond the identification of specific talent, with lots of manual input. Their AI sourcing bot is able to identify and connect to academic talents in healthcare, not just in virology and medicine but in all of healthcare as Biovac has a mission to improve healthcare throughout the world. Talents are identified based on their publications and contacted by a virtual recruitment assistant. The AI assistant is able to write highly engaging messages based on their publications and ask them to join Biovac's talent community. This is an exclusive community that has access to much of Biovac's research and other facilities and a chance to get invited to the Biovac scientific conferences. As members they also receive, if they so desire, personalized AI-based coaching as if they were employees, to help them further their careers. Although the community is exclusive and Biovac removes non-active members or members that work for competitors, it has grown very large over time. The community has become the primary source of hiring and fully automated candidate nurturing keeps the participants engaged. Different participants in the community have different privileges based on the combination of both the quality and the frequency of their contributions to the Biovac community and the scientific community at large.

Of course, most people that join the talent community never start their career at Biovac. The company knows that there will always be more talent that is not working for you than there is working for you. So it also has the most renowned talent exchange, lending talent to and from academia, suppliers and other selected partners in the supply chain. Senior researchers are allowed to return to academia, just like it will give academics the chance to set up a new product line without them losing their tenure at their university. This talent exchange is also open for other senior knowledge workers that are not in R&D. They regularly exchange logistics managers and production coordinators with product designers and software engineers with other organizations in the supply chain.

The hiring of support staff, basically every job that does not relate to either R&D or production, is done using the following mantra: Only if a human can add value, should a human be involved. Biovac has a decent-sized TA department, but every talent advisor is augmented with excellent technology. The talent advisor's main role is to advise the hiring managers on what talent they need for a role. The most important part of the talent advisor role is intake. Together with the hiring manager the talent advisor decides on the skills and personality traits of the desired candidate. The talent advisor is responsible for assisting the hiring manager on having a team that is complementary and making sure the new hire is a fit with the company and team values while adding skills or traits. After the intake is done, this information is added into the hiring system where the AI writing tool will automatically write a job description, only to be checked by the talent advisor. Based on the input, the system will also automatically develop an assessment profile, again to be checked by the talent advisor. The system will than check if there is any talent available with the required skills and traits either inside the company or in the talent pool that has been set up for silver medallists and has been automatically nurtured over time. If there is a suitable candidate the AI virtual assistant will automatically contact this person asking if the position that is open might interest him or her. If that is the case (s)he is automatically asked to book a call with the talent advisor who takes the process from there. If there is no suitable candidate within the company or the talent pool or if no candidate is interested the talent advisor will be notified. When the talent advisor is notified (s)he will receive all the relevant information about recruiting for this role: the difficulty to hire someone for this role, the number of candidates that the AI sourcing engine seems to be able to find and the most successful sources of hire for this, or a similar, role in the past. Based on this, the talent advisor can choose to start the AI sourcing engine and receive potential candidates or advertise on the suggested channels. Although there are AI sourcing-programs that also do the first contact with the candidate, Biovac has chosen not to deploy these yet as they want to optimize their internal AI virtual assistant first before using it for external sourcing. Any interested external candidate will need to either take an assessment provided by Biovac or share their skills passport with the appropriate assessment data. As these skills passports are only just gaining traction few candidates currently have one, but after they have finished the assessment, whether they pass or fail for the job at Biovac, the data is theirs to keep and upload to their skills passport so they might share this later when applying at another organization.

The talent strategy is a bit different for the production locations. Although most of the work in the production locations doesn't require a masters or bachelor's degree, it does require very high levels of both conscientiousness and agility. Mistakes are unacceptable in the production of these sensitive products. Workers also need agility because after the bird flu pandemic Biovac created many production locations with many local supply lines in the world. This meant these locations were not running at maximum capacity most of the time, but needed to be able to scale up quickly in case of another pandemic. The many different locations in the world of course have different strategies depending on the specific labour market conditions. In the poorer regions of the world, where there is high unemployment and low access to education, Biovac has set up their own training facilities. There is little to no advertising necessary to get enough applicants and all applicants are screened with modern game-based assessment tools that screen for potential. The best applicants for different positions will be trained by the company and these regions have a strong internal growth model. The silver medallists that do meet the criteria are invited if in a later stage new training opportunities arise. In the wealthier regions of the world, Biovac uses a slightly different model. For certain jobs in the production facility, like maintenance engineer, a degree of sorts is required. For other positions the assessment model and training programme is also applied. If there is a shortage for certain roles that do require a degree Biovac is able to use the assessment and training model in these countries as well and, depending on immigration laws, Biovac would offer international transfers for employees in high unemployment regions to regions with labour shortages for those specific roles.

Using the assessments to select the trainees has reduced the dropout rate in the training programme to close to zero over time while selecting the most talented individuals for specific roles at Biovac. This enabled them to have relatively fewer staff compared to competitors as fewer mistakes were made and problems were fixed faster and better, leaving room for paying above-average wages.

The Biovac talent strategy is key to the success of the company and has the full support of the C-suite executives. As Biovac itself exists because other big pharmaceutical companies didn't see or recognize great talent, the company has set a policy of screening in rather than screening out. Although it's easier with its current size, even in the younger years they would create positions for people they considered very talented, especially in the R&D side of the company. The position they have taken on talent is similar to that of venture capital firms to investment opportunities. It's not only about those you bring in; they also look at missed opportunity costs if a great talent wasn't spotted or did apply and wasn't selected. Because Biovac sees missed opportunity as costs as well, their TA budget is above average. Not only is there sufficient manpower, but there is also more than enough budget for technology. Biovac uses almost no agencies and if an agency is used this is from the TA budget so there are no hidden costs. The total budget for TA is significantly higher than many competitors, but the total cost when hours spent by line managers and mis-hires is taken into account isn't. The first-year churn is minimal compared to their main competitors, for example.

The early years

When Frank was still the head of TA, he saw the opportunity for talent intelligence, talent exchanges and internal talent markets for a company like Biovac very early on. In his previous job as an TA professional in academia he never had the budget or the management buy-in to do it right, but his ambitions had always been to set up a system combining talent intelligence, internal talent markets and external talent exchanges. He had the vision and one of the founders knew this, so hired him as the head of talent acquisition and later promoted him to the head of talent when the company was big enough.

Talent intelligence was mainly focused on the R&D department and helped them where amazing research was done by academics in more remote areas of the world. They were able to pioneer this in unrepresented ways because of the open character of academic publications. They quickly saw this as the ultimate opportunity to hire those talented individuals that would help the company become as dominant as it has and invested heavily in this from the start. The combination of internal data on desired skills and expected growth of employees combined with external data on researchers in the areas they were still lacking helped them open up research facilities in places no pharmaceutical company had invested before. They joined forces with universities in countries like Congo, Burundi and Mongolia which had been ignored by the traditional companies. These early cooperations led to a lot of internal knowledge on the culture and laws of these countries that helped Biovac considerably when it set up production facilities there.

They quickly opened an internal talent market as they knew this hub and spoke model had its limits when it comes to sharing talent and knowledge.

Giving researchers all over the world the opportunity to share their knowledge and be hired, either for a period of time or permanently, by other locations for research projects helped not only with hiring, as their hubs all over the world were seen as stepping stones for a career anywhere in the world; it also created an amazing talent pool for otherwise ignored talent. Very soon after the initial success of the internal talent market, Biovac management asked why this was only an internal talent market. If their goal was to make the world a safer place, shouldn't they support other organizations with the same goals? And what better way to support this goal than by exchanging talent and helping solve the truly important problems in medicine and health? The internal talent market was opened up for external partners making it a talent exchange.

First this was done with the select universities that Biovac was already working closely with, but the actual exchange of talent was limited as there were many teething problems. These resolved when Biovac started opening the talent exchange to other partners in the supply chain, other research firms, suppliers and even governments. One pivotal moment for the talent exchange was when one of the neighbouring countries where Biovac had a laboratory had a pandemic scare of Ebola and Biovac selflessly stepped in to aid the government with implementing the right measures to mitigate the problem, isolating the strain and quickly developing a cure. The local government of the country where Biovac was located, through the talent exchange, requested Biovac talent to set up a playbook for when a pandemic hit their country. Biovac loaned their best virologists to help set up this policy, which was beneficial to the government, who got the best possible advice at little cost, the employees, who learned on the inner workings of the government while felling they were able to make a serious contribution to the world, as well as the company that got more skilled and more motivated employees, next to lots of positive press. After this the talent exchange started taking off and it became an eco-system of different organizations, all of course selected by Biovac, exchanging talent, either temporarily or part time, which benefited all organizations and employees.

As well as the talent intelligence and exchanges Biovac also pioneered with technology for talent attraction. As many academics that they wanted to hire were sceptical at first of joining such a small and young company, Biovac quickly devised a long-term nurturing strategy. This comprised of three technologies that were still in the pioneering phase at the time they started using them. The first was the second generation of programmatic advertising. This technology didn't just optimize for clicks and conversion, it was able to identify the mental stage, based on the traditional AIDA model of marketing, a candidate was in. As Biovac was such an unknown company at the time this usually started with explaining how they were going to change the world, getting their attention. Once the technology saw they grabbed a person's attention it would look to create an interest, for example in specific parts of Biovac's portfolio and the sharing of their knowledge. The goal was to have people subscribe to the knowledge community and there the candidate nurturing would take over. Those that did not subscribe, but did show an interest would get advertisements showing the career potential or the joy of working at the company, trying to create a desire to work there. If they showed any interest they would be shown relevant jobs persuading them to action. Of course in the early days this technology failed often, but in time it got much better at identifying people based on their behaviours on external websites.

For those signing up for the knowledge-sharing community a fully automated candidate-nurturing system would spring into action. As this community was wholly owned by Biovac they were able to measure exactly who looked at what and the system would follow up automatically with relevant content if something was available. The community quickly began to grow and it became clear it had the risk to succumb to its own success. So Biovac decided to create different levels of participants based on both engagement as well as talent. The top-level participants were given extra perks, from event visits to access to unique knowledge or early access to new papers. These candidates were almost treated like they were part of the Biovac family already. The lurchers, those members that didn't contribute and only consumed, were booted off the community after a warning. Frank also designed a very simple bot that checked the official affiliations of all participants, making sure they hadn't started a position at a competitor. Because although Biovac prided itself on being an open company, its intellectual property was of course it's most valuable possession.

One other key aspect of this strategy was the AI virtual assistant they pioneered with. Although very limited in scope when launched, this bot would proactively start a conversation with candidates that were on file. Either silver medallists or people in the community were asked by a chatbot about their status in the labour market for example. This virtual assistant quickly morphed from just a chatbot to a voicebot being able to call those without Facebook or WhatsApp. Of course candidates were always asked for permission to contact them as they were asked their preferences when the voicebot started. When many people replaced WhatsApp with TeleChat, a new messaging app that really protected their privacy, the AI virtual recruiting assistant actually became more popular as they were now able to get messages from those bots that were verified and most candidates loved Biovac's knowledge-based approach.

As Biovac was pioneering with AI-based virtual assistants for candidates, the same technology seemed to be applicable internally and so it quickly started pioneering this as well. They teamed up with knowledge partners for both personal coaching as well as team coaching.

Their personal coaching bot helped their employees that wanted to grow select the areas they wanted to develop in and combined those with the training programmes offered. At first this project wasn't successful as it was a cheap version of a human being. The personal coach bot wasn't really good at helping with the choices that had to be made and the mental aspect of keeping someone on track during the development programmes wasn't a big success either. It wasn't until Biovac started using digital assessments for much of the recruiting that this personal coaching bot started to take off. Because of all the data input on potential ability it was able to suggest training and jobs that employees would have never thought of before, but suited them well. Because of the unsuccessful pioneering work they also had a lot of data on what the bot did to motivate people and what did and didn't work. This data turned out to be correlated with certain traits and now the bot was able to tailor its style of coaching to the personal character traits of the employee.

The team-based coaching bot was a lot quicker to be successful. The bot was able to measure, both by simply asking and by linguistic analyses of the answers, team interaction and engagement. It was able to screen for potential issues in a team or between a team and its manager and escalate those to the appropriate person. If it seemed like there were issues arising in a team, the team leader would be told he needed to check in with the team more and given tips on how to go about this. If the team bot did not see the atmosphere improve the talent department would get involved and figure out if anything was wrong and if so what the issue was. Biovac used this team coaching bot to make sure small fires were put out quickly before issues escalated. It also helped managers with coaching tips and feedback styles.

The later years

As with all companies in hyper growth, things went wrong when Biovac started opening up lots of facilities in too short a time all over the world as a response to the abundant financing after the bird flu pandemic. As it was able to offer vaccines to its employees, there was no shortage of applicants. As many processes were not easily implemented in different locations, for example because local languages weren't supported, local laws didn't allow it or most applicants used different technology than Biovac was used to, it meant lots of manual labour by the talent team. This resulted in the entire focus of the talent team being on the new locations and neglecting the regular teams. When one of the AI nurturing systems went rogue and started messaging ridiculous messages, damage to the brand was done before it was shut down.

As with many problems, time solved some of it. When the new production locations were up and running Biovac started using the most modern digital assessments. Something that others had been doing for some time, so Biovac wasn't a pioneer of this and was able to benefit from the extensive research done in the past years by these suppliers with other companies. Many of these platforms were using explainable AI, audited yearly on fairness set by international governing standards to assess the qualities needed to succeed in a job. The speed of developments in the first part of the decade was enormous, making it possible to select based on cognitive and psychometric traits. These digital assessments made it possible to select almost bias free on value fit, while looking at the necessary traits to be able to do the job at hand. The talent advisor's role was to look, together with the hiring manager, at non-essential traits and decide the traits to be added to the team. The assessments also showed potential, mainly based on cognitive traits, helping Biovac hire not just on current fit, but also on future growth of the hire. These assessments considerably helped Biovac to hire internationally in more remote areas where access to education was limited and they needed to train their own staff. It soon realized this was applicable for many US sites too so they used the same methodology to hire high school drop-outs and train them as engineering staff for their production facilities.

Although the employer brand had taken a hit when the virtual assistant went rogue, most academics decided to forgive Biovac after they allowed some academic IT researchers to review everything that happened and let them publish on the incident. An apology was issued and the learnings were shared in a peer-reviewed research paper.

Unfortunately there were also other issues to deal with. Biovac had never considered bias and discrimination a big issue as they were so diverse and distributed. But several incidents of all sorts of discrimination in different locations hurt their brand again. Frank quickly took action and after a thorough review that led to some people getting fired, he decided to implement bias-alert tools that would screen for potential hiring manager biases as well as promotion biases. Biovac was able to use these alerts on a level that most companies couldn't yet, as they had the appropriate assessment data as well. These alerts were first set to look at the core HR system to check for potential bias. The algorithms compared compensation based on gender, as most other bias data wasn't stored and it also looked at internal growth and promotions. Biovac soon used the same algorithms on their applicant system, but decided to up the ante by looking at the assessment data. If a hiring manager wasn't hiring according to the fit scores for the role either one of two things could be happening. There was a problem with the algorithm calculating the fit scores or there was a hiring manager bias. Biovac found that cultural differences had a major impact on this, but stayed true to their values and eventually had to let go of some really successful managers that simply would not give fair and equal treatment to all.

Because diversity became an issue during this period of growth they also looked at tools that would be more inclusive at the very start of the process. Using the now well-established AI writing tools they were able to not only save time, but also write better and more inclusive job descriptions, especially for the support staff and production jobs. They combined this with the well-developed tools of dynamic job descriptions and career pages, which would adjust to the desires of the candidate reading them. These tools, automatically writing job descriptions based on a set of inputs and adjusting them to the reader's desires, complete with the adjustment of the visual communications that fit the reader, were introduced only a few years earlier and made many mistakes in their early days. One major problem was the targeting of who was reading the job description. Using AI and many data points, including social media profiles, the margin of error had gone down to under 1 per cent. Recent improvements meant that the targeting wasn't just done on gender, location and ethnicity, but also on personality. The combination of AI writing tools and dynamic job description content didn't just show the benefits you would want as a young, white, male college graduate or a working mum of colour combined with photos of the co-workers that you could identify with and references of them, they now also adjusted the writing to your personality. The highly analytical candidate would get data about the company in numbers, while the people person would get the stories about co-worker hobbies. The security-seeking candidate would be served the latest data on the company finances and the attrition rates while the highly ambitious candidate would read about the potential for growth in the company. This led to a massive increase of applicants on all jobs, but luckily the assessments were able to handle much of the volume that wasn't fit for the job and the candidate-nurturing pipelines that had been in place for ages were able to give the silver medallists a good experience and keep them engaged with the company.

This is a fictional scenario on talent acquisition in the near future.

8

'What hath God wrought?'

The future of recruitment and HR

This chapter title is a quote from Samuel FB Morse when he sent his first telegram. We might use these same words when we talk about ChatGPT and the advances in artificial intelligence. There have been several major technology driven transitions that have changed the world, challenged established norms and opened new ways of thinking and working.

The last major transition was the invention of the internet which opened the world to information and opened millions of minds to new ideas and information that was locked in libraries or only available to a small number of people. It has led to changes in society, education, politics and how we work.

Before the internet, the transformative technologies were physical, machine based rather than digital. The steam engine was one of these and its development revolutionized travel and led to the growth of railroads and mass manufacturing making more products available to more people as lower costs. Factories needed large numbers of skilled workers which led to the creation of the modern educational system, the invention of human resources and modern recruitment.

The recruitment practices of the past decades were designed to serve this manufacturing world. These practices mirrored and served mass manufacturing by hiring large volumes of replaceable workers. This need led to the development of the recruiting profession.

Now, the number of employees an organization has is becoming less of a benchmark of economic success or prestige. The sale of Instagram to Facebook in 2012 for $1 billion even though they only had 13 employees was the first sign of this new paradigm. The quantity of people is not the main source of increasing revenue anymore; it's the quality of people and the tech they are equipped with. The rise of AI, which can replace or augment people, has changed the kind of person an organization needs. In a factory a great worker might have been able to work 20 per cent or maybe even 40 per cent faster than the average worker. In the knowledge economy a great worker can work 20 to 40 times smarter, that's 2,000 per cent to 4,000 per cent. This gives organizations a need to focus on personalizing work and allowing workers more independence.

Work will most likely continue to take up the biggest portion of our day, but it can be shaped to provide more enjoyment and fulfilment than in the past.

The future of recruitment marketing and branding

One specific area we want to emphasize in this chapter is recruitment marketing and employer branding, as that's the area of talent acquisition that will be one of the first impacted by generative AI.

The future of recruitment marketing is mass personalization. With the use of AI and large language models, more and more messages will be tailored to the specific desired content and tone of the candidate. Of course all within the boundaries of the employer brand dictated by the company values.

Ads for jobs on social media will be tailored in tone of voice as well pictures shown to the desire of the candidate. Job ads, the job descriptions that are meant to excite the candidate, will be written not just in a tone of voice that the potential candidate will like, but also with the information that would convince that specific candidate. A person that's more risk averse will get information on the financial stability of your organization combined perhaps with your pension plan. A more risk-taking person will get information on the grand vision of your company and the future prospects. A potential candidate that has a high moral stance will have information about your sustainability efforts. Ad campaigns won't be single ads, but hundreds or maybe even thousands of ads that are similar, but not the same, running all at once. This will be based on the personality of the candidate, based on information derived from their social media presence. Although it's questionable this form of personality profiles will ever be good enough for selection, it's much better than just throwing out one or two ads to all types of people. And with advertising you're not harming anybody when using an inaccurate personality profile as right now, we're not using them at all so the ads are not catered to the different individuals.

The content on your corporate careers website will also automatically adjust to the candidate's preferences. This can be the photos of the team that are shown, the wording that is used and even the content that is prioritized. Just like you have a different first page at Amazon than I do, based on previous purchases and other behaviours, so will your corporate careers website change. From the jobs that are shown to the photos, the language of the job ad and the benefits that are highlighted.

Talent communities will become more common, and talent pipelines and the use of bots to keep in touch with candidates will change talent acquisition from a game of chance to a strategic resource. Here AI and language models will assist in making this a pleasant candidate experience, engaging with talent until the moment for both parties is right to join. AI will help determine the 'hire readiness' of a candidate based on their behaviour in the talent community and their reactions, or lack thereof, on content provided by a different AI.

The future of direct sourcing

A second area we want to emphasize in this last chapter is direct sourcing as this too will be impacted strongly and quickly by (generative) AI.

For the searching part of sourcing AI has been implemented in several products for some time, using the feedback loop of who gets invited and who doesn't to qualify the candidates this specific user wants to see.

Language models and machine learning have already built databases of synonyms in job titles and suggests alternative titles when searching. In the near future AI models will not just search synonyms, but also skill matches. Based on either Onet and or its European counterpart Esco, skills are derived from jobs and skill matching is made possible. So you can source candidates based on transferable skills. The next step is that you can ask your AI assistant who might be ready for this position, looking at internal and external talent based on previous promotions and external data from, for example, LinkedIn, and have made career moves towards the job you are sourcing for. As we all know careers are never linear and very few people end up in the job they actually studied for, so having an AI sourcing assistant that helps us overcome the human linear thinking will become common. Of course, this AI assistant might also start recommending internal candidates without even asking it for promotions or other moves. Internal mobility and talent acquisition will merge into the same function, using the same AI tools.

For the communication part of the sourcing function generative AI will also play a big role in the near future. It is already used to write better outreach messages to candidates that are sent by the sourcer, but soon it will be able to do the first outreach without even a human touching it. The hiring manager will give it a profile or perhaps even just enter the person that's leaving or that they want to 'clone', perhaps with a few options of 'more analytical skills', for example, and an AI sourcing bot will search and do first outreach. This outreach will be tailored to the personality of the candidate, based on its social media presence, just with the recruitment marketing ads.

What about artificial intelligence?

Artificial intelligence, such as ChatGPT, has already changed everything. It has changed how organizations operate, how many people they need to succeed and how they see and value people. Google CEO Sundar Pichai was interviewed on 60 Minutes (a US television news and information show) and compared the invention of AI to the creation of fire, claiming it surpassed even great leaps in technology like electricity.

The interesting fact about this new technology is that generative AI, like ChatGPT, seems to benefit the lower-skilled workers the most according to research by MIT and Stanford.[1] Although much more research is necessary. There is a big question unanswered in this case – will generative AI be good enough to actually completely, or partly, replace customer service agents, for example? This remains to be seen, but it's certainly not unthinkable.

As previously discussed with the example of the chess tournament, no AI is perfect, yet. The teams that win freestyle tournaments use multiple AIs and combine the outcomes with human judgement to choose the best move. This, of course, goes against current doctrine in organizations, as pretty much every organization tends to buy one piece of technology and decides that's it. We already have a tool for that, so either we replace it or we keep it. But never do we have two, or more, systems running in parallel. This might be a business principle that needs to be revisited.

But how will recruiting change?

For this we first need to see how organizations will change, as recruitment is linked directly to organizational demands for talent.

Computers will soon speak at a level where humans cannot tell if they are talking to a machine or a human. They will have vastly increased knowledge of human social behaviour after time spent analysing social media and online interaction. They will have analysed vast amounts of data and be highly skilled in many areas of expertise. With complete memory recall, vast amounts of information, and the ability to integrate and merge disparate data sources, the power of AI is almost limitless. This power will be integrated into programs and apps that will guide and inform us. While human judgement will still be valued and necessary, the traditional duties of many professions, including recruiting, will likely be replaced with automated tools.

'A machine can do the work of 50 ordinary men, but no machine can do the work of an extraordinary man', Elbert Hubbart wrote in the beginning of the 20th century, and this still holds true today more than 100 years later. The only question is how to define an extraordinary person.

One other extremely important aspect of the changing world of recruitment is the importance of recruiting for a team. As mentioned before in the freestyle chess tournaments, well-oiled teams win matches. Something you will know if you're a sports fan, it's not always the team with the best players that wins; they can easily get beaten by a team with lesser players who act more as a team. Although recruiting for team fit has always been a mantra for many recruiters and companies, the reality is it is usually a lot of hot air. Value add and cultural add have been terms introduced in recent years, but in reality little has changed. Competencies are still based on a job profile, not the profile within the team. For actual team recruitment a 360-degree assessment of strengths and weaknesses in both cognitive as well as psychometric qualities needs to be done in order to spot actual value adds. This, combined with a fit on core values and a psychological safe environment, makes for high functioning teams.

Team recruitment and quantum computing

Quantum computing is some time away, but it would be remiss if we did not mention it in this chapter. Although the first quantum are operating, they don't scale and aren't very useful yet, but they do hold great promise and the billions of dollars invested in them over the past few years shows the belief big tech giants like Google and Microsoft have in them.

Just a brief explanation of quantum computing. Basically, really smart people managed to design a quantum bit or Qubit. This is basically a super bit. A normal bit is what makes computers talk and every bit is either a 1 or a 0. A Qubit can be both at the same time. Think of it as opening a combination lock. If you have four numbers that all have 10 digits, you have 10 to the 4th possibilities totalling 10,000 possible combinations. Even for a computer, going though all 10,000 takes some time. But a Qubit can be every one of these 10 numbers at once, so basically four Qubit will break every combination in seconds.

The impact of Qubits on the world, once they get them stable, will be huge as it unlocks a computer power, for research purposes mostly, that we have not seen before. The expected influence on recruitment will, from what we can see now, mainly be on the element of team composition. Let's explain this in sports language. Think of a basketball or a football team, either 5 or 11 players. They all interact with each other and it's not easy to optimize between them. If you replace one player, for example in football the defensive midfielder, this influences the entire team. So having a player that is better in passing, but less in positioning for example, might help in certain aspects of the team and some teammates higher on the pitch, but hurt other midfielders and the defenders that now have to do more defensive work. In current analyses it's possible to look at the effect of changing one player at a time. With quantum computers it's possible to look not just at one player's interaction with the team, but to all the alternatives for all the positions on the field. The same is for teams in organizations. It can answer questions about the best fit for the team, but also for other positions in the teams and perhaps even for changing team members between teams in a company.

Quantum computing will change the way we look at teams, individual strengths and weaknesses, complimentary skills and personalities like never before. The research into high performing teams has been limited by the lack of possibilities to research interactions between a great deal of team members all at once. Most research until now has focused on the team culture and that is important, but we might also learn who flourishes in what culture and how a such a high performing culture can be created naturally.

Although this is a long time ago, many say at least in a decade or perhaps decades, quantum computing will revolutionize the way we look at teams and hence recruitment. Because the sales part of recruitment has now mainly been focused on the job and the company, with quantum computing it will be about the team, your role in the team and the specific traits you bring to that team in order to sell the job to the candidate.

The value of talent

In the new paradigm, talent will be valued very differently. In the old factory model workers were seen as interchangeable. So the most talented were not on the extremes of the spectrum, but in the middle. Recruitment was about predictable results from a hire, and if a hire was 10 per cent better than the average it was an amazing hire. In the age of AI, the AI will deliver predictable results and soon it will be above average compared to humans as it's much easier to scale good performers. Because of this other talents will be valued more in the new organizations. There are three types of talent with great value in the age of AI and both are currently more on the fringes of the labour market.

1 The editor
2 The pit bull
3 The creative

The **editor** is a person who checks the work of the AI. They are extremely meticulous in checking for every possible mistake and completing the work the AI has done. Editors are people that improve other people's work and have traditionally been very undervalued in organizations as we tended to value the creators, the writers and the art directors more than those that gave the book or campaign its finishing touch. With AI being able to create so much decent content, it will be the finishing touch that makes the difference.

The **pit bull** is very steadfast when it comes to checking sources and the validity of the source used by the AI. These people dig in until they get their answer. The pit bull has a combination between extreme desire for the truth, a mentality to never give up no matter the circumstances and an everlasting desire to know even more. In current organizations these are the people management fears will become whistleblowers.

The **creative** – many think of themselves as such, but here we mean the lonely creative. The people that aren't influenced much by the outside world or at least see the world totally differently to everybody else. These are the Pablo Picassos and Antoni Gaudis of the world that create something that nobody before them envisioned, or Luna Lovegood from the world of *Harry Potter*, who sees things others don't. Often seen as 'crazy' people that are unmanageable and certainly not replaceable.

With AI doing the work of ordinary people, the ones we are currently recruiting for that are easily replaceable, organizations will need these three types of workers to add value to the AI. With changing organizations to fit the changing times, just like factories were developed when the steam engine came on the scene, recruitment needs to change with it to fill the changing needs for talent.

Your talent strategy

Just like in the age of the factory model where there was no one talent model and one recruitment model that fit all, the future of recruitment is not a one size fits all either. What we've tried to show you throughout this book is that there are several seemingly contradicting developments, but that's only when you don't have a North Star and a talent strategy. What the scenarios are meant to show you is that there are many roads leading to Rome, but you need to take one and stick with it. Changing directions will keep you driving in circles, never reaching any kind of destination. Your strategy needs to fit both your market as well as your company culture. There are plenty of examples of major competitors where one has a 'develop your own' and the other a 'hire experienced employees' strategy and both are very successful. It's the competitors that are in the middle and do a bit of both that tend to fail.

The future of recruitment and HR is integrated, with a total talent strategy that is closely linked to the corporate strategy. Talent is more important than ever, and as money has become so cheap access to capital doesn't make a difference anymore, and the head of talent, or the CHRO or the Chief People Officer or whatever you like to call this position, is at least as important as the CFO in the near future. So it's time for the head of talent to be as strategic as the CFO.

STRATEGY
Every talent acquisition function will need a talent strategy that answers key questions.

- What is your general philosophy about employees?
- What types of people are going to build the future your organization wants?

- What is your philosophy about automation and outsourcing people functions? What gets automated and what doesn't?
- What does the future of work look like in/for your organization?
- What new jobs are likely to emerge?
- Where is your R&D and business strategy heading?
- What potential skills will your organization need in the next five years that don't currently exist?
- Do your HR polices support the strategy and provide incentives?
- How does this strategy fit in with the corporate strategy?
- How do the strategic objectives translate in people and skills?

Without answers to these questions, it will be hard to direct AI or your recruiters to success.

TACTICAL CHOICES

Based on the strategy it's time to dissect this to tactical choices.

- Do you invest heavily in sourcing or in marketing?
- Do you develop the new skills internally or hire them?
- If you go for the hire strategy, are those permanent hires or temporary hires? And do you differentiate between skills? Are some skills better to have as permanent hires and other skills as gig workers?
- If you go for the development strategy, how will you do this? And do you differentiate between certain skills, are some better to upskill and others to reskill? Do you focus on reskilling or upskilling?

The power of AI

Data will help guide answers to these questions. The future of recruitment and HR is data-centric and AI-powered. The age of guess work, where over 50 per cent of all hires fail,[2] is over. As mentioned before, Google CEO Sundar Pichai has compared the invention of AI to the creation of fire, claiming it surpassed even great leaps in technology like electricity. Whether you believe he is right or not that AI will have the impact of fire or electricity, it's something no organization can ignore.

Today most recruiters don't really know the skills required to excel at a job and hiring managers are often fuzzy as to which skills really are important and which are just nice to have. It is also challenging to describe the skills required in an unambiguous, measurable way. AI will change this and be able to assess the qualities needed to excel, and these skills and qualities will probably be different than expected.

Soon, when AI is able to do so much, it will be the people that make the difference. AI can probably answer 95 per cent of all customer calls, but for that last 5 per cent, or maybe even 1 per cent, you will need a human to fix a problem, make an exception or just listen with empathy. These will not be just any customer support person, but rather a person who is able to genuinely think outside the box and has good judgement for the situation.

Rather than being completely replaced by AI, recruiters will need to adapt their skills and focus on areas where they can add value beyond what machines are capable of doing. One area where recruiters can continue to play a critical role is in building relationships with candidates and understanding their unique needs and preferences. While AI may be able to identify candidates with the right skills for a particular job, for the foreseeable future it cannot select the best person to both fit in a team and complement team skills.

Recruiters can also work closely with hiring managers and business leaders to understand company culture, values and goals. They can help shape job descriptions that accurately reflect these attributes while also appealing to top talent. Additionally, recruiters can leverage their networks within specific industries or regions to help identify high-quality candidates who may not be actively seeking new opportunities.

When it comes to attracting talent AI will fundamentally change the world of recruitment. As new search engines like Google's Bard or Microsoft's AI-powered Bing give answers instead of links, the trust in matching and 'the one right answer' will increase in the next couple of years. AI-matching algorithms will rule job searches, and in order to match correctly, the data about both the job and the organization must be unambiguous and true. Don Tapscott said at the rise of social media: 'if [organizations] are going to be naked, you'd better be buff. As sunlight is a big disinfectant and transparency will kill lies.' Unfortunately events in the past years have shown he was wrong as disinformation has spread throughout social media like never before. From allegations of meddling in US elections by Russia[3] to a smear campaign by the UAE,[4] misinformation seems to prevail in the current societies. This is also true about companies who greenwash or downplay their damage like the tobacco industry once did. The question is if AI will be fooled by this misinformation as well or if we can break the filter bubbles many humans live in.

When it comes to selection of the best candidate, the world will never be the same. Since the introduction of digital or virtual recruitment, from video interviews and take-home assignments, we've seen some cheating. There have been several cases reported of people showing up to their first day who didn't look at all like the person interviewed and sometimes didn't even speak English at all, as someone else did the interview for them. But now a person can have an AI agent either doing the test or assisting them on the interview. But that shouldn't be an issue.

If AI can beat your selection process either one of two things are the issue:

1 Your selection process is bad and needs to be redesigned.

2 AI can actually do the work, so you shouldn't be hiring a human for this job.

So as a recruiter you need to design a process that's AI proof. Different jobs will have different processes, but luckily there will be plenty of data to help you understand what to measure for.

The future skills of a recruiter

Exponential changes are occurring in candidate and worker attitudes, technology and artificial intelligence advancements. Although there are always people unemployed and looking for a job and jobs that cannot be filled. This is because there is also a huge imbalance of skills. Those with few skills and little education find it harder to find decent, well-paying jobs while those with skills seek higher pay and different working conditions.

This puts recruiters in a tough spot. How do they satisfy their hiring managers and also the candidates? How do they influence change in how hiring managers approach this market? How do they market or convince candidates to work at their organization?

Recruiters need to adapt to the changing market. As Darwin said, the key to survival is not necessarily being the strongest or fittest, but having the ability to adapt. It takes recruiters with up-to-date skills, technical acumen and business understanding to thrive in this marketplace. It also takes developing new skills, understanding the latest technology and embracing new processes. Figure 8.1 illustrates a few of the most critical new skills.

Over the years, corporate recruiters have evolved using three major sets of competencies. The first is the ability to deal with corporate bureaucracy and legal issues. These recruiters are formidable navigators of the corporate landscape. They know every hill and valley, every bomb and sinkhole. They produce legally required, nicely prepared, backward-looking reports and know every nuance of HR law.

Recruiters with these competencies likely work for the same firm for many years. The skills are unique to a particular company and do not transfer well. Their internal knowledge and ability to get things done in systems resistant to getting things done makes them valuable, but only *in* that system. This ability fails to help the recruiter navigate a talent-constrained marketplace or understand or know how to use emerging technologies. It leads to the rigid application of techniques that used to work but may not work today.

The second is the ability to screen and interview candidates. This is often considered a primary skill, and recruiters take great pride in their interviewing prowess. They may have spent years taking classes and developing skills in good interviewing. Most of their time is spent scheduling, screening and interviewing. While this may seem value-added, it does not scale and can be replaced mainly with artificial intelligence and various tests that have higher reliability and predictive value.

The third skill is a helper or pair of hands for the hiring manager. They focus on wooing the candidate and hiring manager and making a good impression. The recruiter meets candidates, gives them a tour of the facility, takes them to the hiring manager and perhaps even offers them a coffee or lunch. They become the liaison or interface between the company, the hiring manager and the candidate. This also does not scale and is something the hiring manager should probably do.

None of these three competencies help deliver scarce skills or influence hiring managers to think differently about the changing talent landscape.

In order to thrive in the new reality a recruiter will need several skills.

What six skills does a productive recruiter need to have?

1   **Skill 1: They know how to use data**
    These recruiters are experts at understanding data and using it to influence hiring managers, show objective reasons why someone is a top performer, make better decisions about where to focus time and effort, and find the best people for a particular job family. They are familiar with descriptive and predictive analytics and work with data scientists and analysts to

extract data that helps make better recommendations. They are always seeking to correlate and understand better the relationships between performance, skills and experience. Their recommendations are based on data and as free from bias as possible. They use this data to decide which candidates to present and to influence hiring managers.

2 **Skill 2: They build market and talent intelligence**
According to Toby Culshaw, talent intelligence is 'the augmentation of internal and external people data with the application of technology, science, insights, and intelligence relating to people, skills, jobs, functions, competitors, and geographies to drive business decisions'.[5]

Having this knowledge is power. By gathering market and talent data and analysing and charting it, recruiters can develop talent maps and use those maps to meet, engage and create relationships with the most desirable talent inside your firm and externally.

3 **Skill 3: They build relationships and teams**
The ability to build relationships is essential and close to the top of the pyramid of skills. They spend inordinate amounts of time talking, reading, networking and learning about the areas they are responsible for and the people considered the best in the field. This is what all great recruiters do. They leverage diverse people to find the best candidate for a position or solve a problem. Rather than go it alone, they create teams of stakeholders to speed the process and ensure they have located the best people. These recruiters spend time inside and outside their organization and get to know people at all levels and professions that might be useful to their firm.

4 **Skill 4: They understand and embrace technology**
Technology is already crucial to recruiting success. Applicant tracking systems, HRIS systems, social networks and recruiting websites are the base of older and more mature recruitment technology. On top of this base are increasingly powerful tools powered by artificial intelligence that can find, screen, assess, communicate with and onboard people at all levels. Great recruiters embrace and learn the technology and make it do what they want. If a recruiter is not technically agile and informed, she cannot be successful in the long run.

5 **Skill 5: They are flexible and agile**
As mentioned above, survival goes to those who best adapt to changing situations. As businesses change, new technologies emerge, work goes hybrid and talent remains hard to identify and hire, being willing to accept change and deal with it positively is critical.

FIGURE 8.1 Key recruiting skills

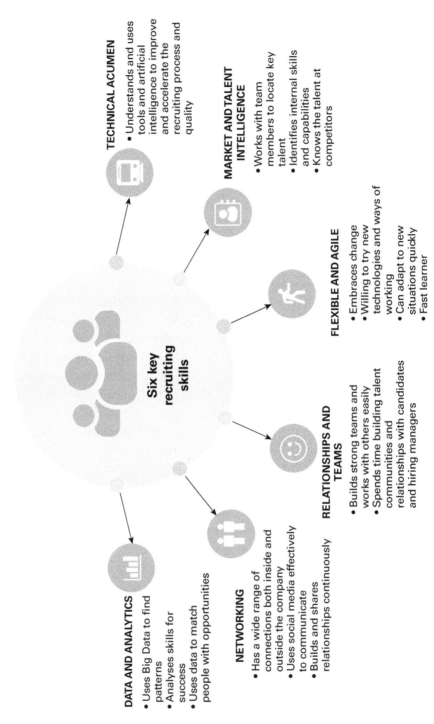

Six key recruiting skills

TECHNICAL ACUMEN
- Understands and uses tools and artificial intelligence to improve and accelerate the recruiting process and quality

MARKET AND TALENT INTELLIGENCE
- Works with team members to locate key talent
- Identifies internal skills and capabilities
- Knows the talent at competitors

FLEXIBLE AND AGILE
- Embraces change
- Willing to try new technologies and ways of working
- Can adapt to new situations quickly
- Fast learner

RELATIONSHIPS AND TEAMS
- Builds strong teams and works with others easily
- Spends time building talent communities and relationships with candidates and hiring managers

NETWORKING
- Has a wide range of connections both inside and outside the company
- Uses social media effectively to communicate
- Builds and shares relationships continuously

DATA AND ANALYTICS
- Uses Big Data to find patterns
- Analyses skills for success
- Uses data to match people with opportunities

6 Skill 6: They are networkers

These recruiters have large networks of friends, social media connections, past candidates, experts, other recruiters and colleagues who can provide leads, refer candidates and provide valuable intelligence about the market.

The future recruiter will develop skills that are not easily done by artificial intelligence. They gladly give up the traditional skills of screening, scheduling, assessment and reporting to focus on adding actual value.

Of course not every recruiter needs to excel in each of these skills. There have always been and will always be specialties within the TA profession. Jobs are always a combination of skills and with these new skills in mind, there will emerge several new jobs within talent acquisition. Here we describe the new jobs that we'll see in talent acquisitions.

Talent advisor

A talent advisor is made from the combination of networking, relationship-building and data analytics. A talent advisor truly understands the business of the hiring manager and where it is going. The talent advisor is able to translate the vision of the business to skills required by the new recruits. And when a recruiter understands the skills to be able to find a way to objectively assess these skills. This means a recruiter needs to have some understanding of organizational psychology as well as data analyses. Being able to objectively show a hiring manager the skills of candidates and how they differ makes the recruiter a talent advisor and a sparring partner on building the best team.

Talent attraction specialist

The combination between talent intelligence and data analytics combined with the understanding of technology makes for a talent attraction specialist. Based on the talent intelligence, the talent attraction specialist determines where candidates can be found and how they can be persuaded to join the company. Using data to either source or advertise and understanding the target audience to gather what it is that will persuade a candidate to join the organization and emphasize that in either the ads or the outreach messages is a skill that's very important in future times of massive skill shortages and a labour market where the candidate has the power. Of course the talent attraction specialist needs to use the right technology in order to scale this.

Candidate engagement officer

The combination between relationship building, networking and being agile and flexible makes for a candidate engagement officer. This person needs empathy and project management skills above all. The candidate engagement officer helps the candidate navigate the process. The more we automate, the more important it is to have a human touch to keep the candidate engaged, especially in a candidate-driven market.

Recruitment operations manager

The combination of being flexible, understanding technology and using data makes for a good recruitment operations manager. This is a job that already exists, but currently only in the largest organizations. This role will become more common in the future. The recruitment operations manager makes sure the process and the technology supporting the process is up to date and offers the best candidate, recruiter and hiring manager experience. They also signal issues in the process and help improve the recruitment process on important metrics.

Conclusion

In this last chapter we try to look into our crystal ball, but predicting is hard, especially about the future. In this book we've tried our best to combine technological trends with social and demographic developments to come to intersections that are feasible. We've tried to look at different areas of the world, as both societal and labour norms as well as demographic developments are very different in different parts of the world.

As we are entering the age of AI and algorithms, we're also entering the age of talent. The truly talented in any occupation will be as valuable as the best players in sports. With AI and algorithms being able to do so much of the work, it's the Michael Jordans, Lionel Messis and Tom Bradys of your company that will make the difference. But those super star players need a great team to support, as Messi showed when he played at Paris Saint German. No super star can win without the proper support – whether that support comes from humans or technology, but it's probably both.

Every person in talent acquisition needs to think about their role and the skills needed for this role in the now changing world of talent acquisition.

For many decades talent acquisition hasn't really changed and kept failing at its goal, given the 30–50 per cent bad hires we've produced. That's about to change because of big data, algorithms and AI. Talent acquisition is about to finally change, and the truly talented in the industry will embrace this change and thrive.

Endnotes

1   Fanatical Futurist (2023) MIT and Stanford ChatGPT study shows low skilled workers benefit the most, 25 April, www.fanaticalfuturist.com/2023/04/mit-and-stanford-chatgpt-study-shows-low-skilled-workers-benefit-the-most/ (archived at https://perma.cc/46LR-FCKD)

2   Dr John Sullivan (2017) Ouch, 50% of new hires fail! 6 ugly numbers revealing recruiting's dirty little secret, 11 April, drjohnsullivan.com/articles/hr-retention/ouch-50-new-hires-fail-6-ugly-numbers-revealing-recruitings-dirty-little-secret/ (archived at https://perma.cc/V4GE-9HBW)

3   U.S. Senate Select Committee on Intelligence (2019) Senate Intel Releases Election Security Findings in First Volume of Bipartisan Russia Report, 25 June, www.intelligence.senate.gov/press/senate-intel-releases-election-security-find-ings-first-volume-bipartisan-russia-report (archived at https://perma.cc/7L9H-KG9U)

4   The New Arab (2023) UAE 'paid Swiss firm' over €5 million on alleged 'Muslim Brotherhood smear campaign' in Europe, 11 July, www.newarab.com/news/uae-paid-millions-brotherhood-smear-campaign-europe (archived at https://perma.cc/4UPB-LTE7)

5   Toby Culshaw (2022), *Talent Intelligence: Use business and people data to drive organizational performance*, Kogan Page, London

INDEX

Looking for another book?

Explore our award-winning
books from global business
experts in Human Resources,
Learning and Development

Scan the code to browse

www.koganpage.com/hr-learning-
development

Also from Kogan Page

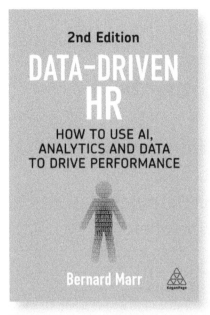

ISBN: 9781398614567

ISBN: 9781398610828

ISBN: 9781398610040

ISBN: 9781398607231

www.koganpage.com